# THE
# DICTIONARY
## OF
# CRICKET

# THE
# DICTIONARY
## OF
# CRICKET

BLOOMSBURY BOOKS
LONDON

© Michael Rundell 1985
This book is copyright under the Berne Convention. No reproduction
without permission. All rights reserved.

First published 1985


**George Allen & Unwin (Publishers) Ltd,**
**40 Museum Street, London WC1A 1LU, UK**

This edition published 1989 by
Bloomsbury Books an imprint of
Godfrey Cave Associates Limited
42 Bloomsbury Street, London WC1B 3QJ
under license from George Allen & Unwin (Publishers) Ltd

ISBN 1 870630 92 0


Printed in Yugoslavia

# The Dictionary of Cricket – Introduction

The language of cricket is as complex and fascinating and eccentric as the game itself – and, to the uninitiated, just as mysterious. It is made up partly of words unique to the game of cricket, like *googly* and *yorker*, and partly (much the greater part, this) of common English words used in a specialised way, like *square*, *point*, and *walk*. Like any other living language it is in a state of continuous, very gradual evolution. Some of cricket's ancient terms, like *notcher* and *bat's end*, have already been obsolete for over a hundred years. Others, like *bumper* and *stumper*, are beginning to sound distinctly old-fashioned and may now be regarded as obsolescent. Sometimes, too, it is the thing itself, rather than the word, that has become extinct: the *draw* stroke, a great favourite with 19th-century batsmen, has not been seen for nearly a century, and it is almost as long since a *lobster* last bowled for England. But all the time, as older words have fallen by the wayside, new ones have evolved to take their place: the *flipper*, the *chinaman*, and the *bat-pad* fielder are all products of the 20th century, and many quite everyday cricket terms, like *swing* and *seam*, only acquired their specialised meanings in fairly recent years.

To a great extent these changes in the language reflect changes in the game itself, which in turn are often conditioned by developments in the wider world. A very modern word like *sledging*, for example, describes a rather dubious form of gamesmanship which many would regard as symptomatic of a more general social malaise – a decline, in fact, from the days when every fellow played 'a straight bat' and refused to contemplate anything that was 'not cricket'. But others will feel that the situation is not quite so cut and dried, and may reflect that in the halcyon days of the 1930s an English team was accused by its opponents of 'unsportsmanlike' behaviour for adopting the tactics of *bodyline*.

This rich and inventive language deserves a fuller treatment than it has traditionally received from the brief 'glossaries' that are often appended to books about cricket. The only serious attempt to catalogue the game's vocabulary is the long-out-of-print *Language of Cricket* by W. J. Lewis (OUP 1934). Lewis's book, an invaluable source of information and in many ways a model of lexicographic rigour, operates within a very restricted framework and so only partially fulfils the promise of its title. *The Dictionary of Cricket* has a wider brief and aims not only to define the vocabulary of the game and provide examples of the words in use, but also to supply any additional information – whether technical, legal, historical, or etymological – that will contribute to a fuller understanding of each item.

As a matter of policy, little or no prior knowledge is assumed in the reader, so recent 'converts' who have not yet cracked the game's mysterious code are well catered for. But the book's breadth of coverage will, I hope, make it just as useful and just as interesting to those with a more established acquaintance with cricket–readers who know very well what a deep backward square leg is, but may nevertheless want to know more about the physics of swing bowling or the origins of the term chinaman.

Two points about procedure should be made here. First, the majority of definitions are accompanied by quotations showing how the word is actually used, and these quotations are for the most part derived from a collection of sources listed at the back of the book. Secondly, like the 1980 edition of the *Laws of Cricket*, the book 'refers to the male person only, for convenience and brevity': the use in definitions of 'he', 'his', etc. is not intended to suggest that the world of cricket is populated exclusively by men.

Finally, I would like to thank all those people who have given valuable advice and encouragement at various stages in the compilation of the book, especially: Dr Jean Branford, Jeremy Burford, David Frith, Mary Lou Grimberg, Charlie Lewis, Peter Roebuck, and Mark Stevens; John Newth and Derek Wyatt of George Allen & Unwin; and my ever-supportive wife Maggy.

# A

**ACB** *abbr* Australian Cricket Board

**ACCA** *abbr* Anglo-Corfiot Cricket Association

**account** *n* – **open one's account** to score the first run or runs of one's innings; get off the mark:

> 'Each batsman opened his account with a single in Sharma's next over' (Berry 1982, p 145).

**across** *adv & prep* **1** (of the ball) moving away from the batsman at a considerable angle to the line of the wickets:

> 'Gooch and Gatting had both played against him [Whitney], and they reported that he . . . only slanted the ball across; they had not seen him swing it in' (Brearley 1982, p 113).

Compare AWAY, BACK 2.

**2** (of a batsman) striking or attempting to strike the ball with the bat held in a horizontal rather than vertical plane, so as to cut across the ball's line of flight:

> 'With lunch eight minutes away, he aimed across Maninder Singh's spin and top-edged a simple catch to Kirmani' (Ian Brayshaw, *The Times* 27 December 1983).

See CROSS BAT.

**action** *n* the manner in which a bowler delivers the ball, especially with regard to such features as the height of the arm and the 'fairness' of the delivery:

'Foster . . . has a well coordinated and high action' (Henry Blofeld, *Guardian* 31 May 1983).

'That winter Lock worked on his action, and from then onwards it was only his occasional faster ball which offended' (Frith 1984, p 131).

**action-break** *n* (old) break imparted to the ball by a fast or medium-paced bowler, either as a 'natural' product of the bowling action or by means of 'cut', as distinguished from break produced by finger- or wrist-spin:

'There are two kinds of break, known as "finger-break" and "action-break"' (Ranji 1897, p 75).

As Ranji explains, at the point of delivery a right-arm bowler 'flings his body, right arm, shoulder, and leg forward, but rather across towards the left. This action gives the hand a sweep across the ball, making it spin in its flight outwards from left to right.'

**ACU** *abbr* Association of Cricket Umpires.

**afini palla** (Corfu) *lit 'to leave the bat'*: used to indicate that an innings has been declared closed.

**aim** *vb* to execute a particular batting stroke, without necessarily making contact with the ball:

'Dooland in time passed on to Richie Benaud the secrets of the back-spun, skidding ball which foxed so many batsmen as they aimed pull-strokes well above the line' (Frith 1984, p 124).

**air** *n* – **give the ball air** (of a slow bowler) to deliver the ball with a relatively high curving trajectory, with the aim of deceiving the batsman as to its line, length, and pace; flight the ball.

'He [Gifford] gives the ball air in a deceptive manner for it seems to come at the batsman slower than his bustling approach suggests and they play too soon' (Henry Blofeld, *Guardian* 9 August 1983).

Compare PUSH THROUGH.

**air-break** *n* (old) movement of the ball in the air; swing:

'"Swerve" or "air-break" . . . is valuable to fast and medium-paced bowlers if combined with length' (E. R. Wilson in Badminton Library, *Cricket* (1920 edition) p 58).

**air-shot** *n* a batting stroke in which the bat fails to make contact with the ball:

> *'Five sixes off Willis, interspersed with several air-shots . . . enabled West Indies to turn a probable deficit into an invaluable lead of 32'* (Christopher Martin-Jenkins, Cricketer September 1984).

**all out** *adv* used in recording the score to show that a side's innings has been brought to an end through the dismissal of its batsmen by the bowling side. Strictly, of course, the term is inaccurate, since a side is 'all out' once ten of its eleven batsmen have been dismissed or have retired.

**all-rounder** *n* a player skilled in both batting and bowling or in both batting and wicket-keeping. Neville Cardus argued that the real test for a great all-rounder (leaving aside wicket-keepers) was: 'Would he be picked to play in a Test match for his batting *only*, or for his bowling *only*?' (Cardus 1978, p 138). But these are rigorous criteria, and many of the great all-round performers (like Grace, Rhodes, and Hammond) are in fact principally remembered for their skill in one or other department of the game. In theory a wide range of permutations is possible, such as the stroke-playing number three batsman who also bowls spinners, or the specialist slow bowler who can also bat a bit, lower down the order. But it is a striking feature of the modern game that the all-rounder is most often a front-line fast or fast-medium bowler who is also an aggressive hitter batting at around six or seven in the order. In the case of a wicket-keeping all-rounder, the term 'wicket-keeper-batsman' is probably more usual. See also BITS-AND-PIECES PLAYER.

**amateur** *n* a person who plays cricket as a pastime rather than as a profession; specifically, in the context of first-class cricket in Britain, a player who held amateur status. According to an MCC ruling, amateurs received no remuneration but were entitled to reimbursement of all their expenses. Amateur status was finally abolished at the end of the 1962 cricket season. See also GENTLEMAN.

**analysis** *n* the record of a bowler's performance in an innings or match:

*'Hadlee topped and tailed the innings with four wickets for 14 runs, bringing the New Zealand fast bowler's match analysis to eight for 22'* (Cyril Chapman, *Guardian* 1 May 1984).

The minimum information supplied in an analysis will be the number of wickets taken and the number of runs scored off the bowler (in that order) – thus: 'England 314 (Lillee 7 for 87)'. A slightly more detailed analysis shows the number of overs (including, after a decimal point, the number of balls bowled in any uncompleted over), the number of maidens, the runs scored, and the wickets taken (in that order) – thus: Lillee 31·4–4–89–7'. The most complete form of analysis, as found in the traditional scorebook, is based on data that is entered as each ball is actually delivered. It thus includes information about every ball – whether it was a no-ball or wide, whether runs were scored off it (and how many), and whether a wicket was taken. Traditionally, the figure in an analysis for the runs scored off a bowler does not take into account any extras accruing to the batting side in the course of his spell. But a new convention whereby no-balls and wides are debited to the bowler's analysis has been operating at Test level in some countries since 1983. Compare FIGURES and see illustration at SCOREBOOK.

**angle** *vb* **1** to deliver the ball in such a way that it either comes into or goes away from the striker at a considerable angle to the line of the wickets, the effect being typically achieved by means of swing or cut, and/or a bowling position relatively wide of the wicket:

*'Frank Tyson . . . says it is clear that the pace bowlers have to go round the wicket, bowl just short of a length, and angle the ball in at the left-hander's stumps'* (Scyld Berry, *Observer* 2 January 1983).

**2** (of the ball) to move into or away from the striker at a considerable angle to the line of the wickets:

*'He has been deceived into assuming an inswinger which proved to be a leg-cutter . . . or one which angled the other way off a "green" pitch'* (Arlott 1983, p 38).

**apo podi** (Corfu) *lit 'from the foot':* used to indicate that a batsman is out lbw.

**apo psila** (Corfu) *lit 'from high':* used to indicate that a batsman is out caught.

**apo xyla** (Corfu) *lit 'from the wood':* used to indicate that a batsman is out bowled.

**appeal** *vb* **1** to make a request to the umpire for his decision on any of various matters; especially, to request a decision as to whether a batsman is out:

> *'On no account ought he to appeal unnecessarily. It is bad form, of which no cricketer should be guilty'* (Ranji 1897, p 142).

~ *n* **2** an act of appealing to the umpire:

> *'An appeal of great conviction against Sarfraz for a caught-behind was turned down early on'* (Scyld Berry, WCM May 1984).

The fielding side appeals to the umpire by shouting 'How's that?', or any phonologically similar expletive, and it has been enshrined in the rules of the game since the earliest times that the umpires 'are not to order any Man out, unless appealed to by one of the Players' (*Laws* 1744; Law 27 §1 is the modern equivalent). In practice, however, appeals are most significant in cases where the issue may be open to dispute, as when a batsman appears to be lbw, stumped, narrowly run out, or caught off a fine deflection. There has been some discussion recently about possible ways in which indiscriminate appealing might be curtailed. Concern has been expressed about 'the intimidatory ploy of attempting to grind a favourable decision out of an umpire by weight of appeals' (Michael Melford, *Cricketer* December 1982). The sort of measures suggested would entail a restriction on the right of appeal to those fielders best qualified to judge a particular case – for example the bowler and wicket-keeper in the case of an lbw appeal, or the bowler and catcher in the case of a close bat-pad catch. For the time being, however, the obvious difficulties of enforcing such restrictions have deterred the game's legislators from making any change in the Laws.

Appeals for an umpire's decision can also be made in the case of a ball becoming unfit for play, or in the event of a deterioration of the light:

*'After agreeing to continue to play in unfit light conditions, the Captain of the batting side . . . may appeal against the light'* (*Laws* 3 §8).

**approach-shot** *n* an unorthodox attacking stroke played with a full swing of the bat (the term is borrowed from the vocabulary of golf):

*'He really scarcely made a fine stroke throughout, and he indulged in an extraordinary variety of approach-shots and mishits all over the field'* (Headlam 1903, p 43).

**arm** *n* – **with the arm** (of a ball) maintaining, after pitching, the direction imparted by the swing of the bowler's arm; continuing in its original line of flight without any deviation:

*'By operating round the wicket . . . Yardley probably forced the batsmen to play more often, and at length Lamb, pushing at one*

*which went on with the arm, was neatly picked up at slip'*
(Mike Carey, *Daily Telegraph* 15 December 1982).

*'He [Laker] could appear to spin the ball hard, only for it to float on with the arm for a catch to slip or the wicketkeeper'* (Arlott 1983, p 44).

Like the googly, the ball that goes 'with the arm' is unsettling (and frequently deadly) because it does the unexpected. The effect is most marked in the case of an off-break bowler coming round the wicket, so that the ball goes away from the batsman at a considerable angle. The term tends nowadays to be restricted to spin-bowling contexts, but was formerly used to describe any type of bowling. The basic principle is that 'unless the ball be very loosely held, it is practically impossible to bowl a ball which, after pitching, goes on in exactly the same straight line' (Ranji 1897, p 75). Hence 'the ball that "goes with the arm" . . . is very deadly' (*ibid*, p 106).

**arm ball**  *n* a ball that goes on 'with the arm':

*'Ten runs later, at 230, Gomes was caught at short-leg from Venkat's arm ball'* (Dilip Rao, *Guardian* 18 April 1983).

**Ashes,** the *n* the title held by the current champions in the continuing competition between the national cricket teams of England and Australia. The title is regularly contested in Test series played in both countries, and changes hands only if the current holders lose a rubber. The Ashes do also exist as a physical entity (see below) but these are permanently housed at Lord's irrespective of which country currently 'holds the Ashes'. The name of the title originates from a mock obituary published shortly after England's first-ever defeat by Australia on English soil, when magnificent bowling by Spofforth (who took 14 for 90) carried Australia to a dramatic 7-run victory:

*'In Affectionate Remembrance of ENGLISH CRICKET, which died at the Oval on 29th August, 1882. Deeply lamented by a large circle of Sorrowing Friends and Acquaintances, R.I.P. N.B. – The body will be cremated, and the Ashes taken to Australia'* (*Sporting Times* 2 September 1882).

In the winter of the same year an English team led by the Hon Ivo Bligh went to Australia and 'regained the

Ashes' by beating the Australians in a three-match series. For this achievement Bligh was presented by some English ladies with a small urn containing the ashes of a set of bails they had burned. The urn was kept by Bligh until his death in 1927, when it was bequeathed to the MCC.

**asterisk** *n* a batsman's innings that has been completed without the batsman being dismissed, so called because an asterisk is conventionally used in reporting the score to indicate a not-out figure – thus: England 358 (Botham 149*):

> *'Another asterisk next day – 41 not out in the NatWest triumph at Southampton – undoubtedly influenced his nomination for the England squad'* (Doug Ibbotson, WCM September 1984).

**attack** *n* the bowling resources available to a side; the bowlers considered collectively:

> *'Tavaré was caught sweeping at Zaheer, whose presence in their attack was the measure of its motleyness'* (Scyld Berry, *Observer* 19 June 1983).

**attacking field** *n* any arrangement of fielders that is primarily intended to get batsmen out rather than to prevent them from scoring runs:

> *'Both bowlers had a full attacking field, as in the first innings, dispensing with the run-saving positions for a start'* (Peebles 1959, p 80).

An attacking field is appropriate in any situation in which the bowling side has the initiative, or wishes to seize it, as when bowling with the new ball or to a newly-arrived batsman, or when the wicket is taking a lot of spin. It may also be employed against a side batting last when the bowling side has plenty of runs to play with but needs to bowl the opposition out in order to win. An attacking field is characterised by a tight cordon of close fielders whose job is to take catches, tie the batsmen down by preventing quick singles, and generally to exert psychological pressure. A typical attacking field for a fast bowler would include three or four slips, a gully, a forward short leg, and perhaps a silly point or short extra cover; run-saving positions like third man and long leg will usually be dispensed with, so that any ball which penetrates the inner ring of fielders is likely to bring plenty of runs. Compare DEFENSIVE FIELD.

**average** *n* **1** (also **batting average**) the arithmetic mean of a batsman's scores during a given period (such as a season or an entire career) and at a given level (such as first-class, Test, or one-day games), calculated by dividing the total number of runs he has scored by the number of times he has been dismissed. Thus, Sir Donald Bradman's career batting average in Test matches is 99·94, arrived at by dividing his aggregate score (6996 runs) by the number of times he was out (70). This is conventionally shown in tabular form, thus:

| M | I | NO | R | HS | A |
|---|---|----|---|----|---|
| (matches) | (innings) | (times not out) | (runs) | (highest score) | (average) |
| 52 | 80 | 10 | 6996 | 334 | 99·94 |

Other non-essential information may also be given, such as the number of hundreds and fifties the batsman has scored.

**2** (also **bowling average**) the mean number of runs that have been scored off a bowler's bowling for each wicket he has taken during a given period and at a given level, calculated by dividing the total number of runs scored off his bowling by the total number of wickets he has taken. Thus, Dennis Lillee's career bowling average in Test matches is 23·92, arrived at by dividing the number of runs scored off him (8492) by the number of wickets he took (355). This is conventionally shown in tabular form with figures for matches played, overs or balls bowled, maidens bowled, runs scored, and wickets taken. Other non-essential information may also be given, such as the number of times the bowler has taken five wickets in an innings or the average number of balls bowled per wicket taken.

**away** *adv* moving towards the off-side from a line initially closer to leg or middle stump, usually so as to go off in the direction of slip:

> 'Then Cowans came on and produced two magnificent deliveries which cut away from the batsmen' (Matthew Engel, *Guardian* 3 February 1984).

*'Fred Titmus . . . was never easy to hit, his control of length and line was brilliant, and of course he mastered that away-drifter better than anyone'* (Jim Laker, WCM December 1983).

**away-swing**  *n* = OUTSWING

**away-swinger**  *n* = OUTSWINGER

**AWCC**  *abbr* Australian Women's Cricket Council

**b** *abbr* BOWLED; used in the scorebook, following the name of a batsman and preceding the name of a bowler, to indicate the bowler responsible for or involved in the batsman's dismissal. On its own b signifies that the batsman has been bowled out; other modes of dismissal are signified by additional information, such as 'lbw b Lillee' or 'c Marsh b Lillee'.

**back** *adv* **1** striking or attempting to strike the ball from a position relatively close to the wicket, with most of the weight of the body thrown on to the BACK FOOT (qv):

> *'In playing back to a fast bowler, the thing to remember is, that there is very little time to make the stroke, the margin of error being exceedingly small'* (Ranji 1897, p 169).

> *'The short fast ball of ordinary height he could get back to for a slash behind point'* (James 1963, p 90).

**2** moving in towards the batsman from a line initially closer to off stump:

> *'On a sticky wicket a right-handed bowler who is making the ball break back will often have six men on the on-side'* (Warner 1934, pp 18–19).

> *'Favell was beaten and bowled by a very good ball, which Statham fetched back some way off the pitch'* (Peebles 1959, p 153).

Compare AWAY.

~ *adj* **3** (of a stroke or style of play) made by or characterised by the batsman playing back:

*'The hallmark of good back play is the use the batsman makes of the ground between the creases'* (MCC 1952, p 86).

*'When the score had reached 219 Hughes seemed to lose concentration and was caught behind playing a loose back stroke to Azeem'* (Henry Blofeld, *Guardian* 10 December 1983).

Compare FORWARD 1, 2.

**back-cut** (old) *n* **1** a LATE CUT (qv) or any cut stroke that sends the ball into the area well behind square:

*'Foster got 2 for a back-cut off Trumper, which curved away from Hopkins at third man'* (*Melbourne Argus* 15 December 1903).

~ *vb* **2** to strike the ball when making a back-cut:

*'Noble back-cut Arnold high to the boundary through the slips, perilously near to both Foster and Bosanquet'* (*Melbourne Argus* 12 December 1903).

**back foot** *n* the foot that is usually closer to the stumps when a batsman is standing at the crease; the right foot in the case of a right-handed batsman or the left foot in the case of a left-handed batsman. A 'back' stroke, in which most of the batsman's weight rests on the foot closer to the stumps, is said to be played 'off the back foot'. See also BACK 1 and compare FRONT FOOT.

**back-foot** *adj* (also **back-footed**) played, or tending to play, off the back foot:

*'The score was 21 when Phillips . . . played a wild back-footed drive at a ball from Azeem . . . and was caught behind'* (Henry Blofeld, *Guardian* 10 December 1983).

*'No great batsman is solely a back-foot or a front-foot player'* (Arlott 1983, p 61).

**backlift** *n* the movement by which the bat is brought backwards over the stumps before being swung forward again as the batsman plays a stroke, especially an attacking stroke off the front foot:

*'Lindwall . . . bowled the outswinger, the ball that gets the good players out; his yorker, which he reserved for batsmen with a high backlift, completed his range of deliveries'* (Sir Len Hutton, *Observer* 8 July 1984).

**back spin**    *n* a reverse spin imparted to the ball, causing it to lose pace significantly after pitching, with little or no lateral deviation. The ball is said to 'hang', as it comes on to the bat much more slowly than would have been predicted from its speed in the air.

**back-spinner**    *n* a ball delivered with back spin; like the top-spinner, it is 'very likely to cause a mistimed stroke, because the ball comes off the pitch at a pace different from that of its flight' (Ranji 1897, p 81).

**back up**    *vb* **1** (of the non-striker) to begin to move down the wicket as the bowler delivers the ball in order to optimise the chances of taking a run should the striker hit the ball:

> *'Evans was nearly caught wide on the leg side by Langley . . . then poor Bailey was run out backing up to Evans'* (Cardus 1978, p 209).

On the complicated legal situation arising when the bowler attempts to run out a backing up non-striker before the ball is delivered, see RUN OUT. To avoid problems, players are advised always to begin their advance down the wicket 'as the bowler delivers the ball but not before' (MCC 1952, p 102).

**2** (of a fielder) to move into a position behind another fielder in order to cover him in case he misses the ball; the term is applied especially to a fielder covering either the wicket-keeper or the bowler at the wicket when a ball is thrown in from the outfield:

*'The man who ought to be abused when an overthrow occurs is not the fieldsman who throws the ball but the men who should be backing up and are not' (Badminton 1888, p 250).*

**backward** *adj & adv* indicating a position somewhat behind the line of the batsman's wicket. The term may be used on its own ('standing a little backward of square') or in combination to indicate a modified fielding position that would normally be squarer on to the wicket, such as point or short leg:

*'The day started with a cool breeze blowing from backward square-leg' (Brearley 1982, p 60).*

Compare FORWARD 3 and see FIELDING POSITIONS.

**bad light** see LIGHT

**bag** *n* **1** the number of wickets a bowler takes in a given period, as in a match or series:

*'Tayfield was nursing a knee injury; but his bag for the series, 37 wickets, was a South African record' (Frith 1984, p 145).*

~ *vb* **2** – **bag a brace**: see BRACE.

In both senses, the word is borrowed from the vocabulary of shooting.

**bail** *n* either of the two pieces of turned wood that are laid across the top of a set of stumps to form a wicket. Each bail is 4⅜ inches long and should not project more than half an inch above the stumps. The wicket is 'down' if either of the bails is dislodged from the stumps by the ball or by the batsman (with his bat, body, or clothing). If the wind is exceptionally strong, the two captains may agree, with the umpires' consent, to dispense with the bails altogether.

'Bail' is an old word of French origin meaning a crossbar or crosspiece, and it had entered the English language by the 16th century. It was used (among other things) to describe the movable horizontal part of the little gate, or 'wicket', that served as the entrance to a sheep pen – and it was of course this wicket that, in an early version of the game, was used as a target for bowling at. The earliest (1744) code of Laws specifies a bail of six inches, and ever since then the length of the bails has been governed by developments in the size of the wickets (see WICKET[1]). The most important change, however, was the adoption of two bails instead of one, which followed (though not immediately) the introduction of a third stump in about 1775. The first reference to a second bail appears in an 'unofficial' edition of the Laws published in Maidstone in 1786, though the earliest MCC code (1788) still refers to a single bail. By the beginning of the 19th century, however, the modern two-bail wicket was firmly established.

**bail ball** (also **bailer**) *n* (obsolete) a good-length ball that rises to the height of the bails, especially one that dislodges the bails without disturbing the stumps:

> 'A more moderate pace resulted from the new discovery of a well-pitched bail ball' (Pycroft 1854 in *HM*, p 151).

> 'A bailer bowled Mr A. C. Lucas at 65' (Wisden 1878, p 185).

**Balista** *n* a type of bowling machine invented in the mid-19th century and used for providing batting practice. The Balista was a smaller, lighter, and apparently more sophisticated version of the older Catapulta:

> 'The principle of the new comer resembled very closely that of its prototype, and notwithstanding its comparative lightness, answered all the purposes for which it was constructed' (Box 1868, p 76).

See also CATAPULTA, BOWLING MACHINE.

**ball** *n* **1** the hard leather-covered ball with which the bowler attacks the batsman's wicket in cricket.

**2** a delivery of the ball by the bowler, often with reference to its type or quality:

> 'Hogan, the difficult nightwatchman, hooked the day's second ball to mid-wicket' (Tony Cozier, *Cricketer* January 1984).

> 'I have always been impressed with Marshall, although it is a pity he bowls so many short-pitched balls' (Sir Len Hutton, *Observer* 1 July 1984).

'The foundation of these balls is a cube of cork' (Box 1868, p 106), around which twine is wound to produce a spherical shape, which is in turn covered with two hemispheres of red leather (white if the ball is to be used in floodlit cricket). The leather pieces are stitched together to leave a raised seam, typically having six rows of stitching. The manufacturing process and the materials used have scarcely changed in 250 years. The dimensions of the ball have also remained remarkably constant. Established as 'between Five and Six Ounces' in the original (1744) code of Laws, its weight was fixed in 1774 at between 5½ and 5¾ ounces, and remains the same today. The size of the ball was first specified in 1838 (a circumference of 9 to 9¼ inches) and was slightly altered in 1927 to its present size of $8^{13}/_{16}$ to 9 inches. A new ball is used for each innings of a match, and the ball may also be changed during the course of an innings under certain circumstances: see NEW BALL, REPLACEMENT BALL.

**3 – with the ball** in one's capacity as bowler:

> 'He took a pair of spectacles at Lahore, but he had his revenge with the ball . . . and took altogether nine wickets for 46 runs' (Headlam 1903, p 162).

**balloon** *vb* to hit the ball high in the air but without sufficient force for it to carry a great distance, typically by playing a mistimed shot; the ball 'floats' upwards like a balloon and usually presents the fielding side with an easy catch:

> 'They had England's sixth wicket record for the taking when Botham . . . ballooned Cairns into the covers after they had added 232' (John Thicknesse, *Cricketer* March 1984).

**banana** *n* a ball that moves substantially in the air, describing a wide 'banana-shaped' arc as it swings into or away from the batsman:

> 'He [Dilley] played for England early last June in two one-day internationals against India . . . and bowled medium-paced bananas, which brought him the axe' (Scyld Berry, *Observer* 22 May 1983).

Despite the considerable lateral movement, the banana has a regular and predictable trajectory, and so poses much less threat to the batsman than the ball that swings in or away late. See SWING.

**bang** *vb* (of a fast bowler) to pitch the ball rather short of a length, with a pronounced follow-through, in order to extract the maximum possible bounce, especially if the wicket is slow or lifeless:

> 'The onslaught of Lindwall and Miller had been vehement but not always technically exacting. Too much short stuff to the off was banged down' (Cardus 1978, p 173).

> 'Imran's spell was fascinating because instead of banging the ball in on this lifeless wicket, he swung the ball and moved it off the seam' (Z. H. Syed, *Cricketer* March 1983).

**barndoor** *n* (obsolete) **1** 'a player that blocks every ball' *(OED)*.

**2 – the barndoor game** cautious, totally defensive batting; stonewalling:

> 'It was almost painful to watch a giant of six feet and a half playing the barndoor game when we knew that if he chose . . . he could pulverize the bowling' (G. Giffen, *With Bat and Ball* 1898, p 64).

**3 – the Barndoor Match** the Gentlemen v Players fixture of 1837. In 1837 it was decided that, since the Gentlemen had not won this fixture since 1822, their chances might be improved if the Players had to defend outsize wickets:

> 'The Gentlemen's wickets were 27 in. by 8; the Players' 36 in. by 12 in. This was called the Barn-Door Match' (Box 1868, p 91),

the name implying a target that is so large that it cannot possibly be missed. Despite these precautions, the Gentlemen somehow contrived to lose by an innings.

**barrack** *vb* to shout sarcastic or abusive comments about the performance of a team of player:

> 'The disappointed spectators at Sydney "barracked" at the Australian cricketers for the feeble stand they were making against MacLaren's eleven' (*Daily News* 18 December 1901).

Barracking was at one time an exclusively Australian phenomenon, described by Harold Larwood in the thirties as 'this growth on the body of Australian cricket' (Larwood 1933, p 87). The term apparently derives from the pidgin-Aboriginal *borak*, meaning 'ridicule' (used in the phrase 'to poke borak at') and may ultimately come from a similar Irish word meaning to boast or brag. But although the word is now fully absorbed into general world English, the practice is still associated above all with the denizens of 'the Hill' in Sydney or the notorious 'Bay 13' at the Melbourne Cricket Ground.

**bat** *n* **1** the implement with which the batsman strikes the ball and defends his wicket, consisting of a hitting part (the 'blade') with a flat face and a convex back, attached to a long cylindrical handle. The blade of the bat is made of willow and 'shall not exceed 4¼ inches/10.8cm. at the widest part' (Law 6). The handle of the bat is designed to deaden the shock waves transmitted from the blade by the impact of the ball. It consists of pieces of cane with thin strips of rubber in between, held together by a binding of twine and a rubber grip. The wedge-shaped bottom end of the handle (the 'splice') fits into a corresponding mortise in the blade, and the total length of the bat must not exceed 38 inches/96.5 centimetres. There is no statutory limit to the weight of the bat, but the average weight of a full-size bat is about 2 pounds 4 ounces,

THE BAT: STAGES IN ITS DEVELOPMENT

while big hitters will use bats weighing as much as 2 pounds 12 ounces and occasionally even more.

'Bat' is an Old English word meaning a stick or club, and the earliest types of cricket bat were long, heavy clubs that curved outwards towards the bottom, somewhat like a hockey stick. The shape was determined by the style of bowling then prevalent – fast underarm 'grubs' rolled along the ground. As John Nyren remarks, 'with such a bat, the system must have been all for hitting: it would have been barely possible to block' (Nyren 1833 in *HM*, p 85). But the development of more sophisticated bowling techniques in the late 18th century (see BOWLING) 'gave the bowler so great an advantage in the game, it became absolutely necessary to change the form of the bat . . . It was therefore made straight in the pod' (Nyren *ibid*). The original (1744) code of Laws had prescribed no limit to the size of the bat, and – as batsmen paid less attention to slogging and more to defence – this loophole was soon exploited, when in 1771 a certain Mr 'Shock' White went in to bat against Hambledon with a bat wider than the wicket itself. Within two days the Hambledon committee had drafted an amendment to the Laws in a minute worded as follows: 'In view of the performance of one White of Ryegate on September 23rd, that four and a quarter inches shall be the breadth forthwith. This 25th day of September 1771' (reproduced in R. S. Rait-Kerr, *The Laws of Cricket* 1950, p 33). The amendment was incorporated in the next revision of the code (1774) and the width of the bat has remained the same ever since; the limitation on the length of the bat – a less crucial dimension – was introduced in 1835. Down to about the middle of the last century bats were made all in one piece: the introduction then of the sprung cane handle marks the last important stage in the evolution of the bat.

**2** a batsman:

'By the time I left school at the age of eighteen I was a good defensive bat' (James 1963, p 43).

**3 – off/from one's own bat** from one's own scoring strokes:

'Tom Walker got five runs from his own bat more than the whole XXXIII of Norfolk' (Bat 1851, p 70).

Though no longer used in cricket contexts this phrase has – in its extended meaning – passed into the general language.

**4 – with the bat** in one's capacity as a batsman or batting side:

> *'Their recent improvement with the bat did not continue in Sydney and, without Imran, their bowling was again shown to be much too weak'* (Henry Blofeld, *Cricketer* March 1984).

~ *vb* **5** to use the bat; play as a batsman, especially in the manner specified:

> *'He* [May] *batted superbly throughout the tour, failing only in the last Test Match'* (Peebles 1959, p 203).

> *'The last hour of the third day saw Downton batting coolly and intelligently'* (David Frith, *WCM* August 1984).

**6** to have one's innings, either as an individual or a team:

> *'Hughes had won the toss and batted on an Adelaide Oval pitch which was obviously going to be full of runs'* (Henry Blofeld, *Guardian* 10 December 1983).

**bat-and-pad** see BAT-PAD

**bat gauge** *n* a device used for checking the width of a player's bat, apparently common in the period following the introduction of a regulation width for the bat (see BAT 1). The first bat gauge was 'an iron frame, of the statute width . . . constructed for and kept by the Hambledon Club; through which any bat of suspected dimensions was passed' (Nyren 1833 in *HM*, p 87).

**bat-pad** *adj & n* (also **bat-and-pad**) **1** (relating to) a close leg-side or off-side fielding position in front of the wicket, where a fielder is stationed in order to snap up catches from balls coming off the edge of the striker's bat and deflected by his pads:

> *'At "bat-pad" Mike Gatting dived far away to his right and could not cling on to it'* (Berry 1982, p 131).

> *'A low bounce means a high frequency of lbw appeals and the constant likelihood of bat-pad catches off the spinners'* (Dilip Rao, *Guardian* 6 March 1984).

'To the next ball there was a huge appeal for a bat-and-pad catch against Botham, which he greeted with disdain' (Robin Marlar, *Sunday Times* 31 July 1983).

With the advent of the helmet (even for fielders) the bat-pad fieldsman is becoming an increasingly common sight, and the term is now beginning to be used (as a noun) as a synonym for the more traditional forward short leg or silly point.

~ *adv* 2 as a result of a bat-pad catch:

'*Downton reached a heroic half-century in the 60th over and eventually fell bat-pad off Harper*' (David Frith, *WCM* August 1984).

~ *vb* 3 to dismiss a batsman by means of a bat-pad catch:

'*After . . . Mudassar had been bat-padded by Cook's arm ball, Saleem and Zaheer paid due care and attention and the innings settled down*' (John Thicknesse, *Cricketer* May 1984).

**bat's end** *n* (obsolete) = POINT, so called because the fielder stood a few yards from the striker in the direction of the end of his bat:

'*Col. Lennox . . . took the post of difficulty and danger, off at the bat's end, where he also acquitted himself with singular activity and address*' (*Kentish Gazette* 1791).

**batter** *n* a batsman:

'*Upon coming to the old batters of our club, the name of JOHN SMALL, the elder, shines among them*' (Nyren 1833 in *HM*, p 46).

This was formerly the more common term, but although it is still occasionally used it was largely superseded by 'batsman' in the mid-19th century, and survives now chiefly as a baseball term.

**batting** *n* the performance or ability of an individual batsman or of the batsmen in a team considered collectively:

> 'The Australian batting looked the more extensive on paper, with two batsmen of the calibre of Benaud and Davidson as low as seven and eight' (Peebles 1959, p 68).

**batting average** see AVERAGE

**batting order** see ORDER

**batting points** see BONUS POINTS

**BCCI** *abbr* Board of Control for Cricket in India

**BCCP** *abbr* Board of Control for Cricket in Pakistan

**BCCSL** *abbr* Board of Control for Cricket in Sri Lanka

**beamer** *n* a fast, high full toss aimed at the batsman's head:

> 'The beamer has been universally condemned by cricketers as an unfair delivery since the best batsmen have been unable to pick it up even in bright sunshine when well set' (Brearley 1982, p 73).

Bowling beamers constitutes 'unfair play' under Law 42, and the bowler is liable to the same disciplinary procedures as those governing fast short-pitched balls. See BOUNCER and see diagram at LENGTH.

**beat** *vb* to break through a batsman's defence, though without necessarily dismissing him:

> 'He moved the ball about, predominantly away from the right hander, and early on especially he beat the bat several times without anything to show for it' (Henry Blofeld, *Guardian* 10 December 1983).

> 'Then Madan Lal dismissed both within three balls, Heron touching a simple catch to Kirmani and Paterson beaten by one which kept low' (Tony Pawson, *Observer* 12 June 1983).

**bend** *vb* (old) to change direction after pitching; break:

> 'I had just made 14 off four balls from Lee, who was bowling

*off-turners that did not always bend much'* (Larwood 1933, p 156).

**beneficiary** *n* a player who has been awarded a benefit by his county:

> *'The size of a benefit depended far more upon the county than the beneficiary's value in terms of cricket to both his club and his country'* (Travor Bailey, *Cricketer* March 1984).

**benefit** *n* a method of providing a lump-sum payment to a professional cricketer in recognition of long service. Benefits were formerly awarded to players who were on the verge of retirement after a long career with their county, and the bulk of the money they received came from the proceeds of a single home county match of their own choosing (the **benefit match**). Since the last war, however, it has become usual for players to be given a benefit ten years after being capped by their counties, so that it is not unusual for a player to have two benefits in the course of his career. The significance of the benefit match itself as a source of income has steadily declined as county gates have fallen, and the emphasis has switched to more diverse methods of fund-raising spread over the whole of a player's **benefit season**, such as raffles, lotteries, special games against local clubs, and even celebrity golf matches.

Following an historic ruling by the House of Lords in 1927, the proceeds of a benefit are not subject to tax, but in order to maintain this advantage benefits cannot be formally guaranteed in players' contracts: they are simply understood to be part of the conditions of service. Compare TESTIMONIAL.

**bias** (obsolete) *n* **1** the 'break' put on the ball by a spin bowler:

> *'It is almost impossible for the umpire, standing where he does, to say that a ball wide-pitched will have the right bias to hit the wicket'* (Box 1868, pp 135–6).

~ *adv* **2** with break on the ball:

> *'It mattered not to him [Beldham] who bowled, or how he bowled, fast or slow, high or low, straight or bias'* (Mitford 1833 in *HM*, p 125).

**bite** *vb* (of the ball) to make firm contact with the ground on pitching, typically on a damp or 'green' wicket, enabling the bowler to produce substantial turn or movement off the pitch:

> 'The amount of break that can be effected depends much upon how far the ground is in a state receptive of the spin – how much, that is, it allows the ball to "bite"' (Ranji 1897, p 78).

> 'De Silva . . . got his leg-breaks to bite enough to dismiss Edgar and Coney to diving short-leg catches' (Christopher Wordsworth, *Observer* 19 June 1983).

**bits-and-pieces player** *n* a player who is neither a specialist batsman nor a specialist bowler, and whose ability in each of these departments does not entitle him to be considered a true all-rounder. A typical bits-and-pieces player will bowl medium-paced seamers or defensive 'pushed-through' spinners, and bat 'usefully' in the late middle order. Compare ALL-ROUNDER.

**blade** *n* the solid part of the bat, as distinguished from the handle, with which the ball is struck: see BAT.

**blind spot** *n* a point on the wicket – usually at a good length (see LENGTH) – where the ball, when pitching, causes the maximum difficulty for the batsman, either because he is momentarily unable to see the ball or because he is uncertain whether to play forward or back:

> 'A good-length ball pitching on or just outside the leg-stump is the most likely of all to light upon the "blind spot"' (Ranji 1897, p 80).

**blob** *n* (old) a batsman's score of nought; a duck:

> 'Mr Jardine encouraged me by at once snapping up the adventurous Vic Richardson for a blob' (Larwood 1933, p 104).

**block** *n* **1** the position adopted by a batsman at the start of an innings, with the bat held upright in front of the wicket and just inside the popping crease; guard:

> 'Alan [Kippax], after he took block, shuffled forward in front of the wicket a fraction of an inch at a time till the ball was delivered' (A. B. R. Roche, WCM January 1984).

~ *vb* **2** to stop the ball defensively with the bat:

> 'He blocked the doubtful balls, missed the bad ones, took the good ones and sent them flying to all parts of the field' (Dickens, *Pickwick Papers* 1837, ch 7).

**blockhole** *n* the mark or indentation in the pitch made by a batsman when 'taking block' and serving to fix his position in relation to the wickets and to guide him in assessing the ball's line of flight:

> 'After he [Sutcliffe] had taken guard and marked his block hole mathematically, he would pat the crease decisively 3 or 4 times' (Cardus 1978, p 92).

**board** *n* the scoreboard:

> 'Essex had made the poorest of starts to the day, Gooch and Gladwin both gone with only one on the board' (Norman Harris, *Sunday Times* 3 June 1984).

**body-break** *n* (old) = ACTION-BREAK:

> 'There has been a tendency in late years to rely on the medium-paced swerver rather than the man who relies on his pace combined with body break' ('Second Slip', *Cricketer* Spring Annual 1933).

**bodyline** *n & adj* fast leg-theory bowling, especially as used by the England fast bowlers during the 1932–3 Test series in Australia:

> 'Body-line bowling has assumed such proportions as to menace the best interests of the game, making protection of the body by the batsmen the main consideration' (telegram sent to MCC by the Australian Board of Control, 18 January 1933, the fifth day of the Third Test match at Adelaide).

See LEG-THEORY.

The term carries the clear implication of deliberate intimidation and for this reason Harold Larwood, the spearhead of England's attack in the Bodyline series, always objected to it: 'It was maliciously coined by a cute Australian journalist for the express purpose of misleading . . . The mere use of the term "Body" was meant to damn me and damn me it did' (Larwood 1933, p 18). Exactly which 'cute Australian journalist' coined the term has been a matter for some dispute. England's leg-theory tactics were already attracting comment before the first match of the Test series, and in late November 1932 the *Australasian* (a Melbourne weekly) carried an article by Jack Worrall on the game between MCC and An Australian XI, which had been played at Melbourne from the 18th to the 22nd of

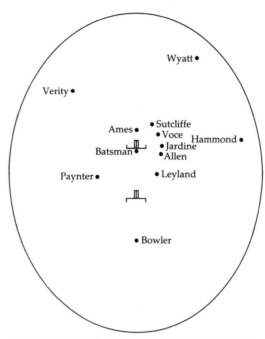

**LARWOOD'S LEG-THEORY FIELD FOR BRADMAN**

November. Worrall's comments included the following:

> 'Voce's half-pitched slingers on the body line provided about the poorest attempt at what should be Test bowling it is possible to conceive'.

The controversy was already in full swing by the time Australia went in to bat at Sydney on the first day of the First Test (2 December 1932). Later that day, the *Melbourne Herald* (Australia's leading evening paper) carried a piece on the game that had been telegraphed from Sydney at lunchtime by its reporter Hugh Buggy. Echoing the phrase used earlier by Worrall, Buggy's article included the expression 'bodyline bowling' and this seems to have been the first use of the term. It is unlikely that Buggy's intentions were malicious – he was probably just using telegraphic shorthand for 'bowling on the line of the body' – but his sub-editor Ray Robinson kept the phrase intact. At any rate it was quickly taken up by the rest of the press, and it probably helped to raise the temperature of the debate.

**bombada** (Corfu) *lit a 'bomb'*: a full toss.

**bonus points** *n* in the English County Championship, points awarded to a team on the basis of its batting or bowling performances in the first 100 overs of each first innings of a match, irrespective of the result of that match. In addition to the 16 points awarded to the winning side (or eight each in the event of a tie), a maximum of eight bonus points may also be scored by each side, as follows: four **batting points**, one for each 50 runs scored over 100 (maximum points being reached when 300 runs have been scored); and four **bowling points**, one point being awarded for the third wicket taken, a second for the fifth wicket, a third for the seventh wicket, and a fourth for the ninth wicket.

**booth ball** *n* (also **boother**) an early form of boundary hit, in which the ball, on reaching the tents or booths dotted around the edge of the ground, was declared dead and a stipulated number of runs was allowed to the batsman. Before the second half of the 19th century there were no boundaries as such, and runs were usually 'run out' in full: the 'booth ball' was an exception to this rule, perhaps on the grounds that the ball would have been expected to travel further but for the 'intervention' of the booth. See also BOUNDARY.

**boot hill** *n* (slang) a very close fielding position in front of the wicket, such as silly point or forward short leg. With its evocation of the Wild West (where the dead were buried on 'Boot Hill'), the term alludes to the extreme hazards of fielding in this position.

**bosie, bosey** *n* (especially in Australia) a googly, so called after its 'inventor' B. J. T. Bosanquet, who used this ball with considerable effect when bowling for MCC on the 1903–4 tour of Australia:

> 'He [Benaud] *varied his attack with a leg-break . . . a well-disguised bosie, and an excellent flipper'* (Jack Fingleton, *Four Chukkas to Australia* 1959, p 36).

**bottom edge** *n* the edge of the bat closer to the ground, *either* at the bottom of the blade *or* on the lower side of a bat held horizontally:

> '*As he hooked at Cowans . . . the ball crashed into the base of his stumps off the bottom edge*' (Robin Marlar, *Sunday Times* 31 July 1983).

**bottom hand**  *n* the lower of the two hands holding the bat (the right hand in the case of a right-handed batsman). The bottom hand gives firmness and solidity to a stroke, and a player is sometimes said to 'give it plenty of bottom hand':

> 'Roger Binny . . . displayed flair and innovative ability despite a dominant bottom hand' (WCM December 1983).

**bounce**  *n* **1** the quality in the wicket that determines the extent to which a bowled ball will rise after pitching. A 'plumb' wicket is characterised by its even and predictable bounce, but on wickets less favourable to batting the ball may rise more steeply than usual or (worst of all from the batsman's point of view) it may behave inconsistently from one delivery to the next, as a result of 'variable bounce':

> 'If the wicket is wet then only a light roller is used as a heavy one will draw up moisture and affect the bounce' (Harry Brind, WCM December 1983).

> 'Pakistan's chances of holding on for a draw on the pitch with the highest bounce in the country were never good (Henry Blofeld, *Cricketer* January 1984).

**2** the extent to which a bowler is able to make the ball rise from the wicket after pitching:

> 'Fowler was quickly undone by Garner's steep bounce' (Michael Carey, *Daily Telegraph* 1 June 1984).

~  *vb* **3** to bowl a bouncer at a batsman:

> 'I could see nothing wrong in bouncing Whitney, who is one of those irritating tail-enders who stop the straight balls and miss the wide ones' (Brearley 1982, p 140).

**bouncer**  *n* a fast short-pitched ball that rises after pitching so as to reach or pass the striker at or above chest height; a bumper:

> 'First Willis bowled a perfect bouncer at Chappell, not too short and dead straight. Chappell, protecting his face, could only lob the ball up for Taylor' (Brearley 1982, p 77).

'Bouncer' is a relatively modern term which has gradually superseded 'bumper' in the last twenty or thirty years. Any short-pitched ball is technically a bouncer, but the term is generally reserved for the ball that comes close enough to the striker to compel him

either to hit it or take evasive action to avoid being hit himself. The bouncer is accepted as a legitimate weapon in the fast bowler's armoury, provided it is used 'tactically' (to surprise or unsettle the batsman) rather than 'persistently' (to terrify him into submission). The first legislative attempts to control the use of bouncers came in the aftermath of the Bodyline series. An MCC directive of November 1934 instructed umpires to treat 'direct attack bowling' as unfair, and defined it as follows: 'Direct attack . . . consists in persistent and systematic bowling of fast, short-pitched balls at the batsman standing clear of his wicket'. The wording of the original ruling (which was incorporated into the Laws in 1939) reflects the contemporary preoccupation with fast leg-theory bowling. The modern ruling, however, provides a broader definition of what constitutes intimidation, as follows: 'Umpires shall consider intimidation to be the deliberate bowling of fast short-pitched balls which by their length, height and direction are intended or likely to inflict physical injury on the Striker' (Law 42 § 8).

Inevitably a ruling of this kind is open to widely divergent interpretations, and the subject of bouncers has become increasingly controversial in a period when at least two major Test teams are committed to a four-man fast-bowling attack. The situation is further complicated by a clause in the law to the effect that 'the relative skill of the Striker shall also be taken into consideration', so that the umpire has also to decide whether a player is to be regarded as a 'recognised' batsman for the purposes of the law. The arrival of the helmet has only made the situation worse, and may have had the paradoxical effect of turning tail-end batsmen (formerly a protected species) into legitimate targets for the bouncer. Further fine tuning of the legislation has so far had only limited success. The 1983 ICC meeting rejected a UK proposal that bouncers in Test matches should be limited to one per over, and in the same year the TCCB abandoned the four-year-old experimental rule that had enforced a one-per-over limit in the English domestic game – partly because 'English players felt that . . . to combat the bouncer they needed to get more practice against it' (Paul Fitzpatrick, *Guardian* 14 December 1983). The idea of drawing a line across the pitch at the halfway point (scornfully rejected by Larwood when it was suggested after the Bodyline tour) is now once again being canvassed in some quarters as a way of precisely defining the bouncer. At any rate, the distinction between the acceptable and unfair use of bouncers seems likely to remain a contentious issue.

Once the umpire is satisfied that a bowler's use of bouncers is 'unfair' he should invoke the following procedure: (1) signal 'no-ball' when a bouncer is bowled and caution the bowler; (2) repeat the process if the bowler again delivers a bouncer, and indicate that the warning is a final one; and (3) in the event of a further infringement, direct the captain to take the offending bowler off (even in the middle of an over), keep the bowler off for the rest of the innings, and report the bowler to the appropriate disciplinary body. It should be noted that the same procedure is to be used in the case of 'fast high full pitches', or 'beamers'. See also SHORT-PITCHED.

**boundary** *n* **1** the limits of the playing area, marked by a line, fence, or rope, or in some other way; reference can be made to particular sections of the boundary in terms of the nearest fielding position (thus, the **third man boundary**, the **mid-wicket boundary**, and so on).

**2** a shot by the batsman that sends the ball across the boundary:

*'He is batting with concentration, too, and rips a beautiful boundary straight past the bowler'* (Moorhouse 1979, p 20).

As a general rule, a ball reaching the boundary scores four runs and one that crosses it without bouncing scores six. These 'allowances' are, however, customary rather than statutory, and the *Laws* make provision for the possibility of local variation (see Law 19 § 2). Boundaries did not feature in cricket until the 1860s and before their introduction all hits had to be 'run out' in full (but *cf* BOOTH BALL). W. G. Grace says that there were no boundaries at Lord's when he first played there in 1864, but they were used in the Eton v Harrow match two years later, and first appear in the Laws in the revised edition of 1884. They seem to have been introduced mainly for the safety of the spectators, who might otherwise be trampled by overzealous fielders chasing the ball into the crowd.

The allowance of six runs for a hit clearing the boundary line did not become general until 1910 – prior to that, the ball had to be struck right out of the ground to score six. A variation of the rules applying in Australia at the turn of the century (until 1906) allowed five runs for a ball that cleared the boundary without bouncing.

**bounds** *n* in the single-wicket version of the game, a line marked on the pitch square with the wicket and to a length of 22 yards on either side of it. When the game is being played between sides of fewer than five players the ball must be hit into the area in front of the bounds before any runs may be scored.

**bowl** *vb* **1** to propel the ball in the direction of the striker's wicket by any fair and legal method of delivery (see BOWLING):

> 'When he has bowl'd one Ball, or more, he shall bowl to the number of Four before he changes Wickets' (Laws 1744).

**2** to complete an over by bowling the requisite number of balls:

> 'The game then changed dramatically in the 12th over, bowled by Cowans, who worked up a good pace' (Henry Blofeld, Cricketer February 1983).

**3** to dismiss a batsman by hitting his wicket with the ball so that one or both of the bails is dislodged:

> 'Cowdrey then bowled Roger Binny, who offered no stroke to a ball that cut back into him' (The News Line 10 January 1985).

**4** to bowl a ball or balls of a particular kind:

> 'Pat Pocock . . . won his first England cap at 21, and bowled crisp off-breaks with a confidence that sometimes troubled his captains' (Frith 1984, p 166).

**5** (of a captain) to put a particular player on to bowl:

> 'I had at times bowled Botham for extremely long spells, as I did in this match' (Brearley 1982, p 67).

**6** (of a team) to field:

> 'It seemed a strange decision when England, with two off-spinners in the side, were ideally suited to bowling last' (Henry Blofeld, Cricketer February 1983).

See also BOWL OUT.

**bowled** *adv* a mode of dismissal in which a batsman is given out if his wicket is put down by a ball delivered by the bowler, 'even if the ball first touches his bat or person' (Law 30 § 1). The dismissal is credited solely to the bowler and entered in the scorebook as 'b [bowler]'.

**bowler** *n* **1** the player who bowls the ball at the striker's wicket:

> 'The Bowler must deliver the Ball, with one foot behind the Crease, even with the Wicket' (*Laws* 1744).

**2** a player who specialises in bowling.

**3** (in combination) a player who bowls balls of a particular type or who has a particular function in the bowling attack (as in 'spin-bowler', 'change-bowler', etc.).

**bowling** *n* **1** the act, manner, or skill of delivering the ball to the batsman.

**2** the performance or ability of an individual bowler or of the bowlers in a team considered collectively:

> 'The Indian hero was Mohinder Amarnath who defied the bowling for three and a half hours for his first innings top score of 58' (Tony Cozier, *Cricketer* May 1983).

It is arguable that the evolution of cricket has to a very large extent been determined by developments in bowling, rather than by developments in batting. In the earliest days of the game the ball was literally 'bowled' along the ground with an underhand delivery and by the mid-18th century the bowler's repertoire consisted of a mixture of daisy-cutters and lobs. But in the last quarter of the 18th century, improvements in bowling technique revolutionised the game. The so-called 'length-ball' – a well pitched-up ball that bounced only once before reaching the striker – was perfected during this period, and its supreme exponent was the Hambledon player David Harris (*b* 1754). Harris's consistently penetrative bowling demanded fundamental changes in batting techniques, and this led to 'a revolution in the game, changing cricket from a backward and slashing to a forward and defensive game' (Pycroft 1854 in *HM*, pp 153–4).

The next major development was the evolution of 'roundarm' or 'straightarm' bowling, in which the ball is delivered with the arm extended more or less horizontally. As early as the 1780s Hambledon's Tom Walker had briefly experimented with something along these lines, but the real pioneer of the new style was John Willes of Kent, who bowled roundarm from about 1803 onwards. It caught on very quickly, and the often-quoted report of a Kent v All England game played in July 1807 seems to imply that not only Willes but most (if not all) of the bowlers in this match employed the new technique:

> 'The straight-arm bowling, introduced by John Willes, Esq., was generally practised in this game, and fully proved an obstacle against getting runs in comparison to what might have been got by the straight-forward bowling' (Sporting Magazine, quoted in Box 1868, p 73).

A rearguard action was mounted, but to little avail. Nyren (1833 in *HM*, p 41) warned that roundarm bowling would reduce 'the elegant and scientific game of Cricket' to 'a mere exhibition of rough, coarse horseplay', but neither the protestations of ex-players nor the attempts at preventive legislation (first in 1816, again in 1828) could halt its advance. The authorities finally capitulated in 1835, with a law that allowed the bowler's hand to be raised as high as the shoulder.

In fact, however, this could only be a temporary solution. It was already clear to many that the effectiveness of the straightarm delivery was greatly enhanced if the arm was raised *above* the level of the shoulder, so that, once roundarm bowling had been legalised, the transition to a modern-style overarm delivery was only a matter of time. Although the stipulations of the 1835 law were twice reinforced (in 1845 and 1858) overarm bowling became widespread, and umpires generally connived. In the notorious incident of 1862, when the England player Edgar Willsher was repeatedly no-balled for bowling overarm in an England v Surrey match, Willsher was simply bowling in his usual fashion. The point about the incident was that the umpire wanted to force a 'constitutional crisis' so that the issue could be resolved once and for all. Two years later the relevant section of the Laws was drastically pruned back, to read simply: 'The ball must be bowled' – thus legalising overarm bowling and bringing to an end a controversy that had raged for over 60 years. As one contemporary philosophically commented: 'The partial enforcement of the law as it stood, and the disagreements which were continually resulting therefrom, rendered almost any change an advantage' (Box 1868, p 119). Although underarm and roundarm bowling remain legal to this day both styles had become virtually obsolete within a generation of the recognition of the overarm style. See OVERARM, ROUND-ARM, UNDERARM.

**bowling average**    see AVERAGE

**bowling crease**    *n* a line marked on the ground at each end of the pitch, from which the bowler delivers the ball. The bowling crease is in line with the stumps and extends on either side of them to reach a total length of 8 feet 8 inches/2.64 metres (Law 9 § 1). The original (1744) code of Laws stipulated that the bowler's back foot (the right foot in the case of a right-handed bowler) should remain behind the bowling crease at the moment of delivery:

> 'If he delivers the Ball, with his hinder Foot over the Bowling-Crease, the Umpire shall call no Ball'.

The introduction of the RETURN CREASE (qv) later in the 18th century led to a redefinition of the no-ball rule, which no longer specifically mentions the bowling crease, though the coaching books still recommend that the back foot should land 'just behind and parallel to the [bowling] crease' (MCC 1952, p 30). The length of the bowling crease was fixed in 1774 at three feet on either side of the wicket, and it reached its present length in 1902. See illustration at CREASE.

**bowling machine**    *n* any of various mechanical devices designed to propel the ball towards the wicket in order to provide batting practice. Early examples of the species are the CATAPULTA and the BALISTA (qv), which were invented in the mid-19th century. But these rather Heath-Robinson contraptions were probably in their day a much less cost-effective expedient than simply hiring the services of a professional bowler. Their modern descendents, however, may well make better economic sense. One well-known bowling machine of the present day can, according to its own advertising copy, 'bowl up to 100 m.p.h., reproduce identical deliveries if required, and impart real swing or spin', as well as being 'instantly adjustable for line, length and speed'.

**bowling points**   see BONUS POINTS

**bowl out**   *vb* **1** = BOWL 3.

**2** to dismiss the batting side, but not necessarily by 'bowling' them:

> 'The trouble with putting the other side in in a Test match is that so much is staked on bowling them out on the first day' (Christopher Martin-Jenkins, *Cricketer* October 1983).

**3** to use up the over allowance of a bowler in a limited-over match:

> 'He [Malcolm Marshall] *took three for four in six balls to rip apart the middle of the Kent batting. But once Marshall was bowled out, Dilley and Ellison . . . hit out'* (Ian Ridley, *Guardian* 2 June 1983).

**box**   *n* **1** a genital protector, usually in the form of a triangular shield made of a strong light material, worn inside the trousers by batsmen.

**2** (old) a fielding position between point and slip; gully or backward point:

> 'Hobbs was caught in that nondescript position which is variously known as "the box" and "the gully"' (*Daily Mail* 29 June 1926).

'Box' was used interchangeably with gully in the earlier part of the century, before gully became established as the 'standard' term.

**brace**   *n* – **bag a brace** to score nought in each innings of a match:

> 'Trumble had followed Arnold's example and had "bagged a brace", having failed to score in each innings' (*Melbourne Argus* 4 March 1904).

'Brace' is of course a contraction of 'brace of ducks' and thus – in the great tradition of English euphemism – a resounding failure is made to sound like a highly creditable achievement. See also DUCK, PAIR.

**brain bucket** *n* (slang, especially in South Africa) a protective helmet.

**break** *n* **1** spin imparted to the ball by the bowler, or the resulting deviation of the ball after pitching (see SPIN):

> 'He [W. G. Grace] would give, apparently, the most tremendous twist to his fingers, making a grunt as though the act of putting on so much break were hurting him' (Cardus 1978, p 47).

**2** the direction taken by a ball that turns after pitching:

> 'He will hit against the break so hard and so often that the poor bowlers wish he would go back to hitting with it' (James 1963, p 216).

~ *vb* **3** (of the ball) to deviate from the original line of flight after pitching, as a result of spin imparted by the bowler:

> 'Immediately after lunch, however, he [Bosanquet] clean-bowled him with a ball which the Warwickshire wicket-keeper thought was breaking from the off and which broke from leg!' (Warner 1934, p 31).

**4** (of the bowler) to cause the ball to break in this way:

> 'I could bowl fast-medium with a high action, swing the ball late from leg and break it with shoulder-and-finger action from the off' (James 1963, p 43).

See also LEG-BREAK, OFF-BREAK, ACTION-BREAK, FINGER-BREAK.

**breakaway** *n* a ball that breaks 'away' from the batsman, moving from leg towards off after pitching:

> 'It means, too, that the demise of the finger-spinner – the right-arm off-break, or left-arm breakaway bowler – is hastened' (Arlott 1983, p 17).

**breakback** *n* a ball that breaks 'back' towards the batsman, moving from off to leg after pitching:

> 'He [W. C. Smith] differed in method entirely from the great majority of slow right-handers, for he relied chiefly on the ball that broke from leg . . . and not on the break-back like most of his class' (Warner 1934, p 43).

> 'Kapil Dev, having survived two slip chances off successive balls from Roberts when he was 86, was out for 88, lbw to a

*vicious breakback from Holding'* (Dilip Rao, *Guardian* 30 April 1983).

The term 'breakback' formerly embraced balls of any pace breaking from off to leg, but in modern usage it tends to be restricted to the faster ball and is thus synonymous with 'off-cutter'. Compare OFF-BREAK.

**bump** *vb* **1** (old) to rise steeply off the wicket after pitching, typically as a result of some irregularity in the surface; steeple:

> *'The wicket . . . played very queerly, the ball never coming off at a true pace and continually bumping or shooting'* (Headlam 1903, p 146).

**2** to bowl a bouncer at a batsman:

> *'Colin Croft . . . is not that fond of West Indian batsmen either, come to think of it, repeatedly bumping them in the nets'* (Peter Roebuck, *Cricketer* November 1982).

**bump ball** *n* a ball hit hard into the ground by the batsman and subsequently taken by a close fielder before it hits the ground again, thus presenting the illusion of a catch:

> *'When an umpire has to decide the question of a "bump" ball or not, he must be guided by its length, its flight from the bat, and the way in which the latter has been used'* (*Badminton* 1888, p 242).

**bumper** *n* **1** a fast short-pitched ball; a bouncer:

> *'There is a very great deal more in Fast-Leg-Theory than the mere delivery of "leg-side bumpers" – a feat, I should imagine, of which any lusty yokel is capable'* (Larwood 1933, pp 181–2).

**2** (old) any ball that rises steeply off the wicket after pitching; a 'bumping' ball:

> *'From the fact of the ground not being a good one, the "bumpers" of Lillywhite could not be mastered'* (*Bell's Life* 18 August 1855).

**bumpy** *adj* **1** (of the wicket) characterised by irregular or unusually steep bounce:

> *'A bumpy wicket is a wicket upon which you may get a shooter one over and a blow on the chest the next, as a pleasing variety to those that come frequently right over your head the first bound'* (*Badminton* 1888, p 309).

**2** (of a ball) rising steeply off the pitch:

> *'The little Lancastrian got 2 for a very clever hook off a bumpy one from Cotter, the ball being negotiated close to his left ear'* (*Melbourne Argus* 27 February 1904).

**bunsen** *n* (slang) a pitch conducive to spin bowling; a 'turning' wicket:

> *'Should they produce what county cricketers know as 'Bunsens', Pakistan can call on something of everything, while England have Nick Cook . . . and Vic Marks'* (Scyld Berry, *Observer* 26 February 1984).

This esoteric item of jargon from the English county circuit is rhyming slang, from 'bunsen burner' = 'raging turner'.

**buy** *vb* – **buy a wicket** to take a wicket by means of bowling and fielding tactics that offer the batsmen the opportunity of scoring quick runs, as by bowling to a deep-set defensive field in the hope of getting catches in the deep, or – in the case of a spin bowler – by flighting the ball rather than 'pushing it through' with a flat trajectory:

> *'He will now try to buy a wicket, Turner's above all, so he brings in his spin and spreads his field wide'* (Moorhouse 1979, p 60).

**bye** *n* (also formerly **bye-ball**) a run scored from a ball (other than a wide or no-ball) that passes the wicket without touching either the striker or his bat. Any runs accruing in this way (whether actually run or coming from a boundary) are credited to the batting side as byes, under 'extras', but not to the individual batsman, and the umpire signals a bye to the scorers by raising his arm above his head with the hand open.

Byes are not specifically mentioned in the original (1744) code of Laws, but seem already to have been a feature of the game by that time: the scores of the famous Kent v All England match played on 18th June 1744 include a record of the byes made by each team. It is likely that the term originally subsumed what were later distinguished as leg-byes, and when wides were first introduced they too were counted as byes. See EXTRAS.

# C

**c** *abbr* CAUGHT; used in the scorebook, following the name of a batsman and preceding the name of a fielder, to indicate the manner of the batsman's dismissal and the player responsible for it. In earlier times dismissals by catching were credited to the catcher alone; thus, in the Kent v All England match of 1744,

> *'Lord J. Sackville C by Waymark 5'* (Nyren 1833 in *HM*, p 86).

But since the early 19th century it has been usual to mention the bowler as well (thus 'c Marsh b Lillee'). See also C AND B.

**call** *vb* **1** (of the umpire) to declare that a bowler has made an unfair delivery; no-ball a bowler:

> *'Larwood opened the bowling to Woodfull and was "called" first ball for dragging his feet'* (*Melbourne Argus* 21 November 1932).

**2** (of a batsman) to shout to the batsman at the opposite end in order to indicate whether a run should be taken. The coaching books stress that, every time a ball is bowled, batsmen should call a clear 'Yes', 'No', or 'Wait'.

**~** *n* **3** an act of doing this, or the responsibility for doing this in a given situation:

> *'If the striker hits the ball in front of the wicket it is his call; if he hits it behind the wicket it is his partner's call'* (Henry Blofeld, *Guardian* 19 July 1983).

After the first run has been taken, the call for any

subsequent runs should be made by the player who will be running towards the end most immediately threatened.

**c and b** *abbr* CAUGHT AND BOWLED; used in the scorebook, following the name of a batsman and preceding the name of a bowler, to indicate that the batsman has been dismissed by a catch taken by the bowler of the ball.

**candidate** *n* (old) a batsman who is out for nought in his first innings and is thus in line for getting a 'pair' by scoring a second duck:

> 'Mr Jardine made a good catch in the slips to get rid of Vic Richardson who thus became a "candidate" and was duly elected in the second innings!' (Larwood 1933, p 151).

**cap** *n* **1** a notional award, in respect of a place in a particular team, made to a player each time he is selected to play for that team:

> 'Bob Taylor, in his 23rd season, maintained his remarkable consistency and won his 50th England cap during the series against New Zealand' (Wisden 1984, p 341).

**2** (also **county cap**) an award made in English first-class cricket to a player who is considered to have completed his 'apprenticeship' and become an established member of his county's playing staff; the change in status also has financial and contractual implications, and the minimum rates of pay for 'capped' players are considerably higher than for 'uncapped' players.

~ *vb* **3** to award a cap to a player:

> 'Since the war a benefit has been normally awarded after some 10 seasons as a capped player' (Trevor Bailey, Cricketer March 1984).

> 'Australia had made three other changes, capping the NSW slow left-armer Murray Bennett and recalling . . . Greg Matthews and . . . Andrew Hilditch' (WCM February 1985).

**captain** *n* **1** the player chosen as the leader of a cricket team.

~ *vb* **2** to act as the captain of a cricket team:

> 'Lloyd played a dominating innings and captained astutely,

*much more willing to experiment and adapt than his less experienced opposite number'* (Christopher Martin-Jenkins, *Cricketer* August 1984).

The captain is responsible for the overall strategy of his team in a match. His duties include marshalling the bowling attack, setting the field in consultation with the bowler, determining batting tactics and the timing of declarations, and of course – if he has won the toss – deciding whether to bat first of put his opponents in. In addition, each of the captains in a match is 'responsible at all times for ensuring that play is conducted within the spirit of the game as well as within the Laws' (Law 42 § 1). It is therefore up to the captain to ensure that none of his players indulge in time-wasting, 'sledging', argument with the umpire, or other undesirable behaviour.

**carpet** *n* the ground:

> *'Voce, who is usually such a good field, put two possible chances on the carpet when O'Brien was in the thirties and forties'* (Larwood 1933, p 152).

**carry** *vb* **1** (of a ball struck by the batsman) to continue in flight without touching the ground, especially so as to reach and be caught by a fielder:

> *'There is much less walking and rather more appealing, but people do not claim catches which do not carry'* (Peter Roebuck, *Cricketer* November 1982).

**2 – carry one's bat (out)** (of a batsman) to remain undismissed when one's team's innings has been completed or declared:

> *'The South African innings was soon over for 91, Nourse batting at no. 8 carrying out his bat for 18'* (Warner 1934, p 202).

> *'Nothing looked more certain than that Tavaré would carry his bat . . . but he was unexpectedly bowled as he tried to straight drive a near full toss'* (Richard Streeton, *The Times* 29 October 1982).

The phrase tends nowadays to be restricted to an opening batsman who has batted right through his side's innings, but earlier writers favoured a less exclusive interpretation which reflects the origin of the term. It comes from the time when a batsman who was dismissed left his bat behind at the wicket for the player coming in next, a practice reflected in several now-obsolete phrases like **to give up one's bat** or **to throw down one's bat**, which were once used to indicate a batsman's dismissal:

> 'He had delighted to hear the stumps rattle, and to see opponent after opponent throw down his bat and walk off' (Mary Mitford, *Our Village* 1830, ch IV).

**cart** *vb* to hit the ball or attack the bowling with unrestrained power:

> 'Understandably, he was not the Hughes who carted Mortimore for 24 in an over and drove Bedi for 26' (Terry Cooper, *WCM* September 1984).

**castle** *n* the wicket that a batsman is defending:

> 'Milton and Graveney carried the score to 91 before Milton very unluckily touched his own castle in playing back a little hurriedly at a ball well up to him' (Peebles 1959, p 95).

**Catapulta** *n* a primitive type of bowling machine invented in 1837 by 'Felix' (Nicholas Wanostrocht) and used for providing batting practice. According to its inventor, 'the history of this machine in its original form is traced back to the time of the Romans' (Felix 1850, p 33), and in fact the basic operating principle is the same as for the Roman war engine of the same name. In the case of Felix's Catapulta, however, the ball is not hurled by the arm that swings forward but is 'made to rest upon a stage and struck from it after the manner of a billiard ball' (*ibid*, p 34). The machine also incorporated a variety of adjustable mechanisms that enabled the ball to be 'propelled with the greatest exactitude as respects both pitch and pace' (Box 1868, p 76). Thus, for example, 'a plate upon which the ball rested would, by a lateral movement upon a screw, enable the attendant to deliver it either on, or off, at pleasure' (*ibid*). The manufacture and retailing of the machine was in the hands of Mr W. H. Caldecourt, from whom it could be bought (in 1850) for '11*l*.11*s*. complete with the latest improvements' (Felix 1850, p 8). See also BALISTA, BOWLING MACHINE.

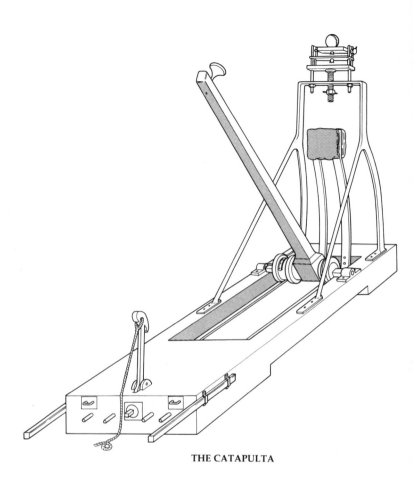

THE CATAPULTA

**catch** *vb* **1** to take and keep hold of the ball after it has been hit by the batsman and before it has made contact with the ground:

> *'It flew fast to fourth slip, where Gower . . . caught the ball above his head'* (Brearley 1982, p 117).

**2** to dismiss a batsman by catching the ball in this way:

> *'The next ball had Burke dabbing outside the off stump and caught by Evans'* (Peebles 1959, p 76).

~ *n* **3** an act of catching the ball and thereby dismissing the batsman who hit it:

> *'Allen hit well with Voce in and was unfortunate to miss his 50, Bradman bringing off a magnificent catch'* (*Cricketer* Spring Annual 1933).

**4** a ball hit by the batsman that gives the fielding side a reasonable opportunity of making a catch; a chance:

> *'If possible, it is best to get to a catch in time, and take it standing still with both hands'* (Ranji 1897, p 20).

A catch is only valid if the ball has touched the striker's bat or his hand holding the bat (see CAUGHT). This is essentially the position outlined in the original (1744) code of Laws, but there is some evidence to show that, at an earlier stage still, catches *behind* the wicket did not carry the penalty of dismissal (R. S. Rait-Kerr, *The Laws of Cricket* 1950, p 3). It is in any case reasonable to suppose that catching was a less prominent feature of the game during its most primitive phase, when the ball was rolled along the ground to the batsman. The most recent amendment to the regulations governing catches deals with the novel situation of the ball becoming trapped in the cage-like structure at the front of some helmets, and states that 'a Striker may not be caught if a ball lodges in a protective helmet worn by a Fieldsman' (Law 32 § 2(b)).

**caught** *adv* a mode of dismissal in which a batsman is given out 'if the ball touches his bat or if it touches below the wrist his hand or glove, holding the bat, and is subsequently held by a Fieldsman before it touches the ground' (Law 32 § 1). The catcher must be within the field of play – with no part of his body grounded over the boundary line – throughout the act of making the catch. The dismissal is credited to the bowler and is entered in the scorebook as 'c [catcher] b [bowler]'. A batsman cannot be out caught off a no-ball. See also CATCH.

**caught and bowled** see C AND B

**caught behind** *adv* dismissed by a catch taken by the wicket-keeper:

> 'Hookes played a loose stroke to be caught at extra cover off Baptiste, who also had Border caught behind' (Tony Cozier, *Cricketer* January 1984).

**centurion** *n* a batsman who scores a century:

> 'Martin Crowe, at 21 years 123 days, became the third-youngest New Zealand Test centurion' (*WCM* March 1984).

**century** *n* a batsman's score of 100 runs or over, made in a single innings:

> 'Chappell now holds the unique record of having scored a century in his first and last Test innings' (Simon Wilde, *WCM* March 1984).

See also DOUBLE CENTURY, HALF-CENTURY.

**chance** *n* an opportunity for dismissing the striker, especially from a stroke that gives the fielding side a reasonable chance of taking a catch:

> 'His century was marred by two chances early in the game' (Headlam 1903, p 121).

> 'It was ironic that the great Viv Richards should make only six, and that after surviving a chance to the wicket-keeper off Terry Alderman' (Dilip Rao, *Guardian* 2 April 1984).

**chanceless** *adj* made without any opportunity for dismissal being given:

> 'Mohsin and Shoaib . . . put on 173 chanceless and scintillating runs' (Robin Marlar, *Sunday Times* 25 March 1984).

**change** *n* (old) = CHANGE-BOWLER:

> 'They are generally moderate bowlers . . . who are often very valuable to their side as changes' (*Badminton* 1888, p 194).

**change-bowler** *n* a bowler, typically not a specialist, whose principal function is to relieve the regular bowlers or to enable a front-line bowler to change ends:

> 'After they had taken 17 in two overs from the change bowlers, Gatting and Smith, Gower . . . had to act quickly and bring back the quicks' (Matthew Engel, *Guardian* 4 January 1984).

W. G. Grace, regarded in his day as 'the best change bowler in England, bar none' (*Badminton* 1888, p 215) took nearly 3000 wickets in his career. But a modern change-bowler, though occasionally effective as a partnership-breaker, is looked to principally for containment. See also FIRST CHANGE.

**change ends** *vb* to bowl from the opposite end of the wicket to that from which one bowled previously:

> 'A Bowler shall be allowed to change ends as often as desired, provided only that he does not bowl two overs consecutively in an innings' (Law 22).

The current law has been in force since 1889. Originally the bowler was allowed to change ends 'but once in the same Innings' (*Laws* 1744), but when he did change he could bowl two overs in succession. In 1870 the law was amended to allow the bowler two changes per innings, provided still that no more than two overs were bowled consecutively. The modern rule, by which consecutive overs were finally banned, was established – significantly enough – at the same time as the first increase in the length of the over. See OVER.

**chinaman** *n* **1** (especially in Britain) a ball bowled by a left-arm wrist-spin bowler that breaks from off to leg when bowled to a right-handed batsman; the 'stock' ball of a left-arm wrist-spinner.

**2** (especially in Australia) a ball bowled by a left-arm wrist-spin bowler that breaks from leg to off when bowled to a right-handed batsman; the left-arm wrist-spinner's googly. Compare GOOGLY.

Left-arm wrist-spin was pioneered in Britain by the Yorkshiremen Roy Kilner (in the twenties) and

Maurice Leyland (in the thirties); while the Australian 'Chuck' Fleetwood-Smith (who also played in the thirties) was 'the founder of prodigious left-arm googly bowling in Australia' (Frith 1984, p 108), where the art flourished with practitioners like Jack Walsh and George Tribe. The origins of the term itself cannot be established with any certainty. The earliest *OED* citation for 'chinaman' is from 1937, and it is commonly supposed to have been named after Ellis Achong, a Trinidadian left-arm bowler of Chinese descent who played six Tests for the West Indies between 1929 and 1933. David Frith reports the story of Walter Robins, who, when stumped off Achong's bowling, is said to have 'turned to Learie Constantine and thundered, "Fancy getting out to a bloody chinaman!"' (Frith 1984, p 113). This sounds a little too good to be true, and it seems more likely that the term derives from the (somewhat racist) connotations of inscrutability or deviousness which have traditionally attached in English to the words 'Chinese' and 'Chinaman' (cf next entry).

**Chinese cut** *n* **1** a batting stroke made unintentionally when the batsman, attempting to play an attacking shot, fails to read the line of the ball and deflects it off the inside edge of the bat:

> *'His first over with the new ball cost 16 runs, eight of them from a stroke known to me in my schooldays as the "Chinese cut", an attempted forcing shot off the back foot on the off-side where the ball is edged past the stumps down to fine leg'* (Brearley 1982, p 117).

~ *vb* **2** to hit the ball when playing a Chinese cut:

> *'Cheerful ones merely smile sadly as some clown of a batsman misreads a googly and Chinese cuts it'* (Peter Roebuck, *Cricketer* November 1982).

**chop** *n* a form of cut, usually played to a ball that keeps unexpectedly low, in which the bat is held horizontally and brought sharply down on the ball just after it has passed the batsman. 'The action is, as it were, an exaggeration of the cut' (Ranji 1897, p 186) and somewhat resembles the wielding of an axe – hence the name. See CUT 1.

**chucker** *n* a bowler whose action is regarded as 'unfair' in that it approximates to throwing rather than bowling:

'Jack Saunders . . . described by his Test captain Joe Darling as "the dirtiest chucker Australia ever had", took 79 wickets at moderate cost in 14 Tests between 1902 and 1908' (Frith 1984, p 75).

**clean bowl** *vb* to bowl a batsman out with a ball that knocks his wicket down without first touching his bat or body:

'At the follow on Davis immediately struck again, clean bowling McEvoy' (Eric Hill, *Daily Telegraph* 10 August 1984).

**close** *n* = CLOSE OF PLAY:

'At the close England found themselves very handily placed with the West Indies 239 for seven' (Matthew Engel, *Guardian* 14 July 1984).

**close of play** *n* the prearranged time at which a day's play finishes. The exact time varies widely according to local rules and conditions, but two generally applicable points of law should be noted, viz that 'The last over before an interval or the close of play shall be started provided the Umpire, after walking at his normal pace, has arrived at his position behind the stumps at the Bowler's end before time has been reached', and that 'An over in progress at the close of play on the final day of a match shall be completed at the request of either Captain even if a wicket falls after time has been reached' (Law 17 §§3,5).

**closure** *n* the voluntary closing of an innings; declaration:

> 'When eight wickets had fallen and 306 was on the board,
> Hollins declared the innings closed. The closure, as it turned out,
> was very neatly timed' (Headlam 1903, p 187).

**coffin** *n* (slang) a cricketer's holdall for clothing and equipment:

> 'Colchester is one of these places where you change by rota, the
> rooms being too tiny to tolerate 11 cricketers and their "coffins"'
> (Peter Roebuck, *Cricketer* November 1982).

**collar** *vb* to dominate completely the bowling of an opposing team or player:

> 'Pringle bowled better at the end of the innings, so that Essex
> were never collared as Gooch was to collar Middlesex' (Robin
> Marlar, *Sunday Times* 24 July 1983).

**country** *n* the area of the field furthest from the wicket; the deep:

> 'The amount of runs that can be saved or given away during two
> long inningses by a fieldsman in the country . . . is astonishing. It
> would do no one any harm to write up a memorandum of the fact
> above his bed [!]' (Ranji 1897, p 17).

**county championship** *n* the premier competition in British cricket, involving (currently) 17 first-class county teams which play a total of 24 three-day games. The championship is based on a league system in which points are awarded to the winning team in any given match, while either side may also score BONUS POINTS (qv) for their batting and bowling performances in the first innings. Games involving English county teams have been played on a regular basis since the beginning of the 18th century, and several of the present county clubs have existed in their present form since the mid-19th century. The modern county championship, however, dates back only as far as 1890. From the 1860s onwards, an unofficial competition had been encouraged by the sporting press, which usually determined the 'champions' on the basis of the team that lost the fewest games. This 'championship', with a more sophisticated scoring system, was officially constituted in 1890, and the first champions were Surrey. A major reorganisation of the championship programme in 1969, following the introduction of one-day competitions in the early sixties, considerably reduced the number of three-day fixtures. From 1977 to 1983 the championship was sponsored by Schweppes, and since 1984 it has been sponsored by Brittanic Assurance.

**cover** *n* **1** = COVER POINT:

> *'He* [Constantine] *goes to British Guiana with the inter-colonial team, does nothing to speak of with bat or ball, but . . . emerges as one of the most brilliant covers ever seen in the West Indies'* (James 1963, p 108).

~ *vb* **2** to stand behind and deeper in the field than another fielder in order to stop any balls which pass him:

> *'In those days of fast bowling they would put a man behind the long-stop, that he might cover both long-stop and slip'* (Nyren 1833 in *HM*, p 62).

The term is used extensively in early descriptions of field placings to define the functions of a number of deep fielders. The idea survives nowadays only in the term cover point.

**3** to put covers over the pitch, the bowlers' run-ups, or any other part of the field as a protection against rain. The Laws state that 'The pitch shall not be completely covered during a match unless prior arrangement or regulations so provide' (Law 11 § 2). In practice, however, local playing regulations do in general provide for the covering of the pitch for most of the time when it is not being used. For example, the TCCB's playing conditions for English first-class cricket state – in a rule first established in 1980 – that the pitch should be covered 'on each night of the match and, if necessary, throughout Sunday' and 'in the event of play being suspended on account of bad light or rain'. While no doubt making life easier for the batsman, this arrangement 'virtually eliminates the element of weather-chance which in the past made English cricket so absorbingly unpredictable' (Arlott 1983, p 76). And, as many commentators have ruefully observed, the virtual disappearance of the 'sticky' wicket has contributed to the continuing decline in slow bowling.

**cover drive** *n* a form of drive, usually played to a good-length ball pitching just outside off stump, by which the ball is sent past cover point. See DRIVE.

**cover-drive** *vb* to strike the ball when making a cover drive:

> *'Gifford opens from the pavilion end and is cover-driven for 4 off his first delivery by Williams'* (Moorhouse 1979, p 65).

**cover-nips** see NIPS

**cover point** *n* (also **cover**) an off-side fielding position (or the player occupying it) anywhere in an arc between point and extra cover, deeper than point but close enough to the batsman to save the single. The fielder in this position was originally referred to as 'The Man who covers the Point and Middle Wicket' (Boxall 1800, p 62). See also COVERS, EXTRA COVER, and FIELDING POSITIONS.

**covers** *n* the entire area patrolled by cover point and extra cover:

> *'They added 32 runs in 34 minutes, with Vengsarkar twice crashing the ball through the covers'* (Dilip Rao, *Guardian* 26 October 1983).

**cover slip** see SLIP

**cowshot** *n* a cross-batted heave, typically played to a ball pitching outside off stump, in which the batsman goes down on one knee and pulls the ball round from off towards the leg-side boundary; a stroke resembling the sweep, but having a more 'random' quality and usually associated (hence the name) with the uncomplicated 'rustic' slogging of the genuine tailender:

> *'If the crowd were keen on naught but Surrey's chances in the match, a cowshot by Hutch would cause as much satisfaction as Hobbs' master-stroke'* (Cardus 1978, p 38).

**cow corner** *n* the part of the leg-side boundary towards which the ball is propelled by a cowshot, roughly between long leg and deep square leg:

> *'Surrey . . . only avoided their lowest ever score (12) by an edge through the slips and a wild swipe to cow corner'* (Peter Roebuck, *Cricketer* November 1983).

**cradle** *n* an apparatus used for catching practice, consisting of a concave, roughly boat-shaped frame fitted with wooden slats; balls are thrown at the cradle with a low trajectory, especially in order to provide practice in slip-catching.

**crease** *n* **1** any of the lines marked on the ground at each end of the pitch and used to indicate the limits of a batsman's ground or the area within which a bowler may fairly deliver the ball. These are the BOWLING CREASE (qv) and the POPPING CREASE (qv), both of which

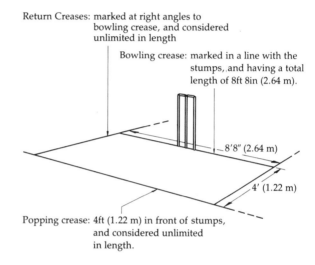

Return Creases: marked at right angles to bowling crease, and considered unlimited in length

Bowling crease: marked in a line with the stumps, and having a total length of 8ft 8in (2.64 m).

8'8" (2.64 m)

4' (1.22 m)

Popping crease: 4ft (1.22 m) in front of stumps, and considered unlimited in length.

are mentioned in the original (1744) code of Laws, and the RETURN CREASE (qv), which makes its first appearance in the 1774 code. The basic meaning of crease is 'a furrow in a surface', and originally the creases were actually cut in the turf. According to Charles Box (1868, p 111), 'the practice of cutting the creases was kept up at Marylebone till within the last five years, much to the detriment of the ground'.

**2 – at the crease** having one's innings; batting:

'Neale . . . only recaptured Wednesday's fluency in patches during his six hours and one minute at the crease' (Peter Ball, The Times 27 July 1984).

**cricket** *n* **1** the game itself:

'John Denwick of Guldeford . . . being of the age of fyfty and nyne yeares . . . saith upon his oath that hee hath known the parcell of land . . . for the space of Fyfty years and . . . that hee being a schollar in the Free schoole of Guldeford, hee and several

*of his fellowes did runne and play there at Creckett and other*
*plaies' (Guild Merchant Book,* Guildford 1598).

**2** the manner or quality of play at cricket:

*'Gower and Botham apart, the batsmen . . . gave the impression*
*that far too little thought had gone into England's cricket'*
(Henry Blofeld, *Cricketer* February 1983).

~ *vb* **3** to play cricket:

*'At Harrow I was always cricketing – rebelling – fighting –*
*rowing'* (Lord Byron, *Letters & Journals* 1830).

Speculation as to the origins of the game, and the etymology of the word itself, has been going on for over 150 years without coming up with any very conclusive answers. The term cricket is variously thought to be derived from the target aimed at and the implement used in defending it. In the former case it is argued that the word is related to Flemish or Low German *krick-stoel*, a long low stool (resembling the earliest types of wicket in shape), and the theory to some extent rests on the likely connection of cricket and stool-ball at an early stage in their evolution. The more popular interpretation connects 'cricket' with the Old English *crycc* or (more plausibly) Middle Flemish *crick*, a staff for leaning on (from which 'crutch' is also derived). Neither theory is at all conclusive, and it would be unwise to argue with the *OED*'s verdict of 'Etymology uncertain'.

As for the game itself, strenuous efforts have been made to demonstrate its extreme antiquity, and references of the most tenuous kind have been seized upon to support some fairly speculative theories. The best-known and perhaps most plausible of these is a reference in Edward I's Wardrobe accounts for 1299–1300 to 'Monies disbursed for the said Prince's playing at *Creag* and other sports'. But the almost total absence of corroborative evidence for the medieval period – such as references in legal documents and literary works – casts serious doubt on the idea that cricket, in anything remotely like its present form, was being played as early as this. The first genuinely reliable reference (quoted above) is dated 1598 and refers to a period about 50 years earlier, so that it is reasonably safe to assume that cricket was being played in the south of England by at least the early 16th century.

It is in the 17th century that references to cricket begin to come thick and fast. Royalist propaganda directed at Cromwell condemns the 'dissolute and dangerous course' of his youth, when he had been 'famous for foot-ball, cricket, cudgelling, and wrestling'. Cricket, then, was already being played in London when Cromwell was a boy (the early 1600s). Later in the same century it seems to have made the transition from being a pastime indulged in by children (or, according to a more bucolic version, Kentish shepherds) to a game played by adults and, increasingly, patronised by the nobility and gentry, who were especially interested in its potential as a medium for gambling. By the end of the 17th century it was a well-established game played in both urban and rural settings. For technical developments, see individual entries, especially BAT, BOWLING, WICKET[1].

**cricketal** (also **cricketical**) *adj* (obsolete) of or relating to cricket:

> 'The juncture was critical, not cricketal' (R. A. Fitzgerald, *Wickets in the West* 1873, p 288).

> 'The "Hawks" was the first of a number of clubs, run upon more or less similar lines . . . partly social and partly cricketical' (Ranji 1897, p 349).

**cricketer** *n* a person who plays cricket.

**cricketress** *n* (obsolete) a woman who plays cricket:

> 'All Alfred Mynn's sisters were famous cricketresses' (*Pall Mall Gazette* 2 June 1890).

**cross** *vb* to hit the ball across its line of flight with a horizontal bat:

> 'I do not consider it good play to cross the ball from one side to the other' (Boxall 1800, p 41).

> 'To cross a ball is the worst of all bad play' (Nyren 1833 in *HM*, p 26).

**cross bat** *n* a bat held in a slanting or horizontal position so that, in the execution of a stroke, it moves *across* the line of flight of the ball rather than straight down it:

> 'Some of the most effective scoring strokes are those played with a relatively "cross", i.e. horizontal, bat' (MCC 1952, p 88).

The cross bat is used exclusively for attacking shots, such as the hook, pull, or cut, and was at one time regarded with the utmost suspicion. In his *Young Cricketer's Tutor* (1833) John Nyren extols the virtues of the upright bat and repeatedly warns his youthful readers against the heretical cross-bat strokes. Nyren's philosophy looks a little stodgy nowadays, but its rationale is of course the fact that a straight bat moving directly down the line of the ball presents a larger surface area, and for a longer period, than a horizontal bat moving across the line. The cautious approach of Nyren and his contemporaries should be viewed in the light of the very unpredictable wickets on which they had to play. And the gradual softening of 'official' attitudes towards the cross bat probably has a lot to do with the great improvement in playing surfaces in the second half of the 19th century. Compare STRAIGHT BAT.

**cross-bat** *adj* (of a stroke) played with a cross bat:

> 'Bowlers do not always bowl a length, and from balls of bad length runs are often most effectively . . . made by cross-bat strokes' (MCC 1952, p 88).

**cross-batted** *adv* 1 with a horizontal bat:

> 'The cut, whether off the front or back foot, is played cross-batted and . . . the margin of error is proportionally small' (MCC 1952, p 95).

~ *adj* 2 = CROSS-BAT

**crumble** *vb* (of a wicket) to disintegrate; a 'crumbling' wicket is one that is beginning to break up, typically towards the end of a long match in dry conditions, and its loose surface encourages spin and produces variable bounce:

> 'Crumbling results either from the nature of the turf and soil or from the wear and tear of long inningses' (Ranji 1897, p 86).

**curator** *n* (Australia, New Zealand, & West Indies) the person responsible for the maintenance of the ground and the preparation of wickets for matches; groundsman:

> 'The New Zealand Board collected a gratifying $NZ40,000, and the much-abused curator, Wesley Armstrong, declared proudly

*afterwards: "That pitch is good enough for another five days!"'*
(Derek Hodgson, *WCM* March 1984).

**curl** (old) *n* **1** movement of the ball in the air or off the pitch; swing or break:

*'His delivery was fast under-hand, and he had a good deal of curl from leg'* (Pullin 1900, p 27).

*'I have not been able to discover, any more than the bowlers themselves, why or how curl in the air takes place'* (Ranji 1897, p 107).

~ *vb* **2** (of the ball) to change direction by moving in the air or off the pitch; swing or break:

*'He [Lamborn] was once bowling against the Duke of Dorset, and, delivering his ball straight to the wicket, it curled in, and missed the Duke's leg-stump by a hair's breadth'* (Nyren 1833 in *HM*, p 54).

*'It is a well-known fact that a new ball will invariably curl more than one which has had thirty or forty runs scored off it'* (Warner 1934, p 60).

**curly** *adj* (old) (of the ball) moving in the air or off the pitch; curling:

*'Neale was out to a curly one from Williams after making a very attractive 55'* (Headlam 1903, p 155).

**cut** *n* **1** a batting stroke in which the ball is struck towards the off-side in an arc between cover and slip, with the bat held at an angle closer to horizontal than perpendicular. The cut is an attacking shot, typically played to a fast ball pitching rather short of a length outside the off stump, and it is executed by moving the back foot across towards off stump and bringing the bat down on the ball as it passes the batsman. A successful cut depends to a large extent on the power of the batsman's wrists and 'like all wrist strokes, charms the spectator by accomplishing great results at the expense of apparently little effort' (*Badminton* 1888, p 6). Cuts are usually classified as either 'square' or 'late', depending on the point at which the ball is struck. See also FORWARD CUT.

**2** the practice or technique of cutting the ball in bowling:

*'This time Willis, Cowans and Dilley found that speed and bounce were less important than swing and cut'* (Christopher Martin-Jenkins, *Cricketer* September 1983).

~ *vb* **3** (of the batsman) to strike the ball to the off-side with a more or less horizontal bat when making a cut:

*'If you are in a position to cut and the ball should bump, it is wise to leave it alone, for the danger of being caught at third man is very great' (Badminton* 1888, p 62).

*'Enter Botham, to overtake Fletcher in two overs by straight-driving and cutting ten runs off Kapil Dev'* (Berry 1982, p 113).

**4** (of the bowler) to cause the ball to move off the pitch into or away from the batsman by drawing the hand rapidly across the seam at the moment of delivery:

*'Even in the last over he* [Lillee] *cut one back at high speed to go over Emburey's stumps'* (Brearley 1982, p 148).

The term is used only of faster bowlers and has evolved fairly recently to distinguish this method of imparting 'break' to the ball from the wrist- and finger-spin used by the slower bowlers.

**5** (of the ball) to deviate from its original line of flight after pitching; in modern usage, used only of faster balls, but formerly applied to balls of any pace:

*'Aided by a turn or motion of the wrist, the Ball may be made to cut or twist, after it has grounded, and will perplex most Strikers'* (Lambert 1816, p 15).

*'When Boycott had reached 44 in 50 overs, he played at Williams . . . and was lbw when the ball cut back into him'* (Henry Blofeld, *Guardian* 1 September 1983).

**cutter** *n* **1** a batsman skilled in cutting the ball; an exponent of the cut (CUT 1):

*'In Dujon he was confronted by one of the few remaining cutters in the game'* (John Woodcock, *The Times* 27 July 1984).

**2** a relatively fast ball that cuts after pitching (CUT 5); a leg-cutter or off-cutter:

*'Cutters require a jerk with the hand as the fingers come across the ball'* (Alf Gover, *Cricketer* November 1984).

**cut through** *vb* (of the ball) to continue in its original line of flight after pitching, without significant lift or deviation but with some (apparent) quickening of pace, typically on a wet wicket:

*'Going in on the wet cutting-through wicket, Massie hit the incapacitated bowlers all over the field' (Badminton* 1888, p 318).

**dab** *n* **1** a tentative prod with the bat, usually towards a ball outside off stump and often made involuntarily:

> 'After Allan Lamb had been grabbed left-handed at short leg . . . Gower played a horribly noncommittal dab' (Scyld Berry, *Observer* 22 January 1984).

~ *vb* **2** to attempt to hit the ball when making such a stroke.

**daisy-cutter** *n* a fast underarm ball delivered so that it skims along the surface of the pitch:

> 'Mr Thornton went on with the quick daisy-cutters, and down fell the players' wickets' (F. Gale, *Echoes from Old Cricket Fields 1871, p 49*).

The term is self-explanatory and was originally used to describe 'a horse that in trotting lifts its feet only very slightly from the ground' (*OED*).

**danger area** *n* that part of the pitch which, according to the Laws, must be protected from damage by the bowlers. It comprises 'the area contained by an imaginary line 4 ft./1.22 m. from the popping crease, and parallel to it, and within two imaginary and parallel lines drawn down the pitch from points on that line 1 ft./30.48 cm. on either side of the middle stump' (Law 42, note (c)). The umpires are empowered to intervene in order to prevent bowlers 'running down the pitch after delivering the ball' (Law 42 § 11). Damage to the pitch within the 'danger area' can give an unfair advantage to the bowling side, who may be able to exploit patches of rough in order to get the ball to turn or bounce unpredictably.

**dead** *adj* (of the ball) no longer in play according to the laws of the game, for any of a wide variety of reasons. The ball becomes dead, for example, when a batsman is out, if it gets lost, or if it becomes lodged in the clothing of either the batsman or the umpires. Most importantly, there is always a stage between one delivery and the next when the ball is temporarily 'dead', either because it has crossed the boundary or because it has become 'finally settled in the hands of the Wicket Keeper or the bowler' (Law 23 § 1(a)). In all such cases the ball's 'deadness' is implicit, and it is not actually pronounced dead by the umpire. There is, however, a further set of circumstances, outlined in Law 23 § 2, in which the umpires may intervene and *declare* the ball dead – most notably in cases of unfair play, as for example, when a member of the fielding side 'wilfully obstructs a Batsman in running' or 'incommodes the Striker by any noise or action while he is receiving a ball' (see Law 42). In cases such as these the umpire calls 'dead ball' and signals to the scorers 'by crossing and re-crossing the wrists below the waist' (Law 3 § 13). Once the ball becomes or is pronounced dead, it remains out of play until the bowler starts his run-up to deliver the next ball, and so long as the ball is dead no wicket can be taken and no runs scored. Finally, it is worth noticing that the ball does *not* become dead if the wicket is put down by a fielder without thereby dismissing the batsman, or if an unsuccessful appeal is made: in both cases the batsmen may still attempt to take runs and the fielding side may still attempt to run them out. Compare **in play** (see PLAY).

**dead bat** *n* a bat used purely defensively, either in making a forward blocking stroke with no backlift, or held loosely in a backward defensive position:

'The more the ball is turning, the more do they rely on their back play, unless of course they are able to smother it by playing right forward with a dead bat' (MCC 1952, p 72).

'Bailey continued according to plan, which meant the forward stab or the dead-bat back stroke to all except the most eminently scorable balls' (Peebles 1959, p 83).

**dec** *abbr* DECLARED

**declaration** *n* an act of declaring an innings closed before all ten wickets have fallen:

> 'His declaration left Australia 232 to win in a little under two hours plus twenty overs' (Brearley 1982, p 32).

**declare** *vb* (of the captain of the batting side) to close the innings before all ten wickets have fallen:

> 'The Captain of the batting side may declare an innings closed at any time during a match irrespective of its duration' (Law 14 § 1).

The law allowing declarations is a surprisingly recent one, dating back only as far as 1889. It had of course always been possible for a batting side to end its innings quickly – if the state of the game demanded it – by deliberately getting themselves out, and the hit wicket rule provided an invaluable fall-back for real emergencies (see HIT WICKET). Such a situation would not, in any case, have arisen very often on the 'sporting' wickets of the 18th and early 19th centuries. But the dramatic improvement in playing surfaces from the 1860s onwards produced too many matches in which the only alternatives were an inevitable draw or the undignified spectacle of batsmen throwing their wickets away in order to revive the game. The growing controversy over the acceptability of this practice was resolved when the MCC ruled 'that on the last day of a match, including one-day matches, the in side should at any time be empowered to declare the innings at an end'. The time limit was progressively relaxed over the next twenty-odd years so that by 1910 a declaration could be made at any time after the start of the second day of a three-day match. There was no further change until 1947 and, after a number of minor adjustments, the law reached its present form in 1957. See also FORFEIT.

**declared** *adv* used in recording the score to indicate that a side's innings has been voluntarily declared closed (thus, 'West Indies 502 for 6 declared').

**deep** *adj & adv* **1** occupying or indicating a position a relatively long way from the batsman's wicket:

'Fowler might have been caught at short leg if the fielder had been two yards deeper' (Robin Marlar, *Sunday Times* 31 July 1983).

Also used in combination to indicate a modified fielding position that would otherwise be somewhat closer to the striker, such as third man, mid-wicket, or extra cover:

'Chappell went for the hook and Lamb at deep backward square-leg judged the catch perfectly' (Henry Blofeld, *Cricketer* February 1983).

Compare SHORT and see FIELDING POSITIONS.

~ *n* 2 – **the deep** the area of the ground that is relatively far from the wicket; the outield.

**deep field** *n* 1 any part of the field close to the boundary; the deep.

2 (old) a fielding position (or the player occupying it) close to the boundary in the area behind the bowler's wicket; long field:

'Gauvinier . . . mis-hit and skied it, and deep field, running at full speed, brought off a beautiful catch' (H. de Selincourt, *Game of the Season* 1931, ch 1).

**defence** *n* 1 the act or skill of batting as it relates to keeping one's wicket intact rather than to scoring runs:

'When I began there was very little length-bowling, very little straight play, and little defence either' (William Beldham in Pycroft 1854 in *HM*, p 134).

'The art of defence – which is the style of play adapted to stop the ball, as distinguished from the offensive method . . . – may be roughly divided into forward play and back play' (Badminton 1888, p 48).

2 the defensive 'barrier', consisting of the bat and sometimes also the padded leg, with which a batsman attempts to protect his wicket:

'Larkins holed out at mid-on in the second over off Inchmore, who immediately afterwards pierced Boyd-Moss's defence and bowled him' (D. J. Rutnagar, *Daily Telegraph* 15 August 1984).

**defend** *vb* to bat in a defensive style:

*'His ability to read the leg-spin was always evident, and his judgment of when to hit the ball and when to defend was infallible'* (Mike Selvey, WCM January 1985).

**defensive** *adj* **1** (of a batting stroke or a style of batting) adapted to the protection of one's wicket rather than to scoring runs:

*'Back and forward play may be further divided into back and forward play for defensive purposes, and back and forward play with the object of making runs'* (Warner 1934, p 8).

*'When he [Glenn Turner] first appeared his shots were just about limited to a forward and backward defensive push'* (Jim Laker, WCM August 1984).

**2** (of a style of bowling or fielding) adapted to preventing the batsmen from scoring freely rather than to taking wickets; accurate, medium-pace in-swing bowling, and 'pushed-through' rather than 'flighted' spin – both tending to restrict strokeplay – are characteristic features of defensive outcricket.

**defensive field** *n* any arrangement of fielders that is primarily intended to prevent the batsmen from scoring runs rather than to get them out. A defensive field may either be forced upon the fielding side, if the batsmen are able to dominate the bowling and disperse the close fielders, or it may be deployed by the fielding captain for good tactical reasons, as for example when the batting side has plenty of wickets in hand but is chasing a difficult target to win the match. A defensive field is characteristically deep set, with a relatively large number of fielders occupying the 'run-saving' positions (like third man, fine leg, and long on) and a relatively small number in close catching positions. Compare ATTACKING FIELD.

**deficit** *n* the number of runs by which a side trails its opponents at a particular stage in the game, especially at the completion of an innings:

*'A heavy pessimism prompted by an overnight deficit of 373 hung over the Surrey innings from the start'* (Cyril Chapman, *Guardian* 1 May 1984).

**deliver** *vb* to propel the ball towards the batsman; especially, to release the ball from the hand in bowling:

'The classic position at the crease for fast bowlers is side on towards the batsman at the other end just before delivering the ball' (Alf Gover, *Cricketer* April 1983).

**delivery** *n* **1** a ball delivered by the bowler:

'Intikhab Alam . . . began his Test career, when a few days short of 18, by bowling Australia's Colin McDonald with his first delivery' (Frith 1984, p 165).

**2** the manner in which a bowler delivers the ball; a bowler's action:

'He had a high delivery . . . and his balls were provokingly deceitful' (Nyren 1833 in *HM*, p 44).

**devil** *n* (old) a quality of extra pace or 'nip', imparted to a ball by the bowler or deriving from the pitch, which makes the bowling dangerously effective:

'A fairly long run up to the wickets . . . gives more impetus to the ball, and what is popularly known as "devil"' (*Badminton* 1888, p 166).

'The ideal match is a match that does not last more than two days, where the wicket has got a bit of devil in it' (*Badminton* 1888, p 402).

**dig** *vb* **1** (**dig in**) to bowl the ball so that it pitches hard and short, in order to extract the maximum possible bounce from the wicket:

'The main tactic of most fast bowlers seems to be to dig the ball in short and hope for a catch close to the wicket as the batsman fends the lifting missile away from his face' (Christopher Martin-Jenkins, *Cricketer* September 1983).

**2** (**dig out**) to avoid being yorked by a well pitched-up ball by keeping the bat very close to the ground as the stroke is made:

'Then Botham bowled four successive deliveries well up in the blockhole; each one Yashpal dug out and hit hard and straight' (Berry 1982, p 91).

~ *n* **3** (Australia) an innings.

**dip** *vb* (of the ball) to turn or swing in towards the batsman, losing height rather more steeply than expected at the end of its flight:

*'He appeared to be a bit late to a ball from Meckiff which pitched well up to him and perhaps dipped in a shade'* (Peebles 1959, p 122).

*'Popplewell followed five overs later, beaten by one that moved and dipped late'* (John Mason, *Daily Telegraph* 15 August 1984).

**direct attack** *n* fast short-pitched bowling aimed at the batsman; bodyline. An MCC directive following the 1934 season in England states that:

*'County captains shall take all steps in their power to eliminate from the game the type of bowling as now defined, ie direct attack'.*

See BOUNCER.

**dismiss** *vb* to get a batsman or batting side out:

*'It was Garner and Malcolm Marshall who set the inevitable course of the match by dismissing Australia on the first day for 199'* (Tony Cozier, *Cricketer* January 1984).

**dismissal** *n* an act of taking a batsman's wicket or of being involved in the taking of a wicket, as by catching the ball:

*'Tolchard, 37, played four times for England in 1976–77 and is one of only seven wicketkeepers to make 1000 dismissals and score 15,000 runs'* (WCM December 1983).

**do** *vb* **1** (of the ball) to move in the air or off the pitch to the specified extent (in phrases like 'do something', 'do a bit', etc):

*'The best inswinger will start about middle-and-off and "do" enough to hit leg'* (Arlott 1983, p 36).

*'Tavaré succeeded in getting out to him only by trying to steer through third man a ball that did nothing'* (Scyld Berry, *Observer* 12 June 1983).

**2** (of the wicket) to be conducive to movement off the pitch:

*'His [Rhodes'] fine length must always command respect, but unless the wicket does something he should not be dangerous'* (*Melbourne Argus* 12 December 1903).

**dolly** *n* **1** (also **dolly catch**) a ball, struck (or mis-hit) by the batsman, that comes slowly to a fielder, usually with a high trajectory, presenting him with a simple catch:

'Wells received a "dolly" catch and bowl off the splice' (*Daily Chronicle* 17 August 1904).

**2** (old) a slow high underarm ball; a donkey drop.

~ *vb* **3** to hit the ball so as to present a fielder with a simple catch:

'He picked the wrong ball from Pocock for a pull and dollied it to mid-on' (D. J. Rutnagar, *Daily Telegraph* 1 June 1984).

**4** (of the ball) to come off the bat straight to a fielder:

'Colin [Cowdrey] *played at it and got an edge, the ball dollying to Andy Corran at first slip*' (Bomber Wells, *Cricketer* December 1982).

The word first appears as a noun around the turn of the century, but its use as a verb is very much more recent. The origins of the term are obscure, but it is tempting to see a connection with an Anglo-Indian word 'dolly' meaning 'a complimentary offering of fruit, flowers . . . and the like, presented usually on one or more trays' (*Hobson-Jobson* 1886). Since a dolly catch is one that is 'handed to you on a plate' it is probably not too fanciful to see it as an extended use of this Anglo-Indian term, especially as it entered the language of cricket at a time when a large amount of so-called 'Hindustani' vocabulary was being imported into the English language.

**donkey drop** *n* a slow ball with a high, dropping trajectory, usually bowled underarm; a lob, especially one that is easy to hit:

'If he [the lob bowler] *does not take wickets, he will be sure to come in for a lot of chaff from the rest of his side for bowling "donkey drops"*' (Ranji 1897, p 96).

The term is a derogatory one, implying that the bowling of such innocuous balls shows stupidity worthy of a donkey.

**dot ball** *n* a ball from which no runs are scored and no wicket is taken, so called because such a delivery is recorded with a 'dot' in the detailed bowling analysis (see illustration at SCOREBOOK):

*'One day he is trying to get wickets, the next merely attempting to bowl "dot" balls'* (David Acfield, *Cricketer* November 1984).

**double** *n* **1** in English first-class cricket, the feat of taking 100 wickets and scoring 1000 runs in a single season.

**2** any notable all-round achievement by an individual player taking a specified round number of wickets and scoring a specified round number of runs, the number of runs typically being a tenfold multiple of the number of wickets:

*'When 64, Imran had the satisfaction of becoming the fifth player to complete the double of 2000 runs and 200 wickets in Tests'* (WCM February 1984).

Until the late sixties, the 'English' double of 100 wickets and 1000 runs was a reasonably common occurrence: Wilfred Rhodes notched up 16 doubles in the course of his career and, much more recently, players like Fred Titmus and Ray Illingworth regularly achieved the double. The most outstanding all-round performance in an English season was George Hirst's 'double double' of 2385 runs and 208 wickets in 1906 – one of the few cricket records that can confidently be regarded as safe. However, the reduced county championship programme operating since 1969 has severely limited players' opportunities for notching up really big aggregates (particularly of wickets), and until 1984 no one had performed the double since Titmus in 1967. Since any top-class all-rounder qualified for England is likely to be on Test duty throughout the summer, and thus have fewer opportunities than regular county players, the likeliest contenders for the double are star all-rounders from overseas not currently involved in a tour for their country of origin. Thus in 1984 it was the New Zealander Richard Hadlee, playing for Notts, who finally achieved what had begun to look unattainable, finishing the season with a remarkable double of 117 wickets and 1179 runs.

**double century** *n* **1** a batsman's score of 200 runs or over, made in a single innings:

*'Greenidge charged to a glorious 214 not out, reaching his double century with a hook off Foster'* (Cricketer August 1984).

**2** (old) a batsman's score of a century in each innings of a match:

> 'Double century is the scoring of two separate centuries in the same match' (A. E. Knight, *The Complete Cricketer* 1906, p 342).

**double figures** *n* a batsman's score of ten runs or over in a single innings.

**double wicket** *n* the variety of cricket played using two sets of wickets, with overs being bowled alternately from each end; the 'normal' form of the game as distinguished from SINGLE WICKET (qv):

> 'One run at single wicket is exactly equivalent to two at double wicket' (*Badminton* 1888, p 383).

**down** *adj & adv* (of the wicket) in or into a position that results in the dismissal of a batsman. The wicket may be bowled down by the bowler, knocked down by the batsman or his bat, or put down (and occasionally thrown down) by a member of the fielding side making a run-out or stumping:

> 'The wicket-keeper should . . . take the ball before the wicket and, as he receives it, his hands should be drawn back, putting the wicket down with one motion' (Nyren 1833 in *HM*, p 31).

> 'The Striker shall be out bowled if his wicket is bowled down' (Law 30 § 1).

The wicket is considered to be down if either bail is *completely removed* from its position by the ball or the batsman; a temporary disturbance of the bails does not result in the wicket being down. If an unsuccessful run-out attempt has resulted in the removal of the bails, any further run-out attempt off the same ball will require the actual removal of a stump from the ground in order to put the wicket down.

**drag** *vb* **1** to strike across the line of the ball making a sort of extended pull shot:

> 'When he bowled wide of the off-stump, Old dragged him to long-on' (Brearley 1982, p 91).

**2** to play the ball on to one's stumps while attempting to execute a scoring stroke:

'Gower, after six hours at the crease, dragged the ball onto his stumps for 114' (Matthew Engel, *Guardian* 15 December 1982).

'Vishwanath had dragged on, trying to square-cut Botham' (Berry 1982, p 103).

**3** (of a bowler) to keep the back foot in contact with the ground at the moment of delivery, drawing it along the surface and thus effectively reducing the length of the pitch by a considerable amount:

'Larwood opened the bowling to Woodfull and was "called" first ball for dragging over the crease' (*Melbourne Argus* 21 November 1932).

'Dragging' became a controversial issue in the early sixties, as more and more bowlers exploited the loophole in the no-ball regulations. Under the version of the no-ball rule then in force, the fairness of a delivery was determined by the position of the bowler's *back* foot in relation to the bowling crease, and this made it dificult for umpires to state categorically that a 'dragging' bowler was bowling unfairly. The practice put batsmen at an obvious disadvantage and so – since the law as it stood offered no remedy – new legislation was required. The result was the present no-ball law (Law 24 § 3), by which the fairness of a delivery is principally determined by the position of the bowler's front foot (see NO-BALL).

**4** (old) to impart back spin to the ball when bowling.

~ *n* **5** a cross-batted stroke resembling the pull:

'On this type of wicket the drag or short arm pull is largely utilized . . . to any ball short of a length' (Warwick Armstrong, *The Art of Cricket* 1922, p 37).

**6** (old) back spin imparted to the ball by the bowler, causing it to lose pace, or 'hang', after pitching:

'The two other spins which can be put on the ball are what have been called the drag (or back spin) and top spin' (*Cricket* (Badminton Library 1920 edn) p 84).

**draw** *n* **1** a match that ends without either side winning; that is, in the case of a two-innings match, without one side dismissing the other side twice and scoring a higher total of runs; technically a tie does not count as a draw (see Law 21).

One of the earliest references to a cricket match ending in a draw is in the *Daily Journal* of 25 August 1731, which reports an 11-a-side game between the Duke of Richmond and a Mr Chambers. The parties had agreed beforehand to play until 7 o'clock, but when the time came Mr Chambers' side, now in its second innings, still 'wanted about 8 or 10 Notches' to reach the 33 runs they needed for victory. So 'they were obliged to leave off, tho', besides the Hands then playing, they had 4 or 5 more to come in: Thus it proved a drawn battle'. Such an outcome was not only rare at this time (owing to the poor state of the wickets and the consequent low scores) but would also have been most undesirable, since the chief interest of any early 18th century game was in the bets riding on the result. In fact, the word 'draw' itself, in its sporting sense, derives from the practice of 'drawing' or 'withdrawing' the bets made on a contest when its issue was undecided. The following report describes an early cricketing example of this phenomenon, in a match that actually ended in a tie: 'On Wed., Sept 1, on Lamb's Conduit Fields, Richmond, Fulham, and Barnes against London, 3 a side.

| London | 4 | 1st innings | Surrey | 18 |
|---|---|---|---|---|
| | 19 | 2nd innings | | 5 |

23 each, so they drew stakes' (*Whitehall Evening Post* 2 September 1736).

See also TIE.

**2** a batting stroke by which the ball is deflected off the angled face of the bat and passes between the wicket and the batsman's legs in the direction of long leg or backward square leg; it is presumably so called because the ball is gently 'drawn' away from the wicket rather than more forcefully 'pulled':

*'In playing the Draw . . . turn the face of the bat inwards, so as to describe an angle of 45° with the parallelism of the wicket'* (Felix 1850, p 24).

Felix and his contemporaries imply that the draw was a popular stroke in the mid-19th century, but by 1900 it had almost died out:

*'John Wisden . . . was one of the last of the school of batsmen who favoured the old-fashioned "draw" stroke. . . . The stroke is now rarely or never seen'* (Pullin 1900, p 19).

~ *vb* **3** to fail to reach a result in which one side wins:

*'On Wed., June 16, on Dartford Brimp, London drew with Dartford: to play another match on Thur., June 24, in the Artillery Ground' (St James's Evening Post* 27 June 1731).

**4** to hit the ball using the 'draw' stroke:

*'"Drawing" between leg and wicket is not a new invention. Old Small . . . was famous for the draw'* (Pycroft 1854 in *HM*, p 141).

**5 – draw stumps** to remove the stumps from the ground at the end of a match or at the end of a day's play:

*'It had been arranged to draw stumps at 1.30 in order to allow the players to get down to the racecourse and back their fancy in the Viceroy's Cup'* (Headlam 1903, p 117).

See also STUMPS.

**drifter** *n* a slow ball that curves deceptively into or away from the batsman without moving sharply enough to put him on the alert:

*'Zaheer . . . was making the most of the brief respite afforded by the off-spin of Gomes . . . until in the last over before lunch, the 31st, he played round a drifter and was bowled'* (Christopher Martin-Jenkins, *Cricketer* August 1983).

**drinks interval** *n* a break of not more than five minutes during a session of play in which drinks are brought on to the field for the players, usually by each side's twelfth man. No more than one such interval may be taken in each session, and no drinks interval may be taken during the last hour of a match (see Law 16 § 6).

**drive** *n* **1** a batting stroke in which the ball is struck with a full downward swing of a perpendicular bat. The drive is an attacking shot, typically played to a ball of good length pitching on or just outside the line of the stumps, and is executed by advancing the front foot towards the pitch of the ball, and giving the bat a full backlift before bringing it down onto the ball very shortly after it pitches. Quick footwork in 'running out' to the pitch of the ball can enable the batsman to drive even a ball of less than full length. Drives can be made to anywhere in front of the wicket in the arc between cover and midwicket, and are usually clas-

sified according to the direction they take – which is in turn largely governed by the line of the bowled ball:

*'The straighter the ball is pitched in a line with the wicket, the straighter should be the drive, and vice versa'* (Ranji 1897, p 186).

Thus, for example, an 'on drive' is usually made to a ball pitching on or just outside leg stump. See COVER DRIVE, OFF DRIVE, ON DRIVE, SQUARE DRIVE, STRAIGHT DRIVE.

~ *vb* **2** to strike the ball with a full downward swing of the bat when making a drive:

*'There is nothing that more completely demoralises a bowler than a player who comes out and drives when the ball is at all over-pitched'* (*Badminton* 1888, p 78).

**drop** *vb* **1** to fail to take a possible catch, or fail to dismiss a batsman in this way:

*'Pakistan threw away a wonderful chance when they dropped Wessels and Yallop in the first hour of the day'* (Henry Blofeld, *Guardian* 10 December 1983).

**2** to bowl the ball in such a way that it pitches at a particular length, on a particular spot, or in line with a particular target:

*'Bowlers of intellect will (if they discover your propensity to the forward play . . .) drop the ball shorter and shorter, and lead you insensibly into error'* (Felix 1850, p 16).

*'The third prong of the attack was Clarrie Grimmett, dropping the ball as if radar-guided onto a teasing spot'* (*WCM* January 1984).

*'He took three steps, dropped the ball on the leg-wicket . . . and could hit the top of the off-stump three times in an over'* (James 1963, p 61).

**duck** *n* **1** a batsman's score of nought, so called because of the supposed resemblance between a duck's egg (the original term – see below) and the figure '0' in the scorebook. (Interestingly, the analogous term 'love', used in tennis and other games, has a similar derivation – from *l'oeuf*, 'the egg'.)

Like dying or getting drunk, failing to score in cricket is too delicate a subject to be discussed without resort to circumlocution, and the term 'duck' is simply the most popular of the many euphemistic expressions that have been coined to get round any embarrassment. A batsman may get a 'blob' or a 'full moon', or may even be out 'without troubling the scorers' – as if he were doing them a positive favour. At the other extreme, some scoreboards put a representation of a real duck beside the unfortunate batsman's name, as if to heighten the indignity, and this idea has now been taken to its logical (?) conclusion with Australian TV's forlorn-looking cartoon duck, shown trudging back to the pavilion whenever a batsman is out for nought. The only thing worse than scoring nought is scoring nought in each innings, and the language of cricket has a number of suitably indirect expressions to cope with this contingency.

The earliest recorded use of 'duck' is dated 1863, and it is probably no coincidence that the term should have evolved at precisely the time when wickets were just beginning to improve and high scores were becoming less of a rarity: presumably there had been little disgrace in scoring nought during the earlier, low-scoring days of the game. See also BRACE, PAIR.

**2 – break one's duck** to score the first run or runs of one's innings; get off the mark:

> 'What matters is not that he should "break his duck", but that he should still be there and getting a sight of the ball' (MCC 1952, p 105).

**duck's egg** (also **duck egg**) *n* (obsolete) a score of nought; a duck:

> 'The player who plays only because he is a good bat, and never bowls after he has laid his duck egg, has no opportunity of getting four or five wickets with the ball' (Badminton 1888, p 90).

**easy-paced** *adj* (of the wicket) characterised by a relative slowness of pace and evenness of bounce, and thus providing conditions more favourable to batting than to bowling:

> 'Sidebottom looked the most penetrative of the pace bowlers and at 42 he took Cockbain by surprise with a ball dug sharply into this easy-paced wicket' (Paul Fitzpatrick, *Guardian* 31 May 1983).

**economical** *adj* (of a bowler or style of bowling) tending to restrict scoring opportunities, without necessarily taking wickets; conceding relatively few runs:

> 'Selvey . . . has sustained a reputation as an economical new-ball bowler with ability to swing and seam the ball either way' (Alan Lee, *Cricketer* December 1982).

**edge** *n* **1** any of the sides of the blade of the bat, as opposed to the 'meat', sometimes further distinguished as the 'top', 'bottom', 'inside', or 'outside' edge:

> 'In their last 29 overs England hit only three fours, two of those off the edge' (John Woodcock, *The Times* 23 June 1983).

**2** a ball deflected off the edge of the bat; a snick:

> 'We kept a third man and square-leg to stop the edges going for too many runs' (Brearley 1982, p 76).

~ *vb* **3** to deflect the ball with the edge of the bat, rather than hitting it cleanly:

> 'Often in the past fast bowlers have switched their line of attack from over to round the wicket, in order to slant the ball across a right-handed batsman and get him edging into the slips' (Scyld Berry, *Observer* 4 December 1983).

**eleven** *n* a cricket team consisting of eleven players. The Laws state that 'A match is played between two sides each of eleven Players', with the rider that 'A match may be played by agreement between sides of more or less than eleven players, but not more than eleven players may field' (Law 1). Surprisingly, these stipulations date back only as far as the code of 1884. Prior to that it was not unusual to find that, for any given match, the numerical strength of the two sides was specially tailored to produce a reasonably fair contest. For example:

> 'In September 1856 we had the All-England Eleven at Dublin, where they played Eighteen of Ireland' (Pullin 1900, pp 71–2).

An extreme case was the match between 33 of Norfolk and 11 of All England, which the Norfolk players, recording a total of 36 ducks, somehow contrived to lose by an innings (*Norfolk Chronicle* 29 July 1797). This practice, however, is seen by Charles Box (1868, p 61) as a 'departure from what the chief of the Hambledon Club determined to be the proper number'. And it is a fact that, even in the absence of specific legislation, the important matches were nearly always played between teams of 11 players from the earliest times. The earliest known case of an 11-a-side match is in 1697:

> 'The middle of last week a great match at Cricket was played in Sussex; they were eleven of a side, and they played for fifty guineas apiece' (*Foreign Post* 7 July 1697).

**emergency** *n* (obsolete) a player not belonging to a team but brought in to replace a regular member:

> 'He [E. M. Grace] got every wicket in the 2nd innings, in the match played at Canterbury, August 14, 15, 1862, Gentlemen of Kent v. M.C.C., for whom he played as an emergency, and in which . . . he scored 192 not out' (W. G. Grace, *Cricketing Reminiscences* 1899, p 12).

Though defined in the *OED* as a 'substitute', an emergency was clearly not a substitute in the strict sense because, as the quotation shows, he was allowed to bat and bowl. See SUBSTITUTE.

**emperor pair** *n* a 'pair' recorded by an opening batsman who is twice dismissed without scoring in the first ball of his side's innings:

'Gooch, on an emperor pair after Dilley removed him first ball in
his last innings, looked destined for his sixth . . . century when
he was out at 99' (Christopher Wordsworth, *Observer*
15 May 1983).

See also PAIR, KING PAIR.

**end** *n* **1** either of the two areas, each comprising a set of
stumps and creases, that form the extremities of the
pitch; the batsman facing the bowling is at the
'striker's end' and his partner is at the 'non-striker's
end' or 'bowler's end'; and at any given ground each
'end' usually has a name based on some local feature:

'The Umpire at the Striker's end may elect to stand on the off
instead of the leg side of the pitch' (Law 3 § 10).

'As the match went on, the wind veered in front of square so that
later on all four were keen to bowl from the Kirkstall Lane End'
(Brearley 1982, p 60).

See also CHANGE ENDS.

**2 – keep an end up, keep one's end up** to maintain
one's own wicket intact; said especially of a late-order
batsman who plays cautiously in order to enable a
more established player at the other end to continue
his innings.

**ESCA** *abbr* English Schoolboys' Cricket Association

**even time** *n* a scoring rate of one run per minute:

'The innings expires at 284 – too many for Chappell's liking, but
not enough for Willis's after a stand of 161 between Tavaré and
Lamb in better than even time' (Scyld Berry, *Observer*
2 January 1983).

**expensive** *adj* (of a bowler or style of bowling) conceding a
relatively high number of runs per over:

'Back in Australia he was successful but expensive against the
1910–11 South Africans' (Edward Liddle, WCM December
1983).

**express** *n* (old) **1** a very fast ball:

'Other bowling feats with his "expresses" include 7 wickets for 9
runs, 9 wickets for 9 runs, and 9 wickets for 8 runs, in 1871'
(Pullin 1900, p 211).

**2** (also **express bowler**) a very fast bowler:

*'With the terrifying express bowler John Jackson bowling opposite Cris Tinley, the attack, it was said, consisted of "a corkscrew at one end and a thunderbolt at the other"'* (Frith 1984, p 23).

**extra** *adj* **1** used in combination to indicate a supplementary fielding position situated fairly close, typically along an anti-clockwise arc, to one of the established fielding positions:

*'Long-off was moved to long-on, and extra-cover to extra long-on – that is, about half-way between long-on and where square-leg would be'* (Ranji 1897, p 135).

Nowadays the term is scarcely ever used, except in the term 'extra cover', which is now an established position in its own right.

∼ *n* **2** = EXTRA COVER:

*'Cowdrey set the partnership on its way with a four to extra'* (Peebles 1959, p 106).

**3** a run credited to EXTRAS (qv).

**extra cover** *n* (also formally **extra cover point**) an off-side fielding position (or the player occupying it) between cover and mid-off. It can be further distinguished as 'deep' or 'short', in which case the term is often shortened to **deep extra** or **short extra**. See FIELDING POSITIONS.

**extras** *n* any runs that do not result, directly or indirectly, from a scoring stroke made by the striker; specifically, runs credited to the batting side (but not to an individual batsman) in respect of byes, leg-byes, no-balls, or wides. Any additional runs that are obtained other than by actual running (as from a boundary, a lost ball, or an instance of the ball being stopped by a player's helmet) are credited to the striker if he hit the ball, but otherwise to the appropriate category of extras: thus, if the bowler delivers a wide which goes to the boundary without touching the bat, four runs are added to the extras under 'wides'.

The term 'extras' does not appear until the second half of the 19th century, by which time the relevant legislation had more or less achieved its present shape. In the earliest period of the game the only runs that could be scored without hitting the ball were from byes; no-balls, though defined in the original (1744) code of Laws, did not incur any penalty until 1829. When wides were first introduced in about 1810 they were, for scoring purposes, 'to be put down to the Byes', and they did not appear as a separate item until 1828. The final component of the extras appeared in 1850, when leg-byes were for the first time distinguished from 'ordinary' byes. See BYE, LEG-BYE, NO-BALL, WIDE.

**extra-slip** *n* see SLIP

**face** *n* **1** the flat front part of the blade of the bat, with which the ball is usually struck:

> '[In back play] *The ball ought to be met with the full face of the bat' (Badminton* 1888, p 55).

~ *vb* **2** to be in the position of defending one's wicket against the bowler; be the batsman at the striker's end:

> '*Botham protected Willis so well that he had to face only 5 balls in the last 20 minutes, and we added another 31 crucial runs'* (Brearley 1982, p 74).

**fag** *n* **1** a fielder, especially one who is not a full member of a team but whose function is simply to retrieve balls in the deep field:

> '*On a fine day the long row of nets is fully occupied, and the "fags" in the out-field have their hands full indeed'* (Ranji 1897, p 343).

~ *vb* **2** (also **fag out**) to act as a fag; field:

> '*Winchester boys were never allowed to touch a bat till they had been two years in the school, their whole time in play-hours being devoted to compulsory fagging out'* (F. Gale, *The Game of Cricket* 1887, p 134).

The word is an extended use of the English public-school term for a junior boy who does menial jobs for his seniors.

**fall** *vb* **1** (of a wicket) to be taken by the bowling side when a batsman is dismissed:

*'In 58 minutes seven wickets had fallen for 19 runs on a pitch playing little worse than in the first innings'* (Brearley 1982, p 77).

~ *n* **2** the taking of a wicket:

*'A Batsman may leave the field or retire at any time owing to illness . . . He may resume his innings at the fall of a wicket'* (Law 2 § 9).

The term derives from the idea of the wicket being 'down' when a batsman is dismissed.

**farm** *vb* – **farm the bowling, farm the strike** (of the batsman) to control the extent to which one has the strike, by such expedients as taking singles off the last ball of each over, especially in order to ensure that a weaker batting partner is not exposed to the bowling for any longer than is necessary:

*'The young giant received but two balls while his captain farmed the bowling for just under half an hour'* (Peebles 1959, p 184).

*'Smith farmed the strike and Chatfield, when he had to play, did so efficiently enough to wallop Marks for two successive on-side sixes'* (Matthew Engel, *Guardian* 13 February 1984).

**fast** *adj & adv* **1** denoting a bowler, a ball, or a style of bowling characterised by high speed; 'fast' is one of the three basic types according to which bowlers are conventionally categorised (the other two being slow and medium-pace) and a really fast bowler is reckoned to be capable of propelling the ball at speeds approaching 100 mph (160 kph):

*'Weighing up the tour generally, it is obvious that our fast bowlers have won us the games; in particular, Larwood has been a great factor'* ('Second Slip', *Cricketer* Spring Annual 1933).

*'Nothing shows up suspect technique in batting more than top class fast bowling, and the West Indians have that in abundance'* (Tom Graveney, *Cricketer* August 1984).

~ *adj* **2** (of the wicket) providing conditions favourable to fast bowling, especially by enabling the ball to continue in its course after pitching without any loss of pace:

*'He should also ponder the pace of the ground, and never forget that wet on the top of a hard ground makes the fastest surface of any'* (Badminton 1888, p 267).

**fast bowlers' union** *n* an unofficial 'brotherhood' of fast bowlers of opposing teams which has a – usually unspoken – agreement, according to which they are guaranteed immunity from bouncers or other forms of intimidation while they are batting. The agreement is upheld by the obvious sanction (also unspoken) that any fast bowler who bowls bouncers at his counterpart can expect similar treatment when it is his turn to bat. The arrangement, though apparently 'sporting', tends to have little effect when there is an obvious imbalance in the fast-bowling strengths of the two sides, and in recent years the bargaining power of the fast bowlers' union seems to have waned. Other factors contributing to its decline are the arrival of the helmet and the near-extinction, in the intensely competitive modern game, of the genuinely incompetent number 11 slogger.

**featherbed** *n* a very easy-paced wicket offering no encouragement to the bowlers and providing favourable batting conditions:

> '*England now start thinking about the three one-day games, which start on Saturday back at Christchurch, which is at least unlikely to be a featherbed*' (Matthew Engel, *Guardian* 16 February 1984).

**feed** *vb* to bowl in such a way as to encourage the batsman to play a stroke which he is known to favour, typically in order to induce a catch to a specially placed fielder:

> '*He is a strong hooker of the ball, but, perhaps because it brought about his downfall at Brisbane, it seemed that the bowlers fed this shot*' (Peebles 1959, p 184).

**fend** *vb* to make a tentative, often involuntary, prodding movement with a raised bat, especially as a means of self-defence:

> '*The main tactic . . . seems to be to dig the ball in short and hope for a catch close to the wicket as the batsman fends the lifting missile away from his face*' (Christopher Martin-Jenkins, *Cricketer* September 1983).

> '*Pakistan's first two wickets fell to Graham Dilley . . . Mudassar was caught down the leg side, Zaheer fended outside his off stump*' (Scyld Berry, *Observer* 19 June 1983).

**fetch** *vb* (obsolete) to score the stated number of runs:

'The Londoners went in first and fetch'd 95; then the Kentish men went in and fetched 80; upon which the odds ran 10 to 3 on the former' (Grub Street Journal 17 July 1735).

**field** *n* **1** the entire area of grass, marked off by a boundary line around its outer edge, on which a game of cricket is played, as distinguished from the 'pitch' or central area between two wickets.

**2** a fielder:

'On smooth wickets you would see Peel at one end, and perhaps Bates at the other, with eight fields on the off side' (Badminton 1888, p 60).

**3** the fielders collectively, especially when considered in terms of the particular configuration in which they are deployed:

'Mr Jardine rang his changes and shifted the field about, but the first pair seemed immovable' (Larwood 1933, p 142).

'He obviously considered the time was come to check a situation which might become dangerous, and for a spell Davidson and Mackay bowled defensively to deep-set, run-saving fields' (Peebles 1959, p 135).

See also ATTACKING FIELD, DEFENSIVE FIELD.

**4 – in the field** as a fielding side:

'Our failure to qualify for the finals was caused not by rainfall in Perth but catastrophic performances in the field' (Vic Marks, Cricketer April 1983).

~ *vb* **5** to be, or be a member of, the side that is attempting to bowl the batting side out:

'Substitutes shall be allowed by right to field for any player who during the match is incapacitated by illness or injury' (Law 2 § 1).

**6** to act as a fielder in the specified position:

'For once the play worked nicely, Hughes timing his hook perfectly so that it carried all the way to Emburey fielding a few yards in from the edge just behind square' (Brearley 1982, p 93).

**7** to stop and return the ball when acting as a fielder:

'Parked out at mid-on, he would never field a ball if he could kick it on to a team-mate' (Frith 1984, p 137).

**8** (of a team) to go into a match with the stated players:

*'Australia brought in Hogg . . . for Maguire, while Pakistan fielded the same side which had drawn the Fourth Test in Melbourne'* (Henry Blofeld, *Cricketer* March 1984).

**fielding positions** (for definitions see individual entries) To those who are uninitiated in the language and lore of cricket, there is nothing more mysterious than a description of a typical field setting: 'Lillee bowled to an attacking field, with three slips and a gully, a silly point, two short legs (one forward and the other slightly backward of square), with only two men out in the deep, at third man and long on'. Yet what looks at first like a foreign language is in fact a logical and highly flexible code that enables a commentator to describe with considerable accuracy any position occupied by a fielder on a ground covering several acres.

The key to understanding the system is the fact that it is made up of two quite distinct elements. The first element comprises a set of basic markers, each of which establishes a broad area or direction in relation to the batsman. These are shown in Fig. 1 and are: *off* and *leg* (or *on*); *square* and *fine*; *backward* and *forward*; *wide* and *straight*; and *deep* (or *long*), *short*, and *silly*.

The second element in the code is a finite set of

*Note:* all positions shown here apply when a *right-handed* player is batting. If the batsman is *left-handed* the off-side and leg-side positions are reversed.

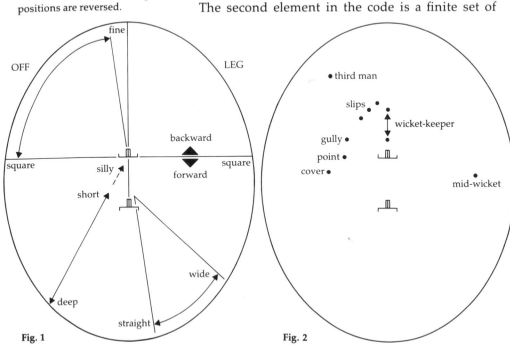

Fig. 1

Fig. 2

terms which, unlike the markers in Fig. 1, denote precise positions in the field: the most common members of this set are shown in Fig. 2. The names of this group of positions have evolved over the years in an *ad hoc* way, and seem to lack the symmetry and logic of the items in the first set. In fact, of course, all these names have their own rationale, but 'wicket-keeper' is the only member of the set that could really be called self-evident, and the *apparent* arbitrariness of all the others helps to make the system as a whole look fairly impenetrable.

These two main sets of terms form the basis of a highly productive system of description. By using individual items or combinations of items from either or both of the sets, it is possible to pinpoint any position on the cricket field. For example: *forward short leg* denotes a position that is in front of the line of the batsman's wicket *(forward)*, not very far from the bat *(short)*, and on the side of the pitch lying behind the batsman as he stands at the crease *(leg)*.

Fig. 3 shows some of the more common positions whose names are formed by combining items from the set in Fig. 2.

Fig. 4 shows some of the more common positions whose names are formed by combining items from *both* main sets.

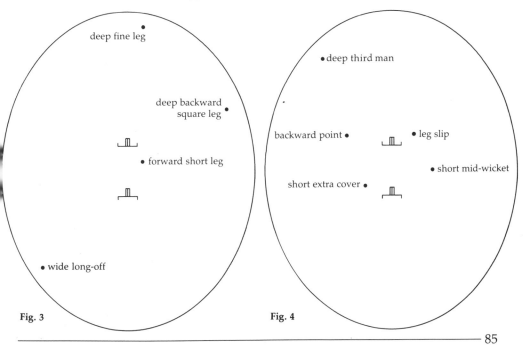

Fig. 3

Fig. 4

**figures** *n* a summary of a bowler's performance in an innings or a match, showing wickets taken against runs scored; it sometimes also includes the number of overs and maidens bowled, but in this case the term ANALYSIS (qv) would be more usual:

> '*His old rhythm and sharpness gradually returned, and he fully deserved his FIGURES of six for 95*' (Brearley 1982, p 64).

> '*On July 31, 1956, Jim Laker, the tall, taciturn Surrey Yorkshireman, completed match figures of 68–27–90–19*' (Frith 1984, p 129).

**fine** *adj & adv* close to an imaginary line separating the off and leg sides of the pitch; the term is restricted to the area behind the batsman's wicket:

> '*Sometimes short-slip is put very fine, sometimes rather wider, as circumstances may require*' (Ranji 1897, p 43).

> '*Cowdrey went ahead with another four off Davidson, which went very fine past backward short-leg*' (Peebles 1959, p 186).

Also used in combination to indicate a modified fielding position that would normally be somewhat squarer, such as third man or backward short leg. Compare STRAIGHT and see FIELDING POSITIONS.

**fine leg** *n* a fairly deep leg-side fielding position (or the player occupying it) behind the batsman's wicket and close to the imaginary line separating the off and leg sides of the pitch. Fine leg is a fairly modern term, rarely found in pre-war writings, which developed out of the older **fine long leg**. See FIELDING POSITIONS.

**finger-spin** *n* spin imparted to the ball chiefly through movement of the fingers, rather than of the wrist. The right-arm bowler's off-break and the slow left-arm bowler's 'stock' ball – in effect a leg-break – are both achieved by means of finger-spin. The right-arm finger-spinner grips the ball chiefly with the thumb and first two fingers and twists it from left to right in a movement that is often compared to turning the handle of a door, with the first finger imparting most of the 'break'. The term finger-spin was formerly less exclusive and was at one time used to denote all forms of slow spin-bowling, as distinguished from faster bowling in which the break was achieved by means of 'cut' or 'action-break'. It was thus often applied to what would now be called wrist-spin: the *OED* has a 1906 citation in which Schwarz, Faulkner, and Vogler – the legendary South African googly trio – are described as 'finger-spin bowlers'. In modern usage the distinctions are more finely drawn. Compare WRIST-SPIN.

**finger-spinner** *n* an exponent of finger-spin:

> *'Now we have adopted the English system of choosing three medium-pacers and a finger-spinner'* (Bob Holland, quoted in *Cricketer* November 1984).

**first change** *adj & adv* **1** bowling as the first bowler brought on to replace one of the two opening bowlers in a side's attack:

> *'NSW's new-ball attack consisted of . . . Geoff Lawson and Michael Whitney, with medium-pacer Trevor Chappell as first-change bowler'* (Phil Wilkins, *Cricketer* May 1983).

> *'The normal rule is that the middle order accelerate after the front-line bowlers . . . have gone, but that is difficult to operate when Marshall is bowling first change'* (Matthew Engel, *Guardian* 5 June 1984).

~ *n* **2** a first change bowler:

> *'Alletson, brought on as first change, took 1 for 7, was taken off and never played in a first-class match again'* (John Arlott, *WCM* March 1984).

**first-class** *adj* **1** denoting cricket played at the highest level, as defined by the ICC; specifically, cricket played in matches of three or more days' duration between two teams of eleven players that are officially recognised as having first-class status. Matches played in the major domestic competitions of all full members of the ICC (that is, England, Australia, West Indies, India, Pakistan, New Zealand, and Sri Lanka) are all accorded first-class status, as of course are any Test matches played between member countries. Well-known first-class competitions include the English County Championship, the Shell Shield in the West Indies, the Ranji Trophy in India, and the Sheffield Shield in Australia. Other less regular fixtures may also be adjudged first-class by the relevant governing bodies: for example, the annual Ireland-Scotland match has first-class status, and so, for the time being (but increasingly controversially), do matches involving Oxford and Cambridge Universities; while in earlier times, the English domestic game boasted a considerable number of 'extra' first-class fixtures, such as matches involving the Free Foresters, Leveson Gower's XI, and of course the Gentlemen and Players. On the other hand, the condition that matches must be of at least three days' duration means that limited-over games – even at international level – do not have first-class status, a fact that has important implications for the players' averages and aggregates, which are always (unless otherwise stipulated) based on their performance in first-class games.

**2** of, concerning, or involved in first-class cricket:

> 'Since then there have been two first-class victories for Sri Lanka – one against a fairly strong Young England team (TCCB XI) and the other against Oxford' (S. S. Perera, WCM September 1984).

**first slip** see SLIP

**fiver** *n* (obsolete) a shot by the batsman resulting in a score of five runs; specifically, a ball hit over the boundary without bouncing, which, under regulations in force in Australia during the first few years of the present century, carried an allowance of five runs:

> 'Braund drove a loose one from Saunders high and straight, the ball landing on top of the bicycle track, almost a fiver' (Melbourne Argus 15 December 1903).

Compare FOURER, SIXER.

**flash** *vb* to play a ball passing outside the off stump with a quick, involuntary movement of the bat, usually withdrawing the bat again hastily in an attempt to avoid making contact with the ball:

> 'England were 193 for six and after two punishing fours Botham flashed at a short one from Thomson and was caught by Chappell at first slip' (Henry Blofeld, Cricketer February 1983).

**flat** *adj* (of a ball bowled by a slower bowler) characterised by a low, straight trajectory rather than a high 'looping' arc:

> 'The standard of wicketkeeping . . . probably is higher than it has ever been in respect of keeping to pace and swing bowling;

and even, which is not easy, to flat, pushed-through spin'
(Arlott 1983, p 54).

**flat bat** *n* a bat held horizontally with its full face presented to
the ball:

> 'Benaud dropped the ball a shade short, and Richardson
> withdrew a pace and lathered it with the flat bat, presumably
> aiming to clear mid-on' (Peebles 1959, p 178).

**flat-bat** *vb* to strike the ball with a 'flat bat', producing a
somewhat unorthodox shot, often when the ball is
neither short enough to cut nor far enough up to
drive:

> 'After flat-batting Thomson over cover point for four he was hit
> a painful blow on the toe by a full toss' (Henry Blofeld,
> Cricketer February 1983).

**flight** *n* **1** the ability to control and vary the trajectory of the
ball, and the consequent potential for deceiving the
batsman as to its length and pace, when considered as
one of the skills of a slow bowler; especially, the
ability to deliver the ball with a high, curving trajectory:

> 'Two runs later Harris went down the wicket to Laker, who beat
> him with flight and turn, and was stumped' (Peebles 1959,
> p 37).

~ *vb* **2** to deliver the ball with a relatively high, curving
trajectory with the intention of deceiving the batsman; give the ball air:

> 'By what is called "flighting" the ball the bowler is out to delude
> him as to where it will pitch, in other words to make the ball look
> as if it will drop farther up than it in fact will' (MCC 1952,
> p 59).

> 'Cyril Vincent . . . played in 25 Tests, excelling at Leeds in 1935,
> when he took eight top England wickets with immaculate
> flighted left-arm spin' (Frith 1984, p 103).

Flighting the ball represents the 'attacking mode' of
slow bowling, in that it is primarily intended to take
wickets even at the risk of severe punishment. Compare PUSH THROUGH.

**flipper** *n* a relatively slow ball that behaves somewhat like a top-spinner and is produced by a particularly convoluted variety of wrist-spin. It is typically produced by gripping the ball mainly with the tips of the first and third fingers and squeezing or 'flipping' it out so that it emerges from the back or side of the hand with an extra helping of top spin on it. If successfully executed it will hurry through without deviation, gaining pace as it pitches and keeping low. The flipper has been described as 'the most arcane and esoteric ball in cricket' (Scyld Berry, *Observer* 11 March 1984) and its 'invention' is usually attributed to Clarrie Grimmett; more recent exponents include Ritchie Benaud and Abdul Qadir.

**floater** *n* a well-flighted slow ball that curves deceptively into or away from the batsman:

> *'Hughes had the better of this contest until the off-spinner deceived him with a perfect floater which he tried to sweep but missed'* (Brearley 1982, p 86).

**fly-slip** *n* an off-side fielding position (or the player occupying it) directly behind the slips and somewhat shorter than third man; fly-slip is particularly effective for trapping a batsman who is inclined to slice the ball over the heads of the slips:

> *'So many runs came from uppercuts over the slips that Willis eventually sent two men two-thirds of the way back to the boundary to act as fly-slips'* (Matthew Engel, *Guardian* 6 November 1982).

**follow on** *vb* (of a team) to have a second innings immediately after the first at the request of the opposing captain, after failing to reach a score within a stipulated number of runs of the opposing team's first innings score, in accordance with the follow-on rule:

> *'Ellison was immediately lbw, cutting against Edmond's spin, and at 59 for five, Kent were in real danger of following on'* (David Green, *Daily Telegraph* 1 June 1984).

**follow-on** *n* an enforced second innings taken by a side immediately after its first innings when its first innings total falls short of its opponents' score by a stipulated number of runs:

> *'Such was the resentment against West Indies captain Jeff*

*Stollmeyer, over his decision not to compel England's follow-on, that he was given police protection'* (Crawford White, *News Chronicle Cricket Annual* 1954, p 6).

The enforcement of the follow-on is at the discretion of the opposing captain, whose side must of course have batted first, and this option is currently available when his team leads by the following margins: 200 runs in a match of five days or more, 150 runs in a three- or four-day match, 100 runs in a two-day match, or 75 runs in a one-day match (Law 13 § 1). If the first day's play is completely lost, the figures are adjusted accordingly: thus the margin would be reduced to 150 in the case of a five-day Test match in which there had been no play on the opening day. The follow-on rule was first introduced in 1835 and was to be applied when the side batting second was 100 runs or more in arrears. The relevant figures were changed from time to time but the main difference from the present Law was that, until 1900, the follow-on was compulsory, rather than being an option available to the opposing captain.

**follow through** *vb* to complete a batting stroke or a bowling action with a follow-through:

> *'Like all other strokes, the cut should be followed through as far as possible'* (Ranji 1897, p 182).

**follow-through** *n* **1** the stage in a batting stroke after the ball has been struck, when the stroke is completed with an upward or lateral swing of the bat.

**2** the stage in a bowler's delivery after the ball has been released, when the bowler completes his delivery stride and, if bowling relatively fast, continues running for several paces; a 'deliberate and fluent follow-through' is listed in the *M.C.C. Coaching Manual* (MCC 1952, p 28) as one of the four requirements for a good bowling action:

> *'Cotter's followthrough was also dramatic, taking him yards down the wicket before his arm's swing finished'* (Edward Liddle, *WCM* December 1983).

**3** a worn or roughened area on the pitch produced by the repeated impact of a bowler's feet as he completes his delivery with a follow-through; such patches should not in theory appear directly between the wickets, since the Laws expressly forbid bowlers running down the pitch after a delivery (Law 42 § 11), but they may still be close enough to be exploited by a resourceful spinner:

> 'Its texture when dry is such that the follow-throughs, even if not part of the main strip, can powder, offering some help to the versatile spinner' (Brearley 1982, p 110).

**foothold** *n* a roughened area on the pitch offering a secure grip for a player's foot, especially for a batsman or bowler:

> 'Lock . . . had persevered in all circumstances and made immediate and effective use of the first signs of wear or dust from the footholds' (Peebles 1959, p 67).

> 'The Umpires shall allow . . . players to secure their footholds by the use of sawdust' (Law 10 § 7).

**footwork** *n* the manner in which a batsman moves his feet when batting, especially as this contributes to effective strokeplay:

> 'Viswanath came in, to meet Underwood's first two deliveries with such precision of footwork that no soothsayer was required to see that a long overdue score was in the making' (Berry 1982, p 102).

**force** *vb* **1** to strike the ball when playing a FORCING SHOT:

> 'Another under-pitched delivery, by no means a long hop but in other conditions short enough to force, played a major part in England's win' (John Thicknesse, *Cricketer* February 1985).

~ *n* **2** a FORCING SHOT:

> 'The force can also be played to the short of a length ball just outside the leg stump which cannot be hooked or pulled' (Wayne Larkins, *Cricketer* September 1984).

**forcing shot** *n* a batting stroke played off the back foot to a ball pitching rather short of a length and typically just outside off stump (or leg stump), in which the bat is swung downwards and forwards from a full backlift, sending the ball into the area between cover and mid-off (or between mid-wicket and mid-on).

**forfeit** *vb* (of a captain) to forgo an innings completely, as provided for under Law 14 § 2 or local playing regulations:

> 'The Kent skipper, Chris Tavaré, forfeited his side's first innings in a bid to make a match of it against Hampshire' (*Guardian* 31 May 1983).

The right to forfeit an innings is a recent innovation, and is typically exercised in an attempt to get a result when a match has been severely curtailed by bad weather. The regulations governing the County Championship in England further stipulate that 'If, owing to weather conditions, the match has not been started when less than eight hours' playing time remains, the first innings of each side shall automatically be forfeited and a one-innings match played'.

**forward** *adv* **1** striking or attempting to strike the ball from a position in which the 'front foot' (the left foot in the case of a right-handed batsman) is advanced down the wicket to the pitch of the ball and carries most of the weight of the body:

> 'The umpire Swarup Kishan took a long time to give his verdict and Lloyd, who had played well forward, departed looking unhappy' (Ian Brayshaw, *The Times* 27 December 1983).

> 'Dyson came half forward to his fourth ball, was beaten for pace and was lbw' (Henry Blofeld, *Cricketer* February 1983).

~ *adj* **2** (of a stroke or style of play) made by or characterised by the batsman playing forward:

> 'David Harris . . . wrought quite a revolution in the game, changing cricket from a backward and slashing to a forward and defensive game' (Pycroft 1854 in *HM*, p 153).

> 'Gatting was placed for the uncontrolled forward strokes of the kind with which Martin Crowe provided Cook his fifth wicket' (Robin Marlar, *Sunday Times* 28 August 1983).

The type of bowling practised in the earliest days of cricket did not encourage the playing of strokes off the front foot:

> 'With the primitive fashion of ground bowling, called sneakers, forward play could have no place' (Pycroft 1854 in *HM*, p 153).

But the more sophisticated style of bowling that evolved towards the end of the 18th century – specifically the well pitched-up 'length ball' perfected by David Harris (see BOWLING) – led to the introduction of the 'straight bat' and to a greater emphasis on forward play. Compare BACK 1, 3 and see also FRONT FOOT.

~ *adj & adv* **3** indicating a position a little in front of the line of the batsman's wicket. Usually used in combination to indicate a modified fielding position that would normally be squarer on to the wicket, such as short leg or square leg:

> 'Chappell avoided a pair when he pushed his first ball uppishly past Cook at forward short-leg' (Henry Blofeld, *Cricketer* February 1983).

Compare BACKWARD and see FIELDING POSITIONS.

**forward cut** *n* a batting stroke in which the front foot is brought forward and somewhat across towards the off, and the ball, typically a short-pitched delivery well outside the off stump, is struck with a horizontal bat into the area between point and cover. Unlike a true cut, the stroke derives much of its force from the arms and shoulders (rather than the wrists) and the MCC coaching book (MCC 1952, p 95) concedes that it 'is really a cross-batted drive or slash'.

**four** *n* an instance of the ball crossing the boundary after bouncing at least once, especially when hit by the batsman but also as a bye, wide, etc, or as the result of an overthrow. The umpire signals a four to the scorers by waving the hand from side to side, and four runs are added to the score of the batsman or team as appropriate. See BOUNDARY.

**fourer** *n* (obsolete) a four:

> 'Warner scored the first fourer by hitting McLeod twice to the mid-on boundary in the same over' (*Melbourne Argus* 18 January 1904).

**front foot** *n* the foot that is usually further from the stumps when a batsman is standing at the crease; the left foot in the case of a right-handed batsman or the right foot in the case of a left-handed batsman. A 'forward' stroke, in which this foot is advanced down the wicket towards the pitch of the ball and carries most of the batsman's weight, is said to be played 'off the front foot':

'Most great batsmen have been ready and able to play off the front and the back foot with equal facility' (MCC 1952, p 72).

See also FORWARD and compare BACK FOOT.

**front-foot** *adj* played, or tending to play, off the front foot:

'Already the ball was coming through sluggishly, which did not suit Gooch's front foot game' (Berry 1982, p 113).

'Malhotra rode his luck for a brief period and played some classic front-foot drives, including three fours off one Holding over' (WCM February 1984).

**full** *n* the point in the trajectory of a well pitched-up ball at which it reaches or passes the batsman while still in flight:

'Lawson tried to york him and in fact Randall played all round a ball which passed his bat on the full and hit the base of the middle and off stumps' (Henry Blofeld, *Cricketer* February 1983).

**full moon** *n* (obsolete) a batsman's score of nought; a duck:

'Two men go in, both of whom in their 1st innings had scored full moons' (Bell's Life, 4 July 1841).

**full pitch** *n* (old) a FULL TOSS:

'The second kind of full-pitch – the one reaching the batsman about the height of his knees – is the most usual of full pitches, and enjoys the distinction of being considered the easiest of all balls to hit' (Badminton 1888, p 144).

**full toss** *n* a ball bowled right up to the batsman so that it does not pitch before reaching the bat. The full toss relieves the batsman of any of the difficulties associated with movement off the pitch and uneven bounce, and unless very fast it also eliminates the crucial problem of assessing the ball's length. It is, therefore, generally regarded as a bad delivery. See diagram at LENGTH.

**gardening** *n* the process by which a batsman attempts to smooth out any irregularities in the wicket, especially by patting the pitch with his bat in between deliveries:

> 'There was a good deal of agitated gardening from the batsmen and Howarth, unusually for him, appeared in a helmet' (Matthew Engel, *Guardian* 3 February 1984).

**gate** *n* **1** the space between the bat and the batsman's leg, especially when the batsman fails to keep bat and pad together when playing a forward stroke:

> 'Zaheer played forward a trifle casually to Matthews and the ball turned through the gate and bowled him' (Henry Blofeld, *Guardian* 31 December 1983).

**2** (obsolete) a set of stumps; a wicket:

> 'Upon the earliest appearance of the game in Ireland, the people applied the word Gate instead of Wicket' (W. Bolland, *Cricket Notes* 1851, p 109).

~ *vb* **3** to dismiss a batsman by bowling him through the 'gate':

> 'Lamb . . . was nicely caught at short leg by Rameez, and when Randall was "gated" by a Qadir googly, the writing was on the wall' (Jack Bannister, *WCM* May 1984).

**gentleman** *n* **1** (especially in Britain before 1962) an amateur cricketer involved in first-class cricket (see AMATEUR):

> 'We think that the Universities, or the laziness of University men, may chiefly be blamed for the dearth of gentlemen bowlers' (*Badminton* 1888, p 378).

**2 – the Gentlemen** (in the period 1806–1962) a team selected by MCC from the body of amateur cricketers to play in one of the regular matches against 'the Players' (see PLAYER):

*'In 1844 the Gentlemen lost the services of Mr. Felix, perhaps their best bat, and Sir F. Bathurst, their second best bowler, and were defeated by 38 runs' (Badminton 1888, p 359).*

The first Gentlemen v Players match was staged in July 1806 at the original Lord's ground, and the annual Lord's encounter (which continued until the abolition of amateur status in 1962) was the high point of the English cricket season before Test matches with touring sides became an annual feature. In addition to the Lord's showpiece, Gentlemen v Players matches were also held annually at the Oval (from 1857 to 1934) and at the Scarborough Festival (from 1885 to 1962), and occasional extra games were staged at other grounds.

**get** *vb* **1 – get** (the ball) **away** to manage to hit a scoring stroke and penetrate the cordon of fielders, especially when playing against tight defensive bowling:

*'Botham, off a short run with Taylor standing up, was dificult to get away, and Hemmings bowled his off-breaks tidily' (Henry Blofeld, Cricketer February 1983).*

**2 – get out** (a) to dismiss a batsman or batting side. (b) to be dismissed; lose one's wicket.

**3 – get up** (of the ball) to rise relatively high off the wicket after pitching; lift:

*'Soon after that, Marsh was lbw pushing half forward at one from Cowans which did not get up' (Henry Blofeld, Cricketer February 1983).*

**give** *vb* – **give out/not out** (of the umpire) to pronounce a batsman out/not out in answering an appeal made by the fielding side:

*'Should a batsman be given out off a no ball the penalty for bowling it shall stand unless runs are otherwise scored' (Law 24 § 11).*

**given man** *n* a player who is not a regular member of a team but is allowed to play for it in a particular match, often being supplied by the opposing side in an attempt to produce a more even contest:

*'On Aug. 28, at Stephens Castle Green, New Alresford beat Bishops Waltham with 2 given men, by 9 wickets'* (*Hampshire Chronicle* 4 September 1775).

The use of 'given men', now long obsolete, was a common feature of the early Gentlemen v Players games, when Players of the highest calibre, such as Beldham and Lambert, were drafted into the Gentlemen's team in an effort to strengthen it.

**glance** *n* **1** (also **leg glance**) a batting stroke in which the ball is deflected from an angled bat into the area between square leg and fine leg. It is played with a more or less straight bat, usually to a ball pitching on or outside leg

stump, and can be made off the front or back foot, depending on the length of the ball. At the moment of impact the face of the bat is angled so that the ball 'glances' off behind square on the leg-side.

This elegant stroke developed out of the rather ungainly DRAW (qv), which had enjoyed a brief vogue in the mid-19th century. Though already established in the 1880s, the glance will always be associated with its most brilliant exponent, K. S. Ranjitsinhji, whose leg-side play mesmerised cricket audiences in Britain at the turn of the century. In Ranji's own version of the glance the back foot seems not to move at all, while the left leg is crossed over in front of the right. Ironically the footwork may be traced back to a rather barbarous method of coaching by which Ranji was encouraged not to 'back away' while at the wicket:

> 'I had to have my right leg pegged down every time I practised during my first two years at serious cricket' (Ranji 1897, p 164).

The terms 'glance' and 'glide' are usually treated as synonymous, but if any distinction can be made it is that 'glide' more strongly suggests simply holding the bat at an angle and letting the ball 'glide' smoothly off it, while 'glance' has a slightly more active ring about it, suggesting a quick turn of the wrists as the ball comes onto the bat.

~ *vb* **2** to hit the ball when making a glance:

> 'Richardson took a single to point off the third ball, and Bailey glanced the fifth for three' (Peebles 1959, p 157).

**glide** *n* **1** a GLANCE, especially one in which the bat is already at an angle at the moment of impact, so that the ball is deflected smoothly off it with little or no movement of the batsman's wrists:

> 'There is another stroke by which good-length balls on the leg-side can be played – the glide or glance' (Ranji 1897, p 190).

~ *vb* **2** to hit the ball when making a glide:

> 'Trumper's eye and quickness are inconceivable, and give him time not merely to hook and glide but to hit the ball with unique power' (A. E. Knight, *The Complete Cricketer* 1906, p 74).

**glove** *vb* to cause the ball to be deflected off one's batting gloves, as by mistiming a stroke, often thus presenting the fielding side with a catch:

'Knowing that the pitch would be slow, I twice hooked him, but nearly gloved another short delivery that bounced like a tennis ball' (Brearley 1982, p 25).

**gloveman** *n* a WICKET-KEEPER:

'In 1929 his Kentish gloveman, Ames, set a new record of 127 dismissals, 48 of them stumpings' (Frith 1984, p 90).

**gluepot** *n* a wicket having a 'glutinous' surface resulting when wet turf is drying under a warm sun; a sticky wicket (see STICKY).

**google** *vb* to cause the ball to break from the off while using an (apparent) leg-break action; bowl a googly:

'Grimmett . . . can spin the ball and google it' (Daily Telegraph 25 April 1930).

**googler** *n* a googly bowler:

'In R. H. Bettington they have a googler who might triumph over the best of wickets' (Daily Mail 9 July 1923).

**googly** *n* a ball bowled by a right-arm wrist-spin bowler that breaks from off to leg; an off-break bowled with an (apparent) leg-break action:

'Abdul Qadir had both Richards and Haynes embarrassed by their inability to read a googly that Jeff Stollmeyer, watching about 120 yards away, spotted the moment it left the bowler's hand' (Christopher Martin-Jenkins, Cricketer August 1983).

Compare CHINAMAN.

The googly is inextricably linked with the name of B. J. T. Bosanquet, who played for Oxford, Middlesex, and England at the turn of the century. Earlier bowlers may indeed have occasionally bowled what were in effect googlies (knowingly or otherwise), but it was Bosanquet who perfected the delivery and used it consistently at the highest level. In Bosanquet's own words, 'the whole secret of it lies in turning the ball over in the hand by *dropping the wrist* at the moment of delivery, so that the axis of spin is changed from left to right to right to left, thus converting the spin from being an ordinary leg-break into an ordinary off-break' (Bosanquet quoted in Warner 1934, p 32).

Bosanquet worked hard at the googly while at Oxford and one of his early triumphs was a haul of 15 wickets in the University's match against Sussex in 1900. His Test career (7 appearances between 1903 and 1905) was brief but memorable. Though not always effective at this level, he turned in the occasional match-winning performance, notably his 6 for 51 in the crucial second innings of the fourth Test of the Australian tour (1903–4), which helped England to win back the Ashes. Bosanquet himself quickly faded from the picture, but his technical innovation had far-reaching, and initially spectacular, effects. The googly was enthusiastically taken up by England's rivals and the South Africans won two successive series against England (1905–6, and 1907) with a Test attack boasting no less than *four* googly bowlers. Even some years later, Sir Pelham Warner wrote that 'the ideal side on a perfect wicket would . . . contain two googly bowlers, one medium right-hander, one left-hander, and one fast right-hander' (Warner 1934, p 39). The decline of slow bowling in the post-war era has made the googly bowler something of a rarity – a fact that merely enhances the effectiveness of a really top-class practitioner, as Abdul Qadir has recently demonstrated.

Finally, there is the perennial question of the word's etymology. The suggestion that it derives from a Maori word, and got its name during an MCC tour of New Zealand in 1902–3, can almost certainly be ruled out because the word 'googly' already existed in Australia in the 1890s, when it was apparently applied to any high, teasing slow delivery (cf Frith 1984, pp 36, 60). The most plausible explanation is that the googly – in both its pre- and post-Bosanquet phases – was a ball that so mystified the batsman that it made him 'goggle' (or 'google', to use an old dialectical variant). This is not wholly satisfactory, but probably as close as we are likely to get.

**goose game** *n* (obsolete) extremely cautious, defensive batting; stonewalling:

> *'Allen and Westcott were wisely content to play the goose-game for a draw'* (Headlam 1903, p 213).

The origins of this term – which was much in vogue around the turn of the century – are shrouded in mystery. The 'Game of Goose' is the name of a now obsolete board game dating back to the 16th century, but there is no evidence to show that extreme caution was the key to winning it. Another possible clue is the former Harrovian custom of playing the last cricket match of the year at the beginning of the autumn term: the game was traditionally followed by a dinner of goose and was called the 'Goose Match'. But again, it is difficult to see why this particular match should have been characterised by defensive batsmanship.

**grass** *vb* to drop a catch:

> 'His only chance came at 34 when a stinging cut against Gilmour was grassed by Hill in the gully' (R. Streeton, *The Times* 29 October 1982).

**greasy** *adj* denotes a wicket that is basically hard and true, on which a small amount of rain has fallen, making movement off the pitch very difficult to achieve, and thus generally favouring the batsman:

> 'A hard fast wicket, made greasy on the top by rain, is the best of all from the point of view of a batsman who knows how to utilise the opportunity' (Ranji 1897, p 84).

Unlike the more treacherous 'sticky' wicket (which requires heavy rain) the greasy wicket is not wholly ruled out by modern regulations on covering the pitch, since some time is likely to elapse between the onset of rain and the point when the wicket is fully covered.

**green** *adj* denotes a wicket with a relatively lush covering of grass that retains early morning moisture well into the day, producing conditions favourable to movement of the ball off the pitch:

> 'Phillip and Foster . . . kept the ball up to the bat and found movement off the seam on a greenish pitch' (Henry Blofeld, *Guardian* 31 May 1983).

The modern practice of covering the pitch outside playing hours, so far from shutting out moisture, actually inhibits its evaporation, with the result that even a fairly well mown strip may effectively be 'green' in the early part of the day, especially in English conditions.

**green top** *n* a 'green' wicket:

> 'Middlesex must have smacked their lips when Kent's captain,
> Chris Tavaré, won the toss and elected to bat on a green top'
> (John Parker, *Observer* 6 May 1984).

**ground** *n* **1** the entire area of land on which a match is played, as distinguished from the 'wicket' or 'pitch' between the two sets of stumps:

> 'The Umpires shall consider the ground as unfit for play when it
> is so wet or slippery as to deprive the bowlers of a reasonable
> foothold' (Law 3, note (c)).

**2** the area behind the popping crease of the wicket at which the batsman is standing, within which he is immune from being stumped or run out:

> 'As Gatting tried to regain his ground he was run out by about a
> foot' (Matthew Engel, *Guardian* 24 March 1984).

> 'A Batsman shall be considered to be out of his ground unless
> some part of his bat in his hand or of his person is grounded
> behind the line of the popping crease' (Law 29 § 1).

The crease itself is *not* part of the batsman's ground. The notation 'out of ground' often appears in 18th century score sheets as a mode of dismissal, presumably indicating a run-out.

~ *vb* **3** to bring the bat into contact with the pitch inside the popping crease, as when completing a run:

> 'Having grounded his bat after the first run, he stood his ground
> as his partner stormed through safely for his second' (Ian
> Brayshaw, *The Times* 27 December 1983).

**4** (of the ball) to make contact with the pitch after being bowled:

> 'The Ball may be made to cut or twist, after it has grounded, and
> will perplex most strikers' (Lambert 1816, p 15).

**grounder** *n* (obsolete) a very short-pitched underarm ball that travels mainly along the ground; a grub:

> 'The old bat used to be heavy at the point – very requisite for
> picking up a Grounder' (J. Pycroft, *Cricket Tutor* 1862, p 8).

**ground fielding** *n* the department of fielding concerned with stopping and retrieving balls that travel along the ground, rather than with catching:

'The ground fielding was again superb, with Fowler chasing and slithering and bringing up clouds of red dust just to turn fours into threes' (Matthew Engel, *Guardian* 21 January 1985).

**groundsman** *n* the person responsible for the maintenance of the ground and the preparation of wickets for matches.

**groundstaff** *n* a staff of players employed at a particular club, originally in order to give members batting and bowling practice:

'Vogler... was accepted on the MCC groundstaff, and in 1906 his bowling might have been penetrative enough for Middlesex to have offered him a contract' (Frith 1984, p 66).

The groundstaff has declined as an institution, and it is only at Lord's that a significant groundstaff is still retained, made up of promising young British and overseas players who, in addition to playing cricket, assist the groundsman, act as stewards at big matches, and so on.

**grub** *n* (also **grubber**) a ball bowled underarm along the ground; although this style of bowling has been more or less obsolete for almost a century, it is not actually forbidden by the Laws of the game:

'In the one-day international at Melbourne in 1981, when New Zealand needed six runs off the last ball of the match to tie it, Greg told his brother Trevor to bowl an underarm grub' (John Arlott, *Guardian* 4 January 1984).

'Armitage then tried a "grubber" all along the ground – Trevor Chappell wasn't the first – and Lillywhite took him off' (Frith 1984, p 27).

**guard** *n* the position adopted by the batsman in which the bat is held upright in front of the wicket and just inside the popping crease. The batsman 'takes' guard – usually at the start of an innings or following a change in the bowler's point of delivery – by asking the umpire (who 'gives' guard) to indicate the line from where he is standing to a stated point on the batsman's wicket, typically middle stump, middle-and-leg, or leg stump; the batsman then marks this position with a BLOCKHOLE (qv), which provides a point of orientation enabling him to assess the ball's line of flight and to determine his own position in relation to the wicket.

**gully** *n* a close off-side fielding position (or the player occupying it) slightly behind the line of the batsman's wicket, between the slips and point. Gully is a fairly recent term for a position that would formerly have been called short third man or backward point. It became established as a regular position in its own right – and thus eventually evolved a distinctive name – following the development of the modern OFF-THEORY attack (qv) towards the end of the 19th century:

> 'A. O. Jones . . . was, indeed, quite exceptional as a fieldsman in any position, but especially in the slips and at short third man, or in the "gully" as it is called nowadays' (P. F. Warner, *My Cricketing Life* 1921, p 229).

The name apparently derives from the more general meaning of gully, and suggests a narrow channel or 'gorge' between point and the slips. See FIELDING POSITIONS.

**hacker** *n* (especially in South Africa) an attacking batsman, especially one with a hard-hitting uncultured style batting in the lower order; a slogger.

**half-century** *n* a batsman's score of between 50 and 99 runs, made in a single innings. See also CENTURY, DOUBLE CENTURY.

**half-cock** *adj* **1** denoting a defensive batting stroke in which the bat is held quite straight, more or less over the popping crease, and the ball is allowed to come on to it:

> 'With his next ball he had Botham well caught by Martin Crowe at short-leg off a half-cock defensive push' (Andrew Longmore, *Cricketer* April 1984).

This is an improvised stroke, made when the batsman has misjudged the pitch of the ball and brought his front foot down the wicket in order to make a forward shot, only to find that 'he cannot reach far enough to smother the ball at the pitch' (*Badminton* 1888, p 51). The arms are then quickly drawn back to effect a stroke that is neither forward nor back.

~ *adv* **2** making a half-cock stroke:

> 'In the next over Richardson, playing half-cock at a brisk outswinger, edged Davidson to third slip' (Peebles 1959, p 71).

**half-hit** *n* (old) a badly-timed shot that sends the ball only a relatively short distance:

> 'Extra cover-point, and sometimes even cover-point as well, may be brought across the wicket and placed for half-hits wide

*on the on – i.e. about half the distance from the batsman that a
deep field would stand' (Badminton 1888, p 112).*

**half-pitcher** *n* (especially in Australia, old) a fast short-pitched
ball; a bouncer:

*'He had to duck for safety as a half-pitcher from Voce flew past
his ear' (Melbourne Argus 17 January 1933).*

**half-volley** *n* a ball that pitches just in front of the popping crease
and comes straight on to the bat, enabling the
batsman to hit it shortly after it bounces with a
minimum of danger or difficulty:

*'His first ball was a long-hop, the second a swinging half-volley:
Wood hit both for fours to leg' (Brearley 1982, p 75).*

Even a ball of good length (ie, slightly shorter than a
half-volley) can by deft footwork be turned into a
half-volley:

*'Batsmen who are quick on their feet often jump out to the pitch
of a ball, and thereby make it a half-volley' (Warner 1934,
p 19).*

See diagram at LENGTH.

The word is derived from the general sporting term
'volley' (from the French *volée*, flight) meaning either a
ball that reaches its target without bouncing, or a hit
or kick at a moving ball (as in tennis or soccer) before it
bounces. Cricket's 'half-volley' is a ball that is 'almost
a volley'.

**hand** *n* (obsolete) **1** a member of a team; a player:

*'The second match between London and Kingston & Moulsey
. . . the Country lost five of their best hands that played on
Moulsey Hurst, but notwithstanding all that, the Country won
their match by 3 notches' (London & Country Journal 25 July
1739).*

**2** (also **hands**) an innings:

*'There were several very considerable wagers laid of the first
hands which were won by the London gamesters by one notch'
(St James's Evening Post 29 June 1732).*

*'Umpires . . . to allow Two Minutes for each Man to come inn
when one is out, and Ten Minutes between each Hand' (Laws
1744).*

**3** the score made by an individual or team in an innings:

'*Andrew* [Freemantle] . . . *would often get long hands, and against the best bowling too*' (Nyren 1833 in *HM*, p 80).

**handled the ball** *adv* a mode of dismissal in which the batsman is given out 'if he wilfully touches the ball while in play with the hand not holding the bat unless he does so with the consent of the opposite side' (Law 33); the dismissal is entered in the scorebook as 'handled the ball' and the wicket is not credited to the bowler.

Although it is exceptionally rare for a batsman to be dismissed in this way – since 1857 there have been fewer than 30 instances at first-class level – the rule against handling the ball is of great antiquity and appears in the original (1744) code of Laws, as follows: 'If the Striker touches, or takes up the Ball before it has lain quite still, unless ask'd by the Bowler, or Wicket-Keeper, it's out'. An early instance of the law in action appears in a match report in the *Kentish Weekly Post*, 8 September 1797, where a member of the Strood Club, a Mr Horn, is recorded as being out 'handling b. in play'. Rather more recently, in the latter half of 1982, Mohsin Khan and Desmond Haynes became respectively the third and fourth players in Test cricket to be dismissed in this way.

**hang** *vb* **1** (also **hang back**) to lose pace after pitching and come on to the bat more slowly than expected, especially as a result of back-spin imparted by the bowler:

'*The ball that hangs or stops a bit after pitching instead of coming on is perhaps the most fatal ball that is bowled*' (*Badminton* 1888, p 77).

'*Then the West Indian* [Kallicharran], *looking comfortable on 55, mistimed a crafty ball from Emburey which hung back and Barlow took a simple catch at cover*' (Robert Armstrong, *Guardian* 3 August 1983).

**2 – hang one's bat out to dry** to hold one's bat loosely, away from the body, as when playing forward or across to the ball but without moving the feet to get in line with it; the resulting loss of power and control makes this a hazardous procedure.

~ *n* **3** loss of pace after pitching:

> 'However short and bad a ball, it should be carefully watched all
> the way in case of an unexpected hang or rise' (Warner 1934,
> p 17).

**hanging guard** *n* (obsolete) a defensive position in which the batsman goes on to the back foot and allows the bat to
'hang' in a perpendicular position so as to cover the
wicket:

> 'Practise going (from the attitude of play) back quickly to the
> hanging guard, and notice if your bat hang well over to cover as
> much of the wicket as it can' (Felix 1850, p 16).

**harrier** *n* (slang) a ball that rises very steeply off the pitch; a
steepler:

> 'Hadlee produced a "harrier", a ball that took off almost
> vertically and ground the knuckles of Lamb's right hand' (Scyld
> Berry, *Observer* 5 February 1984).

The delivery is named after the vertical takeoff Harrier
jet, and the term came into vogue at the time of the
South Atlantic campaign of 1982, in which these
planes featured prominently.

**Harrow bat** *n* a bat that is one size down from the full-size adult
bat, for use by younger players.

**Harrow drive** *n* a batting stroke made unintentionally when the
batsman, attempting to play a normal off drive, fails to
get properly in line and deflects the ball off the inside
edge of the bat, either through the slips or down
towards long leg:

> 'Fletcher had the luck to see two of his nine boundaries come off
> the inside edge, "Harrow drives" or "Chinese cuts"' (Berry
> 1982, p 113).

The term was not always a derisive one, but originally
denoted an orthodox drive through extra cover, which
was thought to be especially characteristic of Harrovian batsmen:

> 'The "Harrow drive" towards extra-cover-point was at one time
> peculiar to the school' (Ranji 1897, p 294).

Its more modern meaning may well have been foisted
on it by Harrow's arch-rivals:

'Mr. Stevens scored several useful 4's by the stroke through the
slips which Etonians call the Harrow drive' (*The Times* 19 July
1923).

**hat trick** *n* (also formerly **hat feat**) the act of dismissing three
batsmen in three consecutive deliveries:

'*Ferrands performed the hat feat by bowling 3 wickets with
successive balls of an over*' (Wisden 1873, p 33).

'*Simpson-Hayward took seven wickets for 34 runs and three of
those with consecutive balls. He was presented by the last
batsman of the trio with a fez, in token of the hat-trick*'
(Headlam 1903, p 175).

The hat trick is so called because of the old custom,
probably originating in the mid-19th century, of
presenting a new hat to a bowler who achieved this
feat (see quote above). A hat trick still 'counts' if the
three consecutive dismissals are spread over two
consecutive overs by the same bowler, or even over
both innings of a match, though in the latter case the
dramatic impact is obviously somewhat diminished.
Like many cricket terms, hat trick has entered the
vocabulary of many sports, and indeed the general
language (as in phrases like 'a hat trick of election
victories').

**headquarters** *n* Lord's cricket ground, considered as the 'headquarters' of the game:

'*England had selected no fewer than five Middlesex players to
play New Zealand at headquarters*' (Jim Laker, WCM
December 1983).

**helmet** *n* a piece of strong protective headgear, sometimes
equipped with a metal grille in front of the face, worn
by batsmen as a protection against fast short-pitched
bowling, and sometimes also by fielders in close
catching positions. Helmets first appeared in the late
1970s and quickly became established – especially
among younger players – as an item of equipment
almost as essential as batting gloves or pads. This has
predictably drawn criticism from the older generation, but it should be remembered that when pads
were first introduced in the mid-19th century they got
a similarly contemptuous reception from older players who had 'managed perfectly well without them'
(see now PAD). But aside from this sort of criticism, a

more serious argument against helmets is the theory that batsmen's unconscious instincts of self-preservation are fractionally impaired by the sense of security that comes of wearing a helmet, and it is certainly true that helmeted batsmen have been hit much more often than their helmetless elders ever were. Players themselves, however, would argue that the helmet greatly increases the batsman's confidence, and it is hard to imagine that the wearing of helmets will turn out to be just a passing fad.

The arrival of the helmet has led to certain adjustments in the Laws. For example, if a ball struck by the batsman lodges in a fielder's helmet (as in the protective grille at the front) the ball becomes 'dead' and the batsman cannot be out (Law 32 § 2b). Similarly, a catch does not count if the ball rebounds off a fielder's helmet, whereas a ball could legitimately be caught if it ricocheted off a fielder's head! (Law 32 § 2e). The old law imposing a five-run penalty in the case of a fieldsman stopping the ball with his hat (introduced in 1798) still stands, and applies equally to the case of a ball being stopped by a helmet left lying on the ground (Law 41 § 1).

**hip** *n* (obsolete) a leg-side fielding position (or the player occupying it) roughly equivalent to the modern square leg. Originally the term indicated the general area square of the wicket on the leg-side, as if starting from the hip of the batsman, whose stance was more 'two-eyed' in the early game:

> 'If the ball is directed to the legs of the Striker, or near Stump, it is frequently hit to the hip' (Lambert 1816, p 13).

See also LONG FIELD.

**hit** *n* **1** an act of striking the ball in an attempt to score runs, as distinguished from a purely defensive push or blocking stroke:

> 'To make this hit [the cut] . . . the ball must be judged to bound well to the off, rather short' (Felix 1850, p 31).

> 'With one of the largest hits seen in Test cricket, Garner hit Hogan out of the ground' (WCM May 1984).

~ *vb* **2** to strike the ball, especially to do so forcefully in an attempt to score runs, rather than playing purely defensively:

*'Before this alteration in the bat defence was almost unknown. The long pod and curved form of the bat, as seen in the old paintings, was made only for hitting'* (Pycroft 1854 in *HM*, p 134).

*'Having endeavoured . . . to enumerate a few principles as to defensive tactics, we will now try and discuss offensive tactics, or hitting'* (*Badminton* 1888, p 59).

*'It was a fine performance, characterised by powerful hitting which brought him long sixes off Marshall, Garner, Holding and Harper'* (Tony Cozier, *Cricketer* June 1984).

As the quotations suggest, this word has undergone a noticeable change in meaning over the last hundred years or so. It was originally used to describe any scoring stroke as distinguished from purely defensive play, but it came increasingly to be applied to the attacking shots played with a cross bat, as opposed to the more 'respectable' straight-batted 'strokes' such as the cover drive. In discussing the on drive played to a ball pitching outside leg stump, Ranji notes that it 'can either be a genuine hit or a very hard forward stroke' (1897, p 188). More recently, the word has become synonymous with batting of unrestrained aggression, and while a classical batsman is admired for his 'strokeplay', a player whose primary instinct is to attack is called a 'hitter'. See also LEG HIT.

**hitter** *n* an aggressive batsman who plays attacking shots whenever possible:

> *'When a hitter is in, and is hitting to all parts of the field . . . the ball may be bowled with a great chance of success'* (*Badminton* 1888, p 110).

**hit the ball twice** *adv* a mode of dismissal in which the batsman is given out 'if, after the ball is struck or is stopped by any part of his person, he wilfully strikes it again with his bat or person except for the sole purpose of guarding his wicket' (Law 34 § 1); the dismissal is entered in the scorebook as 'hit the ball twice' and is not credited to the bowler. If the batsman 'lawfully' hits the ball a second time (i.e. to prevent it hitting his stumps) he is not allowed to take any runs from the shot. 'Hit the ball twice' is one of the modes of dismissal that remain valid even in the case of a no-ball. The rule dates back to the earliest (1744) code of Laws: 'If a Ball is nipp'd up, and he strikes it again wilfully, before it came to the Wicket, it's out'. Allowing for changes in wording, the rule has remained in force throughout the history of the game. It has, however, been very sparingly invoked: with only ten instances since 1864 of batsmen being out in this way at first-class level, 'hit the ball twice' is the rarest of all forms of dismissal, with the exception of the modern TIMED OUT (qv).

**hit under leg** *n* an obsolete batting stroke, similar to the DRAW (qv), in which the front foot is raised off the ground and the ball is deflected off an angled bat under the raised leg and into the area backward of square on the leg-side.

**hit wicket** *adv* a mode of dismissal in which the batsman is given out if 'his wicket is broken with any part of his person, dress, or equipment as a result of any action taken by him in preparing to receive or in receiving a delivery, or in setting off for his first run' (Law 35 § 1). As the wording makes clear, the batsman does not have to strike the stumps with his *bat* in order to be out hit wicket; the effect is the same if, for example, his cap falls off and disturbs the bails. The dismissal is credited to the bowler and is entered in the scorebook as 'hit wicket b [bowler]'. The batsman is not out, however, if he hits the wicket while trying to avoid being stumped or run out.

The earliest (1744) code of Laws includes a hit wicket ruling: 'If he strikes, or treads down, or falls himself upon his Wicket in striking (but not in over-running) it's out'. Unaccountably, the rule was omitted from the code of 1774, but it reappears with a revised wording in 1788, and it has remained essentially unchanged ever since. Early scorebooks show a variety of ways of recording such dismissals, including 'struck himself out' and 'beat down his stumps'. But in those days, long before the introduction of the declaration and the follow-on, the hit wicket rule had an additional significance, in that it was often invoked as a ploy for cutting short an innings, so that many batsmen dismissed in this way had actually broken their wickets deliberately, as in the following report: 'Kingsclere made 71, and Newbury nearly 200 and beat their own wickets down, expecting when the evening had so far advanced as not to admit of any further play, that the game would have been yielded up to them' (*Reading Mercury* 15 August 1791).

**hole out** *vb* to be dismissed by hitting the ball, usually into the deep field, and being caught:

> 'For the next hour he [Viv Richards] *decimated the shell-shocked Indian bowling, scoring 61 off 35 balls with four huge sixes and five fours before he holed out to wide long-on'* (Tony Cozier, *Cricketer* April 1983).

'Hole out' is a golfing expression, meaning to sink the ball into a hole, but in the language of cricket it represents an undesirable rather than a desirable end.

**home** *n* the area between the striker's wicket and the popping crease, considered as the batsman's own territory within which he is safe from being stumped or run out; the batsman's 'ground':

> 'When the Ball has been in hand by one of the Keepers, or Stoppers, and the Player has been at Home, he may go where he pleases till the next Ball is bowl'd' (*Laws* 1744).

> 'They were going along very nicely indeed when a smart pick-up and return by Armstrong compelled Arnold to do his best to get home' (*Melbourne Argus* 19 January 1904).

**home-and-easy** *adj* (obsolete) denotes a type of high, lobbing under-arm bowling, so called because it was pitched well up to the batsman (cf HOME TOSS) and delivered at an 'easy' pace:

> 'He [Lord Frederick Beauclerk] *introduced a slow home-and-easy kind of bowling, which was very effective'* (Mitford 1833 in *HM*, p 132).

**home toss** (also **home pitch**) *n* (obsolete) a FULL TOSS (qv), so called because it is pitched right up to the batsman standing at 'home' in his ground:

> 'The Catapulta could bowl a home toss, a grubber, . . .' (*Bell's Life*, 15 October 1837).

**hook** *n* **1** (also **hookshot**) a batting stroke in which a short-pitched ball is swept round to the leg-side with a horizontal bat. The stroke can be played to any short ball pitching on or not too far outside the stumps, and is executed by moving the back foot far enough across to get right behind the line of the ball; the bat, held horizontally, is then swung across the ball's line of flight, usually sending it into the area between square

and fine leg. The traditional distinction between the hook and the PULL (qv) is that the former is made off the back foot while the latter is a front-foot stroke. Some commentators however, would argue that the hook can be played off either foot; a more obvious – and less contentious – distinction lies in the point at which the ball is struck. The pull is played on the half-volley (or, if slightly later, to a ball that has kept very low), whereas the hook makes contact with the ball well after it has pitched and often when it has reached a considerable height – which is why the hook, if successfully executed, is regarded as the most effective antidote to the bouncer.

~ *vb* **2** to strike the ball when making a hook:

> *'Hooking a fast bowler is fraught with no little danger, for often the ball comes shoulder high to the batsman'* (Warner 1934, p 17).

**hook-stroke** *n* (old) a HOOK:

> 'Remember that sovereign hook-stroke of his; nay, he did not hit the ball – he dismissed it from his presence' (Cardus 1978, p 40).

**how 'dat** (Corfu) used both in appealing (like howzat) and to describe the position of the batsman against whom a successful appeal is made (like 'out').

**howzat** *interj* (also **how's that, how was he**, etc) an interjection used by fielders when appealing to the umpire to give a batsman out. The unabbreviated form is 'how's that, umpire?' but it is unlikely that anything so sedate is ever actually heard on a cricket field.

**hustle** *n* increase of pace by the ball as it comes off the pitch, forcing the batsman to react hastily:

> 'Edmonds . . . knows better than anyone that while the Oval pitch sometimes dusts, it seldom encourages hustle' (Robin Marlar, *Sunday Times* 10 July 1983).

**ICC** *abbr* the International Cricket Conference: a body that exercises general supervision over cricket at the international level. The ICC is responsible for – among other things – approving the details of Test tours and other international tournaments like the Prudential World Cup, conferring Test status on new countries, and discussing proposals for changing the Laws of the game. It was founded in 1909, as the Imperial Cricket Conference, and its original members were England, Australia, and South Africa. India, New Zealand, and the West Indies were admitted to membership in 1926, followed by Pakistan in 1953, while South Africa's membership lapsed on its withdrawal from the Commonwealth in 1961. In 1965 the ICC changed its name to become the International Cricket Conference and a new two-tier membership system was adopted, involving a distinction between 'full members', whose representative sides are qualified to play official Test matches, and 'associate members', comprising those countries 'where cricket is firmly established and organised'. The six countries already belonging in 1965 became full members, and the election of Sri Lanka to full membership in 1981 brought the number of Test-playing countries to seven. The associate members are: Argentina, Bangladesh, Bermuda, Canada, Denmark, East Africa, Fiji, Gibraltar, Hong Kong, Israel, Kenya, Malaysia, Netherlands, Papua New Guinea, Singapore, USA, West Africa, Zimbabwe.

**in** *adv & adj* **1** in or into the position of being the batsman or batting side:

'The Party that wins the Toss-up, may order which Side shall go in first, at his Option' (*Laws* 1744).

'With the score at 57–3, I went in ahead of Gatting, hoping to steady the innings for a while' (Brearley 1982, p 116).

'A cricketer need only look at his scores and references to see how often the out side . . . has prevented the in side from getting the runs required' (*Badminton* 1888, p 197).

**~** *n* (obsolete) **2** a decision by the umpire that a batsman is not out:

'They are the sole Judges of all Outs and Inns [and] of all fair or unfair Play' (*Laws* 1744).

**infield** *n* the part of a cricket field lying relatively close to the wicket as distinguished from the outfield:

'This time Ghai stayed in the infield after the over' (Matthew Engel, *Guardian* 21 January 1985).

**infielder** *n* a fielder occupying a position relatively close to the wicket; a close fielder:

'Both times there is a strident chorus of appeal and Turner is surrounded by infielders with arms and legs splayed in mid-air' (Moorhouse 1979, p 58).

**inning** *n* (obsolete) the innings of an individual batsman:

'If the Notches of one Player are laid against another, the Bets depend on the First Inning, unless otherwise specified' (*Laws* 1809).

See INNINGS.

**innings** *n* **1** a division of a cricket match in which one of the two teams has its turn to bat, or is 'in':

'The pitch may be rolled at the request of the Captain of the batting side, for a period of not more than 7 minutes before the start of each innings' (Law 10 § 1).

First-class matches typically consist of two innings per side, taken alternately except in the case of a follow-on, while one-day games usually consist of one innings per side. The decision as to which side shall have the first innings lies with the captain who has won the toss. A team's innings is considered to be at an end when 10 wickets have fallen or (in certain competitions) when a stipulated number of overs has been bowled; it may also be declared closed by the captain at any time.

**2** the turn of an individual player to bat, especially when considered in terms of the number of runs he scores or the quality of his batting:

> '*Ponsford and Oldfield* [put on] *63 more for the sixth and I was dreadfully sorry that Oldfield's innings should end as it did*' (Larwood 1933, p 130).

> '*At Old Trafford, Botham played an innings of classical power and splendour*' (Brearley 1982, p 120).

**3 – by an innings** indicates the winning margin when one side scores more runs in a single innings than its opponents score in both their innings; a match completed in this way is termed an **innings defeat** (or an **innings victory**, depending on one's viewpoint).

The word 'inning' originally denotes 'an act of going in or bringing in' and is formed in the same way as 'outing', 'offing', and similar words. It is first found in a cricket context in the early 18th century, though an earlier form **going in** is still encountered 50 years or so later:

> '*Mr Colchin . . . displayed his abilities to great advantage on the Middlesex side, bringing at the first going in 42 notches*' (*Middlesex Journal* 13 August 1772).

At first the singular form 'inning' was used to indicate the turn of an individual batsman, while the collective effort of the team was their 'innings' – a plural formed in the normal way. At some later point the form 'innings' ceased to be treated as a plural and began to be used without distinction for both the individual's turn and the performance of the whole team.

**insert** *vb* (of a captain) to put the opposing side in to bat after winning the toss:

> '*The outcome then was a disgracefully substandard pitch on which the inserted New Zealand side was out for 65 (Derek Underwood 6 for 12) in less than three hours*' (Terry Power, WCM March 1984).

**inside** *prep* with the bat moving along a line on the near side of the ball's line of flight, so that the ball passes the outside edge of the bat:

'Howarth played inside a perfect ball which just clipped the off bail' (Matthew Engel, *Guardian* 3 February 1984).

Compare OUTSIDE.

**inside edge** *n* **1** the edge of the bat, when held more or less perpendicularly, that is closer to the batsman; the 'leg-side' edge of the bat:

'Rutherford went stubbornly on, but at 92 he played back at Statham and was caught at the wicket, apparently off the inside edge' (Peebles 1959, p 31).

**2** a ball unintentionally deflected off the inside edge of the bat:

'Jeff Crowe got away with what looked as though it must have been an inside edge to Bob Taylor' (John Thicknesse, *Cricketer* April 1984).

**inside out** *adv & adj* sending the ball into the off-side area, especially between extra cover and point, by playing slightly *inside* the line of it with a downward swing of the bat, so that the ball is deflected off the *outside* edge of the bat:

'It was Gomes who started the Indian decline, first when Yashpal Sharma scooped him "inside out" to one of the three offside fielders' (Christopher Martin-Jenkins, *Cricketer* August 1983).

'The tail folded without much resistance, though Willis played two of his unique sliced, inside-out drives over the off-side' (Brearley 1982, p 85).

**insinuator** *n* (obsolete) a slow flighted or turning ball:

'Thirty runs were wanting; a weak bat advancing; Lord Frederick bowling slow "insinuators"; and a good wicket-keeper on the look-out' (Felix 1850, p 21).

**inswing** *n* movement of the ball in the air, typically from the line of off stump or middle-and-off in towards leg stump:

'The generality of seam bowling is inswing, which is relatively easy to produce; but it can be monotonous and restrictive of strokes' (Arlott 1983, p 38).

Inswing is on the whole easier for the batsman to deal with than outswing, and so less likely to produce wickets. But its effectiveness as a means of containment has made it a valued weapon in limited-overs cricket. See SWING, and compare OUTSWING.

**inswinger** *n* **1** a ball that swings in towards leg stump from a line initially closer to the off:

> *'Edgar struck a typically trenchant 84 and Cairns's mild inswingers brought a handful of wickets'* (Peter Roebuck, *Cricketer* November 1983).

**2** an inswing bowler:

> *'If one of the opening bowlers is an inswinger he* [the batsman] *should open his stance to bring himself in line with the ball from the bowler's hand'* (Alf Gover, *Cricketer* September 1984).

**intimidation** *n* the intentional use of bowling methods that are calculated to cause or threaten injury to the batsman:

> *'Umpires shall consider intimidation to be the deliberate bowling of fast short pitched balls which by their length, height and direction are intended or likely to inflict physical injury on the Striker'* (Law 42 § 8).

There is widespread concern that the present Law, which requires umpires to make judgements about the bowler's intent, is unlikely ever to achieve the purpose for which it was framed. To quote one eminent opinion:

> *'As regards intimidation, the umpires have to be given a matter of fact to determine, and the only one that occurs to me is the line across the pitch, any ball short of which would be a no-ball'* (E. W. Swanton, *Cricketer* March 1984).

See now BOUNCER.

**jerk** *vb* (obsolete) to deliver the ball using an underarm or roundarm action in which the elbow is brought against the side of the body so that the ball is catapulted forward:

> 'The Ball must be bowled (not thrown or jerked)' (*Laws* 1816).

The ban on 'jerking' is elucidated by Felix (1850, p 44): 'Neither the elbow, nor any other part of the arm in the act of delivering the ball, may touch the hip, or ribs, or any other part of the body whereby any increased speed may be communicated to the ball'.

**jerker** *n* (obsolete) a bowler who 'jerks' the ball rather than bowling it fairly:

> 'Brett was . . . neither a thrower nor a jerker, but a legitimate downright bowler' (Nyren 1833 in *HM*, p 44).

See also YORKER.

**Jessopian** *adj* (of a batting stroke or style of batting) characterised by unrestrained aggression; big-hitting and fast-scoring:

> 'Evans led the way with some square-cuts of Jessopian quality, and the 300 was soon up' (Peebles 1959, p 30).

Although one-off adjectives have of course often been coined to describe the style of great players ('Bradmanesque', 'Hobbsian', etc) 'Jessopian' is probably the only one that has become really established, perhaps because it denotes an extreme, uncompromising, and therefore easily categorised style of play. The term derives from Gilbert Jessop, who played for

Cambridge, Gloucestershire, and England from the 1890s until the first world war. Scorned by the purists, Jessop's powerful and often unorthodox hitting established some remarkable records for fast scoring, including: a 50 in quarter of an hour (Gloucestershire v Somerset, 1904), a 150 in 63 minutes (Gents v Players, 1907), and a double century in two hours (Gloucestershire v Sussex, 1903 – a record equalled by Clive Lloyd in 1976 and finally beaten by Raví Shastrí in January 1985).

**jump** *vb* **1** (also **jump out**) to move quickly forward out of one's ground, especially in order to make a drive; by going down the wicket, the batsman is able to convert a ball of full length into a half-volley:

> *'Hopkins jumped at one from Rhodes and missed, but was back before Lilley . . . could get the bails off'* (*Melbourne Argus* 12 December 1903).

> *'The best method of meeting him is to be ever ready to jump out to drive anything the least over-pitched'* (Warner 1934, p 15).

~ *n* **2** an act of advancing quickly down the wicket:

> *'The jump, or the run to drive, was not a stroke they remembered only when they found themselves tied up by a length bowler'* (James 1963, p 210).

**kato** (Corfu) *lit 'down'*: the fielding side. Compare PANO.

**keep** *vb* (also **keep wicket**) to act as wicket-keeper:

> *'Downton has not only kept splendidly, but with an exemplary technique has batted longer than anyone in the series except Lamb'* (Michael Carey, *Daily Telegraph* 13 August 1984).

> *'Keeping is a craft which takes time to absorb'* (Neil Hallam, WCM August 1984).

**keeper, 'keeper** *n* = WICKET-KEEPER:

> *'Amal Silva, the reserve 'keeper and opening batsman, has toured Australia and New Zealand'* (Harold de Andrado, *Cricketer* September 1984).

**keep low** *vb* (of the ball) to fail to rise to the expected height after pitching:

> *'First he dismissed Dyson, whom he forced on to the back foot, with a ball that kept low'* (Brearley 1982, p 93).

**kick** *vb* (of the ball) to rise steeply and unexpectedly high off the pitch; steeple:

> *'It was soon evident from the way the ball kicked and hung that runs would be difficult to get'* (Headlam 1903, p 163).

> *'Three balls later Yallop had gone, beautifully caught at short square-leg from a nasty, kicking delivery'* (Brearley 1982, p 77).

**king pair** *n* a 'pair' recorded by a batsman who is twice dismissed without scoring off the first ball he receives:

> 'He took guard on a King Pair, of course, and was obviously very nervous' (Bomber Wells, *Cricketer* December 1982).

See also PAIR, EMPEROR PAIR.

**knock** *n* a turn at batting by an individual or team; an innings:

> 'They will have to look to compiling well over 400, and very briskly, in their first knock to exert any pressure at all' (John Sheppard, *Sunday Times* 8 July 1984).

> 'Crowe hit eight fours in his attacking knock' (WCM January 1985).

Though more or less synonymous with 'innings' the term tends – when applied to an individual batsman's innings – to be used to describe an attacking spell of batting (such as a brisk, entertaining half-century) and is unlikely to be applied to a prolonged, defensive occupation of the crease.

**Kookaburra ball** *n* a hard, resilient type of cricket ball widely used in Australia, having a wider and flatter seam than a conventional ball, and tending to retain its shine for longer on hard wickets:

> 'The much more dangerous "bodyline" of Lillee and Thomson, bowling with Kookaburra cricket balls which kept their bounce for 40 or 50 overs instead of rapidly going soft like the balls of Larwood's day, also won a series for Australia' (Tony Pawson, *Cricketer* July 1983).

**lap**  *n* **1** a cross-batted stroke – somewhat like a pull – played especially to a ball pitching on or outside off stump and sending it into the area between mid-wicket and square leg.

~  *vb* **2** to strike the ball into the leg-side area when making a lap:

> 'Knott, typically, cut and lapped zealously and helped to add 47 for the sixth wicket' (David Green, *Daily Telegraph* 1 June 1984).

**last over**  see CLOSE OF PLAY

**late**  *adv & adj* (happening or done) at a relatively advanced stage of the ball's flight:

> 'There are very few players, indeed, who can cut late with anything like effect or severity' (Ranji 1897, p 182).

> 'He kept the ball well up, swinging it late from outside the off-stump to middle-and-off' (James 1963, p 92).

> 'There is no smothering a good late outswinger which starts about middle stump; and, if it finds the edge . . . must almost certainly go to slip or wicketkeeper as a catch' (Arlott 1983, p 38).

**late cut**  *n* a cut made by striking an off-side ball at the latest possible moment, after it has passed the batsman and sometimes after it has passed the stumps, sending the ball into the area behind gully. Described by Ranji (1897, p 182) as the 'most telling' of cuts, it demands great power and control in the wrists.

**late-cut** *vb* to strike the ball making a late cut:

> '*Cowdrey reached his fifty when he late-cut Benaud for a couple*' (Peebles 1959, p 159).

**late order** *n* the players batting at or towards the end of a team's batting line-up; the tail:

> '*It was left to a distinctly out-of-touch Lamb to help the late order salvage something*' (Matthew Engel, *Guardian* 4 January 1984).

> '*Ravi Ratnayeke . . . ran through the late-order batsmen with a spell of 4 for 10 from six overs*' (WCM May 1984).

**lbw** *adv* (also **leg-before-wicket, leg-before**) a mode of dismissal in which the batsman is given out if he stops a ball, other than with his bat or hand, which in the umpire's judgement would otherwise have hit the wicket. This dismissal is credited to the bowler and entered in the scorebook as 'lbw b [bowler]'.

In its current state the lbw law prescribes three situations in which a decision may be given against the batsman, subject in all cases to the overriding condition that the ball *would have hit the wicket* had it not been intercepted by the batsman. The batsman should be given out: (1) if the ball pitches in a straight line between wicket and wicket THEN hits the batsman standing between wicket and wicket (or, in the case of a full toss, if the ball would have pitched between wicket and wicket if not intercepted by the batsman); (2) if the ball pitches outside off stump THEN hits the batsman standing between wicket and wicket; and (3) if the ball pitches on the off-side of the wicket AND is intercepted by the batsman outside the line of off stump BUT in the umpire's opinion the batsman makes no attempt to play a stroke. In all three cases a decision can still be given against the batsman even if the point of interception is above the level of the bails.

Apart from a general injunction against 'standing unfair to strike', the original (1744) code of Laws has no mention of lbw as a mode of dismissal; but with the old-style curved bats, requiring a stance well outside leg stump, the problem would scarcely have arisen. The arrival of the straight bat in about 1770 opened up new possibilities for the defence of the wicket and these must have been quickly exploited by

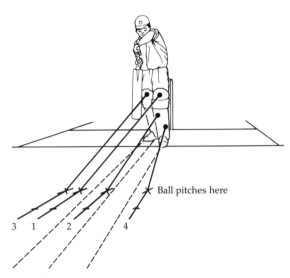

Ball pitches here

3 1 2 4

1 & 2: batsman out
3 : batsman out if not playing a stroke
4 : batsman not out

batsmen, because in 1774 the specific 'offence' of lbw appears for the first time in the Laws: the batsman was to be given out if he 'puts his leg before the wicket with a design to stop the ball, and actually prevents the ball from hitting the wicket by it'. The next 200 years saw a gradual extension in the scope of the law which, effectively, put the bowler in an increasingly advantageous position. The question of the batsman's 'design' was quickly eliminated from the reckoning (1788), so that even accidental obstruction could lead to dismissal; the point of interception was extended in 1823 to include any part of the batsman's body, not just his legs; and, much more recently, the law was further extended in 1937 to include the case of balls pitching outside off stump (condition (2) above). The third type of dismissal (condition (3) above) was introduced in 1970 in an effort to discourage deliberate 'padding up' to the ball, a ploy developed by batsmen to combat the 1937 ruling. Many would argue, however, that *both* modern extensions to the law (1937 and 1970) have given an undue advantage to the off-break and inswing bowlers, possibly to the detriment of more attacking styles of bowling. The conditions for an lbw decision are now defined with considerable precision, but the difficulties for the umpire are as great as ever, and few would disagree with the verdict of a 19th-century commentator that the lbw law is 'the most perplexing and disagreeable of the whole code' (Box 1868, p 135).

**leading arm** *n* the bowler's non-bowling arm, the left arm in the case of a right-arm bowler. At the moment before the bowling arm is brought over to deliver the ball, the 'leading arm' is held upward and forward, pointing down the wicket:

> *'Dilley . . . worked at running in closer to the stumps and getting his leading arm round to fine-leg instead of third man'* (Scyld Berry, *Observer* 22 May 1983).

**leading edge** *n* the edge of the bat that is nearer the bowler as the batsman plays a stroke:

> *'Gooch was caught and bowled off a leading edge next morning for 127'* (Berry 1982, p 138).

**leather** *n* the cricket ball, so called because of the material from which its outer cover is made; the term is best known from the almost clichéed expression 'the sound of leather on willow', but it is also used in other cricket contexts:

> *'They* [the French] *can see no delight in being bowled at over 22 yards, or of getting in the way of "leather" at a much longer range'* (Box 1868, p 22).

> *'They gave us a fine bit of leather-hunting in their second innings, scoring 341'* (W. G. Grace, *Cricket* 1891, p 89).

**leave** *vb* (of the ball) to move sharply away from the batsman, going towards the off-side from an initially straighter line:

> *'The ball that undid Greenidge left him quite viciously as he played back, and had him caught at third slip'* (Dilip Rao, *Guardian* 9 April 1984).

**leg** *n* **1** that side of the pitch on which the striker stands to receive the ball, separated from the off-side by an imaginary line passing between the two wickets, bounded at its outside edge by the fine-leg, square-leg, mid-wicket, and long-on boundaries, and constituting half of the entire playing area. Also called ON. See FIELDING POSITIONS.

**2** (obsolete) a leg-side fielding position (or the player occupying it) equivalent to the modern square leg:

'The Man that stands to the Leg. He stands the on side, little behind the straight line of the popping crease; if he stands to save the runs, he will stand fifteen yards or more from the stumps' (Boxall 1800, p 59).

The unadorned 'leg' gradually gave way to more detailed descriptions like square leg, short leg, and long leg.

~ *adj & adv* **3** on, towards, or relating to the leg-side:

'It may be taken for certain that for every leg ball you see now in first-class matches you saw ten or twenty in former days' (Badminton 1888, p 65).

'One peculiarity of the leg-twisting ball is that when the ground is soft and sticky it is comparatively of no avail' (Badminton 1888, p 113).

'As runs came Larwood packed his leg field; and now had seven men on the leg side' (Melbourne Argus 3 December 1932).

**leg-before,** *adv* = LBW:
**leg-before-wicket**

'Qadir quickly dispatched Foster, leg-before to the sweep' (Robin Marlar, Sunday Times 25 March 1984).

**leg-break** *n* **1** a relatively slow ball that deviates from leg towards off after pitching. Technically, the term can apply to any ball breaking *away* from the batsman, such as a right-arm bowler's googly bowled to a left-handed batsman or the 'stock' ball of a slow left-arm finger-spinner. But for practical purposes leg-break generally denotes the ball bowled by a right-arm wrist-spinner (see WRIST-SPIN). Compare LEG-CUTTER.

**2** deviation of the ball from leg towards off after pitching, caused by spin imparted by the bowler; leg-spin:

'Leg-break is artificial rather than natural, and is much more difficult to produce than off-break' (Ranji 1897, p 78).

**leg-bye** *n* a run scored from a ball (other than a wide or no-ball) that is deflected off some part of the striker's body, apart from his hand holding the bat, when he is attempting *either* to hit the ball with the bat *or* to avoid being hit by the ball. If neither of these conditions is met (ie, if the umpire believes the batsman deliberately used his body to deflect the ball) the umpire should call 'dead ball' and no runs will be allowed. Any runs legitimately accruing as leg-byes – whether actually run or coming from a boundary – are credited to the batting side as 'extras', but not to the individual batsman, and the umpire signals a leg-bye to the scorers by lifting a leg and touching the knee with his hand.

Runs scored from deflections off the striker's body were not distinguished from other forms of bye until 1850, but were certainly a legitimate form of scoring long before that. According to Charles Box (1868, p 124) 'a suggestion was made by Mr. Denison, in the year 1845, to particularize runs obtained off the padded legs', and it is likely that the impetus for this change was provided by the introduction of leg guards in about 1840. See EXTRAS.

**leg-cutter** *n* a relatively fast ball that deviates from leg towards off after pitching, produced by 'cutting' the ball rather than by wrist-spin (see CUT 4):

> 'New Zealand bowled very well, especially Cairns, who varied his inswingers so cleverly with his slower leg-cutter' (Christopher Martin-Jenkins, *Cricketer* September 1983).

Compare LEG-BREAK.

**leggie** *n* (Australia) a bowler of leg-spin; a wrist-spinner:

> 'A decade ago it was normal practice to go into a match with two pace bowlers and two spinners, and they were usually leggies' (Bob Holland, quoted in *Cricketer* November 1984).

**leg glance** *n* (also **leg glide**) a batting stroke, the GLANCE (qv):

> 'He [Ranji] played his famous leg glance with a dead straight bat, merely turning his wrist over at the last possible second, and flicking the ball away' (Warner 1934, p 130).

> 'In the leg glide the left leg will be brought in its forward movement just inside the line of the ball' (MCC 1952, p 99).

**leg guard** *n* (old) either of a pair of padded coverings worn by batsmen to protect their legs; a pad: *(qv)*:

> 'Do not face fast bowling without leg guards' (W. G. Grace, *Cricketing Reminiscences* 1899, p 293).

**leg hit** *n* (old) an attacking batting stroke sending the ball into the on-side area; especially, a stroke played off the front foot to a ball pitching outside leg stump. If the ball pitches fairly close to leg stump it is hit square of the wicket with a straight bat, but if it pitches wide it is played with a cross bat into the area backward of square.

**leg-hitting** *n* (old) the action or technique of hitting the ball to leg, especially when making a 'leg hit':

> 'With good leg-hitting, it would be impossible for the fielders to stand so near in as they do, nor would any captain be such a fool as to ask them to do so' ('Second Slip', *Cricketer* Spring Annual 1933).

**legs** *n* **1** – **off one's legs** (a) with the ball being deflected off one's legs (or pads) and on to the stumps:

> 'A favourite scheme for a slow bowler to get rid of a batsman is by bowling him off his legs' (*Badminton* 1888, p 137).

(b) with regard to one's batting strokes on the leg-side:

> 'With Jack Heron also looking strong off his legs the innings began to gather momentum' (Tony Pawson, *Observer* 12 June 1983).

**2** – **round one's legs** with the ball passing behind one's legs and on to the stumps:

> 'Boycott so completely misread him that he was bowled round his legs by a leg-break while thinking it was a harmless leg-side off-break' (Frith 1984, p 184).

**leg-shooter** *n* (obsolete) a relatively fast ball that pitches on or outside leg stump and fails to rise significantly off the wicket; a SHOOTER (qv) bowled down the leg-side:

> 'We read of the marvellous feat of Mr. T. A. Anson at the wicket when he stumped a man off a leg-shooter of Alfred Mynn' (*Badminton* 1888, p 278).

**leg-side** *n & adj* (on or towards) the side of the pitch on which the striker stands:

> 'The difference achieved by Jardine's tactics of linking Larwood with two other great fast bowlers in Voce and Allen, and giving

*him for periods a packed leg-side field, is clear enough in the*
*bowling figures'* (Tony Pawson, *Cricketer* July 1983).

See LEG.

**leg slip** *n* a close leg-side fielding position (or the player
occupying it) behind the batsman's wicket and fairly
near to the line of flight of the ball. Leg slip is a fairly
recent term for what could also be called fine short leg.
See FIELDING POSITIONS.

**leg-spin** *n* the practice or technique of spinning the ball so
that it deviates from leg towards off after pitching;
especially, the bowling of leg-breaks by means of
WRIST-SPIN (qv):

*'Abdul Qadir . . . was soon to emerge as a torchbearer for*
*leg-spin, an operator who bemused dozens of county batsmen in*
*the best Freeman tradition'* (Frith 1984, p 180).

**leg-spinner** *n* **1** an exponent of leg-spin bowling:

*'The other leg-spinner in the Pakistani party, Wasim Raja, took*
*nine wickets in 117·4 overs'* (Arlott 1983, p 49).

**2** a leg-break:

*'There was not a great deal of flight about his leg-spinners and*
*googlies'* (Frith 1984, p 125).

**leg-theory** *n* a form of attack in which most of the fielders are
stationed on the leg-side, many of them in close
catching positions, and the ball is bowled on or
outside the leg stump with the primary aim of
inducing the batsman to hit a catch. A typical leg-
theory field would include a square leg, a fine leg, two
or three short legs, and perhaps a silly mid-on.

Field settings of this type are used especially by
bowlers of off-breaks or inswingers, and leg-theory
has been a recognised tactic of the game at least since
the late 19th century. But in cricketing lore the term is
inextricably associated with the controversial MCC
tour of Australia in 1932–33 – the so-called 'Bodyline
series' – when England's leading fast bowler, Harold
Larwood, carried the leg-theory attack to its logical,
most systematic conclusion. Larwood bowled extremely fast, often short-pitched balls to a packed
leg-side field, and finished the series with a record
haul of 33 wickets. Larwood's bowling was bitterly

condemned in Australia and allegations of 'unsportsmanlike' behaviour almost brought the series to a premature end. Larwood himself always insisted that his version of fast leg-theory was a legitimate tactic, and he rejected the provocative term 'bodyline' coined by the Australian press. But his claim that leg-theory was *not* a decisive factor in England's 4–1 victory – 'We should have won this game and the others whether I had bowled Fast-Leg-Theory or not' (Larwood 1933, p 135) – is disingenuous and not easily reconciled with the facts. What distinguished Larwood's bowling from previous forms of leg-theory was, first, the extent to which his leg-side field was 'packed' (with as many as six close fielders) and secondly, Larwood's high pace and almost legendary accuracy.

Directly after the tour Larwood warned that any attempt to legislate against fast leg-theory would make cricket 'a less manly game', and in his view 'that would be an Imperial disaster' (!) (Larwood 1933, p 44). By the end of the following year, however, the MCC had issued a directive aimed at curbing 'persistent and systematic bowling of fast, short-pitched balls at the batsman standing clear of his wicket' (see BOUNCER). In a sense this should have made no difference to Larwood, who always claimed that he bowled at leg stump and not at the batsman. Nevertheless, Larwood's version of fast leg-theory, as a fully orchestrated 'set piece', was not employed again in first-class cricket. See also BODYLINE.

**leg trap** *n* the cluster of fielders in close catching positions, in an arc between leg slip and silly mid-on, in a LEG-THEORY field setting:

'*Once, while fielding in the leg-trap, he received a terrific blow on the ankle*' (Cardus 1978, p 92).

**length** *n* **1** the point at which a ball pitches, considered in terms of the distance down the wicket that it travels after leaving the bowler's hand:

'*To be a good judge of a ball's length is a source of strength in any player*' (Badminton 1888, p 51).

'*Rhodes . . . was accurate in his length, had a deceptive flight, and on a sticky wicket could make the ball "talk"*' (Warner 1934, p 40).

**2** the optimum point at which a ball should pitch in order to cause maximum difficulty for the batsman, lying between the point that produces a long hop and the point that produces a half-volley:

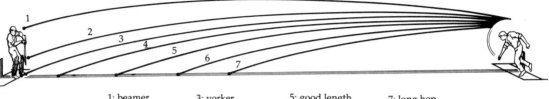

1: beamer     3: yorker     5: good length     7: long hop
2: full toss     4: half-volley     6: short

> *'Spare your vigour at first, now exert all your strength*
> *But measure each step, and be sure pitch a length'*
> (Rev R. Cotton, *'Hambledon Song'* 1778 in *HM*, p 52).

> *'The ball which did him was, however, a particularly nasty one rising sharply from a length'* (Peebles 1959, p 115).

The precise distance that constitutes a good length will depend on a number of factors, such as the pace of the wicket, the age of the ball, and of course the speed of the bowler:

> *'bowlers differ generally in their paces, just the same they differ in their lengths:*

| | |
|---|---|
| Slow Bowling, | *3 Yds and 3 Qrs* |
| Middling Ditto, | *4 Ditto and a Half* |
| Fast Ditto, | *5 Ditto Ditto* |

> *FROM THE STUMPS'* (Boxall 1800, p 13).

Boxall's stipulations remain more or less valid (despite the intervening revolution in bowling techniques), but the best definition of a good length does not depend on precise figures: 'A Victorian cricketer once described it as the ball delivered to such a point on the pitch as produced the agonizing uncertainty in the batsman of not knowing whether to play forward or back' (Arlott 1983, p 38). Compare LINE.

**length-ball** *n* (obsolete) a ball that is pitched well up to the batsman and bounces once before reaching him; a ball of good 'length':

> *'The bowler . . . when he sees a man coming in that he knows will stop all his length-balls with ease, is always in a degree disheartened'* (Nyren 1833 in *HM*, p 23).

The length-ball, as distinguished from the 'grubs' and 'lobs' of the earliest days of cricket, was perfected in the Hambledon era (late 18th century), especially by David Harris:

'Length-bowling . . . was introduced in David's time, and by him first brought to perfection' (Pycroft 1854 in *HM*, p 151).

See BOWLING.

**life** *n* **1** a 'lively' quality in the wicket that makes it particularly helpful to the faster bowlers, providing conditions conducive to pace off the pitch, good bounce, and (sometimes) movement off the seam:

'Lloyd, back after missing Port-of-Spain because of a hamstring injury, expected early life from a well-grassed pitch' (WCM May 1984).

**2** a fortuitous extension to a batsman's innings due to failure by the fielding side to dismiss him when an easy chance was offered:

'On the first day Wessels had played extremely well after his early "life"' (Henry Blofeld, *Cricketer* February 1984).

**lift** *vb* **1** (of the ball) to rise from the pitch more steeply than usual, typically from a good length; unlike a ball that 'kicks' or 'steeples', the lifting ball depends less on irregularities in the pitch and more on the skill of the bowler:

'Hardly had Shah begun to play a few strokes than Sandhu made one lift to have him caught behind' (Tony Pawson, *Observer* 12 June 1983).

~ *n* **2** a capacity for making the ball rise relatively steeply off the pitch:

'Qadir found turn and lift when bowling round the wicket into the rough' (Henry Blofeld, *Guardian* 14 December 1983).

**lifter** *n* a ball that rises off the pitch more steeply than expected, though not as high as a 'steepler':

'A lifter from Willis hit him near the wrist to be taken by Gatting at short-leg' (Brearley 1982, p 61).

**light** *n* the opportunity to discontinue play when the light is judged by the umpires to be unfit, offered to the batsmen at the wicket, who are thought of as deputising for the captain of the batting side:

> 'Play began at 3.40, with 25 overs a side the intention, but only one had been bowled by Dennis when the Kent openers were offered the light' (Guardian 18 July 1983).

> 'England needed . . . to pretend that they had more of the initiative than they did. Hence the furore when Lamb "accepted the light" on Monday evening' (Robin Marlar, Sunday Times 8 July 1984).

The umpires are the 'sole judges' of the fitness of the light for play, but they are required to take into account the wishes of the players. In cases where play has not yet started, or has not yet resumed after a stoppage, play may begin if *both* captains inform the umpires of their willingness to play in the prevailing conditions. But in cases where the light becomes unfit while play is actually in progress, only the batting side are 'offered the light' and given the option of coming off or continuing; and if they do agree to stay at the wicket in poor conditions, they can only successfully 'appeal against the light' if conditions *further* deteriorate from the point at which they agreed to stay on; the use of light meters in recent years has made it possible for umpires to judge more accurately the progressive deterioration of the light. According to the Laws the light should be judged unfit for play when 'conditions are so bad that it is unreasonable or dangerous to continue' (Law 3 note (d)), and recent TCCB guidelines have stressed that 'risk of injury to the batsmen' should be the main criterion in any decision.

**line** *n* the degree of accuracy, with regard to the direction of flight rather than the distance from the wicket at which the ball pitches, with which a bowler propels the ball:

> 'Baptiste, whose line tends to wander, nevertheless finished with another four wickets to bring his total to 17' (David Lacey, Guardian 16 June 1983).

Line is the complement of length and these are the fundamental prerequisites for effective bowling. Compare LENGTH.

**lively** *adj* denotes a wicket that offers assistance to the faster bowlers, helping them produce good bounce together with pace and (sometimes) movement off the pitch; the lively wicket was traditionally thought of as hard and dry, but nowadays liveliness is more likely to be associated with the 'green' wicket that retains a little moisture early in the day:

> 'There is logic in thinking that a side strong in fast bowling should bowl when the pitch is at its liveliest, which it will be on the first morning while moisture lingers after the groundsman's final watering' (Berry 1982, p 128).

**lob** *n* **1** a slow underarm ball with a high curving trajectory. Although lobs of a kind were no doubt bowled during the Hambledon era (when all bowling was underarm) lob-bowling was not seriously cultivated as a specialist skill until the mid-19th century, when other forms of underarm bowling were already obsolescent. The baffling flight of a well-bowled lob could pose serious problems of timing for the batsman, and even if he managed to make contact with the ball he was still not out of danger, since the lob-bowler's 'great aim', according to Ranji (1897, p 94), was 'to bowl balls which are difficult to score off unless hit in the air'. Despite the rapid decline of underarm bowling that followed the legalisation of the overarm delivery in 1864, the bowling of lobs remained relatively common for a further 50 years. Successful exponents included Walter Humphreys of Sussex, who took 148 wickets in 1893, and George Simpson-Hayward who took 23 Test wickets for MCC on the 1909–10 tour of South Africa.

By 1914, however, the otherwise universal abandonment of underarm bowling had turned the 'lobster' into something of a curiosity. His subsequent demise is possibly explained by the fact that batsmen unused to underarm bowling could only cope with lobs by 'throwing the bat'. This made life uncomfortable for the fielding side and could also cost a lot of runs; thus, even when taking wickets, the lob-bowler could be unacceptably expensive. (There is perhaps an analogy here with the more recent decline of leg-break bowling.) The last serious lob-bowler in first-class cricket was Trevor Molony, who took four wickets in his four appearances for Surrey in 1921.

~ *vb* **2** to hit the ball high in the air:

'Botham was retained as opener in the belief that, like Border, he might be able to lob the ball into the outfield, which . . . can be patrolled by only two fielders in the first 15 overs' (Matthew Engel, *Guardian* 27 January 1983).

**3** (of the ball) to fly high in the air off the bat:

'Dyson's long innings ended soon afterwards when he swept at Hemmings and the ball lobbed up off the top edge' (Henry Blofeld, *Cricketer* February 1983).

**lobster** *n* (old) a bowler of lobs:

'He displayed a great turn of speed running out to the lobster, whom he really played extremely well' (Headlam 1903, p 187).

**loft** *vb* to hit the ball high in the air, especially when playing a front-foot shot such as a straight drive:

'In the following over . . . Botham stepped down the pitch and lofted the ball far above the height of St Ann's tower' (Berry 1982, p 145).

**lolly** *n* (Australia) a simple catch; a dolly.

**long** *adj* (now used only in combination) occupying or indicating a fielding position close or relatively close to the boundary. Although formerly used to describe positions all round the ground (see LONG FIELD) the term 'long' has now been largely superseded by 'deep' and survives only in the terms long-off, long-on, and long leg.

**long field** *n* **1** (old) the entire area of the field behind the bowler's wicket, close to the boundary and in an arc between wide long-off and wide long-on; also, a fielder occupying a position in this area:

'Rhodes drove a ball into the long-field very hard and low . . . and Douglas, racing along the boundary caught it in his left hand just as it was clearing the ropes' (Warner 1934, p 79)

**2** (obsolete) any of various deep fielding positions:

'Long field to cover the middle wicket and point is a situation in which the fieldsman will have many hard balls to stop' (Nyren 1833 in *HM*, p 36).

The modern terms long-off and long-on developed

from the now obsolete **long field, straight off** and **long field, straight on**.

**long handle** *n* an aggressive style of batting, so called because of the natural tendency of a batsman playing attacking strokes to grip the bat closer to the top of the handle and thus allow the bat to swing through a greater arc; used in phrases like 'give it the long handle' and 'use the long handle':

> 'As to sticky wickets . . . unless a batsman has an almost superhuman power of watching the ball, the best thing he can do is to "take the long handle" and hit as hard as ever he can' (Ranji 1897, p 204).

**long hop** *n* (also formerly **long hopper**) a very short-pitched ball that does not rise steeply from the pitch but comes through at a comfortable height, giving the batsman plenty of time to play a shot:

> 'Next he sent Kenyon a long-hop which was summarily sent to the boundary' (Cardus 1978, p 155).

> 'A rank "long hopper" may be sent to any point of the compass with a horizontal bat' (Warner 1934, p 17).

The long hop, so called because the ball pitches early and comes on to the bat after a prolonged 'hop', amounts to a free gift for the batsman and has long been regarded as 'the sin of bowlers for which there is no forgiveness' (*Lillywhite's Cricketers' Companion* 1867). See diagram at LENGTH.

**long leg** *n* a deep leg-side fielding position (or the player occupying it) behind the batsman's wicket and anywhere in an arc between deep fine leg and deep backward square leg. See FIELDING POSITIONS.

**long-nips** see NIPS

**long-off** *n* a deep off-side fielding position (or the player occupying it) behind the bowler's wicket and anywhere in an arc between deep extra cover and the area directly behind the bowler. See FIELDING POSITIONS.

**long-on** *n* a deep leg-side fielding position (or the player occupying it) behind the bowler's wicket and anywhere in an arc between the area directly behind the

bowler and the area behind wide mid-on. See FIELDING
POSITIONS.

**long slip**  *n* (obsolete) an off-side fielding position (or the player
occupying it) equivalent to what would now be called
a fairly short third man:

> *'Long Slip or the Man that stands to cover the Short Slip
> [stands] the same distance from the stumps as the long stop . . .
> between the man at the point and the man at the slip'* (Boxall
> 1800, p 61).

See also SLIP.

**long stop**  *n* a fielding position (or the player occupying it)
directly behind the wicket-keeper and close enough
in to save the single:

> *'Long Stop. This man should stand at a proper distance behind
> the wicket, to save a run, if the ball should not be stopped by the
> Striker or Wicket-keeper'* (Lambert 1816, p 42).

Except in the lowest reaches of the game, this position
has been more or less obsolete for almost a hundred
years. In earlier times, however, long stop was a
specialist fielder occupying 'a most important station
in the game' (Nyren 1833 in *HM*, p 34) – which is
hardly surprising when one remembers that the job of
keeping wicket was originally done by the bowlers in
between overs (see WICKET-KEEPER). The importance of
long stop gradually diminished with the emergence of
wicket-keeping as a specialist skill and the increasing
use of protective gear. At the same time, the dramatic
improvement in playing surfaces in the late 19th
century reduced the need for a second line of defence
'because, now that wickets are good, fewer byes are let
by wicket-keepers' (Ranji 1897, p 42). The crack Australian eleven that toured England in 1882 pointed
the way forward, with the brilliant J. M. Blackham
keeping wicket to the 'demon bowler' Spofforth
without a long stop. Before the end of the decade long
stop was virtually redundant:

> *'In these days of slow bowling and fine turf captains of elevens
> do not bother themselves with providing long-stops at all'*
> (Badminton 1888, p 269).

**long-stop**  *vb* (obsolete) to field in the long stop position:

> 'Cambridge had to provide itself with a long stop, and Mr. H. M. Marshall in that capacity has earned undying fame; for long-stopping on Lord's Ground in 1861 and 1862 was no laughing matter' (*Badminton* 1888, p 276).

**look out** *vb* (obsolete) to act as a fielder:

> 'Several players were stationed, to "look out", in different parts of the field' (Dickens, *Pickwick Papers* 1837, ch 7).

**loose** *adj* **1** (of a ball) carelessly bowled and inaccurate in line or length:

> 'With the exception of Hollins, who scored a useful 31, chiefly from loose balls to leg, no one survived for long' (Headlam 1903, p 163).

**2** (of a batting stroke) carelessly played, so that the bat does not hit the ball cleanly:

> 'Border and Hookes . . . were pulling the innings round with a partnership of 123 for the fifth wicket when Hookes played a loose stroke to be caught at extra cover' (Tony Cozier, *Cricketer* January 1984).

**loosener** *n* one of the early balls of a bowler's spell, when he is still 'loosening up' and not yet bowling a good line and length:

> 'Remarkably Chris [Old] did not take a wicket. Replacing him, Botham, with his third ball, which was little more than a loosener, had Wood LBW' (Brearley 1982, p 61).

**lost ball** *n* an instance of the ball becoming lost or impossible to recover. If such a case arises, any member of the fielding side may call 'lost ball', whereupon six runs are added to the score of the batsman who hit the ball (unless of course the ball has become lost without being struck from the bat, in which case the runs are credited to the appropriate category of extras). If, however, the batsmen have already taken more than six runs before 'lost ball' is called, they are allowed all the runs they have completed. The lost ball is then replaced by a ball that has had a similar amount of wear. Though rarely invoked in first-class cricket, the lost ball law still has a job to do in the lower reaches of the game. It was introduced in 1809 and has remained more or less unchanged, except that the original allowance of four runs for a lost ball was increased to six in 1822/3.

**lower** *vb* (obsolete) to account for the wicket of a batsman; take a wicket:

> 'He . . . then retired in favour of one of the regular bowlers, after having, simply by wild erratic fast delivery, lowered three of the best Australian wickets' (Badminton 1888, p 174).

The term arises from the idea of a dismissed batsman's wicket being 'down' (see DOWN).

**lower order** *n* the LATE ORDER (qv); the tail:

> 'Lower-order man Roger Binny . . . with 83 not out and 54 in successive innings, displayed flair and innovative ability' (WCM December 1983).

**maiden** *n* **1** (also **maiden over**) an over in which no runs are scored off the bat:

> 'He played twice for England during Lord Hawke's tour of South Africa in 1898–99, holding the batsmen down at Johannesburg with 24 maidens in his 32 overs' (Frith 1984, p 51).

A maiden is represented in the scorebook by joining the dots in the record of the over to form a letter 'M' (see illustration at SCOREBOOK), and in a simple bowling analysis the second digit indicates the number of maidens bowled (thus 22–7–3–39). The definition of this term has recently undergone a significant change: under new regulations approved by the ICC in 1984, whereby no-balls and wides are debited to the bowler's analysis, an over that includes either of these will no longer count as a maiden. Byes and leg-byes, however, may still be scored off an over without affecting its 'maidenhood'.

~ *adj* **2** being the first instance of its kind:

> 'The startling contrast in pace-bowling strengths of the two sides proved to be the decisive factor in the first Test of Pakistan's maiden five-match series in Australia' (WCM January 1984).

> 'Crowe, having with Wright added 154 in 200 minutes . . . went on to his own maiden Test century' (Scyld Berry, *Observer* 12 February 1984).

The term 'maiden' had long been used in English in two distinct figurative senses – 'unproductive' and 'happening for the first time' – before it entered the vocabulary of cricket. Thus, for example, the idea of a maiden over is prefigured in the phrase 'maiden sessions', defined in Capt Grose's *Dictionary of the Vulgar Tongue* (1811) as 'a sessions where none of the prisoners are capitally convicted'. Similarly, its use in describing the first occurrence of some notable event can be seen in the term 'maiden speech', which considerably predates the equivalent cricket sense.

**maiden ball**  *n* (obsolete) a ball from which no runs are scored:

'*Clarke bowled 64 maiden balls*' (*Lillywhite's Guide to Cricketers* 1854, p 26).

**majority**  *n* (obsolete) a lead held by one side over another, or the margin by which one side defeats another:

'*Oxford won easily in 1894, but Cambridge made it "all square" in 1895, her majority being 134*' (Ranji 1897, p 360).

**mark**  *n* **1** the point from which a bowler starts his run-up, usually marked in some way so that the length and direction of the run-up remains constant:

'*At that moment Michael Holding suddenly marched back past his regular mark, stopped two thirds of the way back to the pavilion and began gliding in off his long run*' (Matthew Engel, *Guardian* 14 August 1984).

**2** – **off the mark** having scored the first run or runs of one's innings:

'*Lloyd edged Miller to slip, but instead of being caught for a duck he was off the mark for two*' (Robin Marlar, *Sunday Times* 3 June 1984).

**MCC**  *abbr* the Marylebone Cricket Club: a body formed in 1787 by members of the old White Conduit Club of Islington, based originally at a ground belonging to Thomas Lord on the northern fringes of London's West End (in what is now Dorset Square) but from 1814 based at the modern Lord's Cricket Ground in St John's Wood. The leading lights in the foundation of the club were the Earl of Winchelsea and the Hon Charles Lennox (the future Duke of Richmond), and with such weighty aristocratic patronage MCC quickly eclipsed Hambledon as the leading club in England. Although only a private cricket club it has always wielded immense authority – albeit largely unofficially – over the conduct and organisation of the game at national and international level, and it is only fairly recently that many of MCC's functions have been devolved to more 'official' bodies like the ICC and the TCCB. Within a year of its foundation MCC had conducted the first major revision of the Laws of the game (1788), and it has been responsible since then for four further revisions, the most recent being published in 1980. It remains today the chief authority on the Laws, and they can only be changed if proposed amendments are approved by a two thirds majority at a special meeting of the club.

**meat** *n* the thick central part of the blade of the bat.

**meaty** *adj* (of a batting stroke) striking the ball forcefully with the 'meat' of the bat:

> 'He let the ball go with fine judgment outside the off-stump . . . punishing anything over- or under-pitched with meaty drives, cuts and hooks' (Brearley 1982, p 17).

**medium-pace** *adj* (also **medium-paced**) denoting a bowler, a ball, or a style of bowling characterised by a speed significantly lower than that of a fast bowler but higher than that of a slow bowler; medium-pace is one of the three basic types according to which bowlers are conventionally categorised, and bowlers of this type generally rely on accuracy of line and length, and movement in the air and off the seam:

> 'In any chapter on bowling it would be impossible to omit the name of George Lohmann, probably the greatest medium-paced bowler that ever lived' (Warner 1934, p 63).

**medium-pacer** *n* an exponent of medium-pace bowling:

> 'The man who kept Wilson out of the England side . . . was the phenomenal Derek Underwood, whose speed through the air was such that many might be tempted to class him as a medium-pacer' (Frith 1984, p 155).

**middle** *vb* **1** to strike the ball cleanly with the middle of the bat:

> 'Lamb strode to the wicket soon after lunch at 58 for two, and from the outset middled the ball on his way to his third Test century' (Robin Marlar, *Sunday Times* 28 August 1983).

~ *n* **2 – in the middle** at the wickets, considered as the scene of the batting or bowling action:

> *'May lacked practice in the middle and this could have had a profound influence'* (Peebles 1959, p 52).

> *'Back in the middle, neither Alderman nor Lillee swung the ball at all'* (Brearley 1982, p 89).

**middle order** *n* the players batting in the middle of a side's batting line-up, after the openers and before the tailenders; the middle order represents the backbone of a team's batting strength and typically stretches from numbers three and four (the 'early middle order') down to numbers seven and eight (the 'late middle order'):

> *'Shastri and Binny were unhurried as they posted 127 for the fifth wicket, though this was rare and pleasing solidity from India's middle order'* (WCM January 1984).

**middle wicket** *n* (obsolete) an off-side fielding position between extra cover and the bowler; mid-off:

> *'The Man that stands Middle Wicket. His place is the off side, not far from the bowler's wicket and about twenty-two yards from the hitter's wicket'* (Boxall 1800, p 50).

See MID-OFF.

**midfield** *n* the part of the field between the area occupied by fielders in close catching positions, and the area close to the boundary patrolled by 'deep' fielders. Fielders in the midfield are usually placed to save the single rather than to take close catches, and typical midfield positions include cover, mid-off, mid-on, mid-wicket, square leg, and short third man.

**mid-off** *n* an off-side fielding position (or the player occupying it) between extra cover and the bowler. Mid-off is normally about 25 to 30 yards from the striker and fairly close to the bowler, but the position can also be modified to be 'deep', 'short', silly', 'wide', or 'straight': see FIELDING POSITIONS. The term mid-off is a contraction of the earlier 'middle wicket off'. The manuals and illustrations of the early 19th century all show middle wicket (not to be confused with the modern mid-wicket) as one of the 'standard' fielding positions of the game at that time. However, an equivalent leg-side position was also occasionally used, so the two 'middle wicket' positions came to be distinguished as **middle wicket off** (= mid-off) and **middle wicket on** (= mid-on).

**mid-on** *n* a leg-side fielding position (or the player occupying it) between mid-wicket and the bowler. Though nominally the mirror image of mid-off, this is in practice a more variable position and its precise location will depend on such factors as the type of bowling, the pace of the pitch, and the style of the batsman. Consequently, 'none of the regular places is more elastic than mid-on' (MCC 1952, p 20). For the etymology of this term, see MID-OFF.

**mid-wicket** *n* **1** a leg-side fielding position (or the player occupying it) between mid-on and square leg. Mid-wicket is normally about 20 to 30 yards out from the pitch at a point midway between the two wickets, but the position can also be modified to be 'deep' or 'short'. See FIELDING POSITIONS.

**2** (obsolete) = MID-OFF:

> 'Mid Wicket stands on the 'off' side, a few yards in front and to the left of the bowler' (G. H. Selkirk, *Guide to the Cricket Ground* 1867, p 31).

Mid-wicket is an ancient cricket term but only acquired its current meaning in the mid-1930s. Prior to that mid-wicket, or 'middle wicket', was simply another name for mid-off, and was indeed the preferred form in most early writing:

> 'He at mid wicket disappoints the foe,
> Springs at the coming ball, and mocks the blow.'
> (James Love, *Cricket: an Heroic Poem* 1746)

The position now called mid-wicket would formerly have been called forward square leg or perhaps extra mid-on.

**military medium** *n & adj* bowling of a steady medium pace. The word 'military' alludes to the brisk, no-nonsense character of this type of bowling, in which efficiency and reliability are the chief virtues:

> 'There now is a vast army in English cricket of practitioners of "military medium"; bowling briskly, seam up, achieving a little movement but, above all, striving for sufficient precision to avoid punishment' (Arlott 1983, p 41).

**miscue** *vb* **1** to fail to 'middle' the ball when playing a shot, so that the ball does not go in the direction intended:

> *'Richards having once hoisted Venkat for six, attempted to repeat the stroke and came to grief, so badly miscuing the shot that he put up a lobbed catch to slip'* (Dilip Rao, *Guardian* 18 April 1983).

The term is of course borrowed from the vocabulary of billiards.

~ *n* **2** an act of miscuing the ball:

> *'With a flourish of the bat that might have decapitated an incautious wicket-keeper, he struck a spectacular miscue. The ball re-entered the atmosphere above Jeff Crowe at point'* (Matthew Engel, *Guardian* 23 January 1984).

**miss** *vb* **1** to fail to catch a ball struck by a batsman; drop:

> *'Right at the start Cowdrey was missed by Davidson at backward short-leg'* (Peebles 1959, p 159).

**2 – play and miss:** see PLAY.

**miss out** *vb* (of a batsman) to fail to score a substantial number of runs, especially in circumstances favourable to batting:

> *'When Victoria came to Sydney there were batfuls of runs to be had, but the ironic fact was that Jackson (11 and 44) missed out . . . and, in the first innings, so did Bradman'* (David Frith, *WCM* January 1984).

**molly grabber** *n* (Australian slang) a fast ball that fails to rise significantly off the pitch but comes quickly on to the batsman, often at a potentially painful height; readers interested in etymology may draw their own conclusions about the derivation of this term:

> *'These men . . . rushed India from 35 for three to 379 for seven, despite the perils of a dead pitch which from time to time produced a snorter or a shooter (Australians might prefer "rib-tickler" and "molly grabber")'* (Peter Roebuck, *Cricketer* November 1982).

**move** *vb* to cause the ball to deviate laterally, either during its flight or after it pitches:

> *'A superb fast bowler with a classically flowing action and fundamental hatred of batsmen, he had the capacity to move the*

*ball either way in the air'* (John Arlott on Dennis Lillee, *Guardian* 5 January 1984).

*'John, moving the ball off the pitch, was a consistent danger'* (Dick Brittenden, *Cricketer* May 1983).

**movement** *n* lateral deviation of the ball, either during flight (**movement in the air**) or after pitching (**movement off the pitch** or **movement off the seam**):

*'He swung the ball out and in late enough for it not to be clear whether the movement was in the air or off the pitch'* (Brearley 1982, p 150).

*'They kept the ball up to the bat and found movement off the seam on a greenish pitch'* (Henry Blofeld, *Guardian* 31 May 1983).

Movement in the air describes the curving arc of a ball that 'swings' into or away from the batsman: see SWING. Movement off the pitch depends on the angle of the seam and the rate and direction of spin on the ball as it makes contact with the ground. The effect, in John Arlott's words, 'is not compellable by the bowler' (Arlott 1983, p 19). Certainly, some bowlers deliberately set out to produce such movement by 'cutting' the ball as they release it (see CUT 4). But in the right conditions (especially on a well-grassed, or 'green', wicket where the ball can 'bite' as it pitches) the ball will tend naturally to move off the pitch from a normal fast or medium-pace bowling action, and even the bowler may not always be sure which direction it will take.

**mow** *vb* to hit the ball from off to leg with a low sweeping cross-batted stroke, somewhat similar to the movement used in mowing grass with a scythe.

**NCA** *abbr* National Cricket Association: the body with official responsibility for cricket in Britain at all levels except those controlled by the TCCB.

**Nelson** *n* the score of 111 runs, made by a team or an individual player and generally believed to be extremely unlucky:

> 'Simon Doggart . . . braved two overs of Clarke and went on to muster 22 before being yorked by Monkhouse at the dreaded Nelson – 111' (John Parker, *Observer* 22 May 1984).

The origins of this term lie in the erroneous notion that Admiral Nelson had *one* eye, *one* arm, and *one* leg; in reality, of course, Nelson lost an arm and an eye but retained the use of both legs.

**net** *n* a period of play on a practice pitch in the 'nets'; a practice session:

> 'Willis had a brief batting net. We have given up attempts to coach him, and now leave him to his idiosyncratic ways' (Brearley 1982, p 75).

**nets** *n* one or more practice pitches, each enclosed by an arrangement of netting, where players practise batting and bowling:

> 'After my knock in the nets and some slip-catching practice, I did the usual pre-match interviews' (Brearley 1982, p. 52).

**new ball** *n* **1** a completely unused ball. In all grades of cricket, 'either Captain may demand a new ball at the start of each innings' (Law 5 § 3). At first-class level, there is also provision for a new ball to be taken while an innings is still in progress, once a stipulated number of overs has been bowled. For the fielding side the advantages of the new ball are that it is 'considered to swing more, and bounce in a livelier fashion, than a more worn ball' (Arlott 1983, p 81). The fielding captain is not of course obliged to take the new ball as soon as it becomes available (it may sometimes be worthwhile, for example, to persevere with an old ball that is turning well), but any *subsequent* new ball can only be taken after the full number of prescribed overs has been bowled with the current ball, regardless of when that ball was taken. See also REPLACEMENT BALL.

In 18th-century cricket, a single ball was used throughout the match, and the original (1744) code of Laws required the umpires 'To mark the Ball that it may not be changed'. The law was amended in 1798 to allow a new ball to be requested at the beginning of each innings, and this arrangement remained intact until 1907. The new rule introduced in that year, allowing a fresh ball to be taken after 200 runs had been scored, represented an attempt to strengthen the hand of the bowlers at a time when batsmen were in a dominant position and the prevalence of high-scoring draws threatened to alienate the public. Since 1945 various stipulations involving runs and/or wickets have been used to determine the point at which the new ball becomes available. Regualtions vary from country to country, subject to a recommended minimum of 75 six-ball overs or 55 eight-ball overs. In the West Indies, for example, the new ball becomes available in Test matches after 75 overs, while in England it may be taken after 85 overs in Tests or 100 overs in county championship matches.

**2 – take the new ball/give a bowler the new ball** to open the bowling/ask a particular bowler to open the bowling:

> 'Marshall not only came out to allow Gomes to get his hundred by holding up one end batting one-handed, he also took the new ball and proceeded to return his best Test figures' (Christopher Martin-Jenkins, *Cricketer* September 1984).

**nightwatchman** *n* a late-order batsman who is sent in to bat ahead of his normal place in the order when a wicket has fallen a short time before the close of play; the nightwatchman is usually the most competent of the non-specialist batsmen and his function is to stay in as long as possible so as to protect the wickets of players higher in the order until the next day's play:

'McDonald was soon defeated by the indefatigable Statham, at which Grout came in as night-watchman' (Peebles 1959, p 117).

**nip** *n* **1** a quality in the wicket, or in a bowler's delivery, that causes the ball to move briskly off the pitch with an apparent increase in pace:

'Though the spinners did manage to turn the ball, they could not get the necessary nip out of the wicket' (K. N. Prabhu, WCM March 1984).

'Afterwards, batting was much easier. Alderman lacked his earlier nip and tended to over-pitch' (Brearley 1982, p 83).

**2** (obsolete) an unintentional glance or snick from the bat:

'A stroke, or Nip, over or under his Bat, or upon his Hands . . . if the Ball be held before it touches the Ground it's out' (Laws 1744).

~ *vb* **3** to make the ball move sharply off the pitch:

'As soon as Lillee found his length he nipped one back from off to have me LBW' (Brearley 1982, p 25).

'Mohinder Amarnath . . . was, apart from his open stance, a model of technical perfection until Holding nipped one through his gate to send the off stump dancing back' (Christopher Martin-Jenkins, *Cricketer* August 1983).

**4** (obsolete) to snick the ball unintentionally:

'If a Striker nips a Ball up just before him, he may fall before his Wicket, or pop down his Bat . . . to save it' (Laws 1744).

**nipbacker** *n* a ball that 'nips back', moving sharply in towards the batsman after pitching:

'It was four for two moments later: Fowler was bowled by a nipbacker and Gower . . . edged to third slip' (Matthew Engel, *Guardian* 26 November 1982).

**nips** *n* (obsolete) the fielding position of point, presumably so called because the fielder was stationed there to catch balls 'nipped up' off the edge of the striker's bat (see NIP):

'In the match between Eton and Harrow 1822 I fielded "nips". It was the position since named "point". There were also cover-nips and long-nips' (Herbert Jenner-Fust in Pullin 1900, p 5).

**no-ball** *n* **1** a delivery judged by the umpire to be unfair. When a no-ball is bowled the umpire calls 'no-ball' and signals to the scorer by extending one arm horizontally. One run is added as an 'extra' to the score of the batting side, so long as no runs are made in any other way, and the no-ball does not count as part of the over. The batsman may attempt to score runs in the normal way off a no-ball, but can only be dismissed by being run out or by hitting the ball twice, obstructing the field, or handling the ball. See also EXTRAS.

~ *vb* **2** (of the umpire) to declare that the bowler has made an unfair delivery, by calling 'no-ball':

'It was, in fact, as a fast bowler that nature first stirred the cricketer in him [C. B. Fry], until Jim Phillips, the umpire, no-balled him for throwing' (Cardus 1978, p 80).

**3** (of a bowler) to bowl a no-ball:

'I was glad that Willis and Dilley chose the other end since they are both prone to no-ball' (Brearley 1982, p 60).

The fairness of a delivery is assessed according to a wide variety of criteria. The most important of these are: (a) the position of the bowler's feet as the delivery is made – some part of the front foot, whether grounded or in the air, must be behind the popping crease, and the back foot must land inside the line of the return crease; (b) the movement of the bowler's arm – the bowler must not *throw* the ball (as by straightening the arm just before delivering the ball: see THROW); and (c) the mode of delivery – the bowler is supposed to inform the umpire whether he intends to bowl underarm or overarm, left- or right-handed, over or round the wicket, and any change of 'mode' made without informing the umpire constitutes an unfair delivery. In addition, the no-ball rule is used as part of the procedure for cautioning a bowler who persistently bowls fast short-pitched deliveries (see BOUNCER). Finally, the fairness of a delivery may also be affected by other factors not directly within the bowler's control: for example, if the wicket-keeper is not completely behind the line of the stumps as the ball is bowled; the ball will be deemed unfair. Or again, if field-setting restrictions are contravened, the no-ball rule is used as a sanction: for example, the regulations affecting English limited-overs competitions state that there should be at least four fielders within a 30-yard radius of the stumps and 'in the event of an infringement, the square-leg umpire shall call "No-ball"'.

The original no-ball rule referred only to the bowler's back foot and prescribed no penalty, the ball being regarded as 'dead' once the call was made:

*'If he delivers the Ball, with his hinder Foot over the Bowling-Crease, the Umpire shall call no Ball, tho' it be struck, or the Player be bowl'd out'* (Laws 1744).

At some time during the first ten years of the 19th century, a change was made to allow the striker 'all the runs he can get', with the proviso that he *could* be dismissed by being run out. The one-run penalty was first introduced in 1829 and 'the first mention of No ball on the score-sheet occurs in the year 1830 in a match between Marylebone and Middlesex at Lord's' (Box 1868, p 153). Since then the rule has been altered in two important respects. Throughout the first half of the 19th century the regulations governing the movement of the bowler's arm were repeatedly invoked, and occasionally modified, in a rearguard action aimed at preventing the spread of roundarm and overarm bowling (see BOWLING). The matter was laid to rest with the legalisation of the overarm style in 1864. More recently, when 'dragging' became an issue in the early 1960s (see DRAG 3) the law relating to the position of the bowler's feet was modified to put the main emphasis on the position of the front foot, rather than (as previously) of the back foot.

**non-striker** *n* the batsman who is at the opposite end of the wicket from the player who is facing the bowling (the 'striker'); his position is referred to as the 'non-striker's end':

*'The non-striker calls for the run whenever the ball has been played behind the wicket'* (Ranji 1897, p 200).

**notch** (obsolete) *n* **1** a run:

*'On Wednesday last a match at* Cricket *was played at Barnes*

Common between the Gentlemen of Barnes, Fulham, &
Richmond on the one side and the Gentlemen of London on the
other, when the Londoners were beat 19 notches' (St James's
Evening Post 12 August 1736).

**2** an incision cut in a stick or tally as an early method of recording the scoring of a run:

'They are sole Judges of all Hindrances . . . and in Case of
Hindrance may order a Notch to be scor'd' (Laws 1744).

'Awakened echo speaks the innings o'er
And forty notches deep indent the score'
(James Love, Cricket: an Heroic Poem, 1746).

~ *vb* **3** to score the stated number of runs:

'All-Muggleton had notched some fifty-four' (Dickens,
Pickwick Papers 1837, ch 7).

**4** to act as scorer; keep the score:

'The umpires were stationed behind the wickets; the scorers
were prepared to notch the runs; a breathless silence ensued'
(Dickens, ibid).

In cricket as in other games, the earliest method of keeping a record was to cut, or 'score', an incision in a piece of wood each time a point was gained. The term 'notch' did not long survive the introduction of more sophisticated recording methods; the word 'score', by contrast, is still very much part of the language.

**notcher** *n* (obsolete) a scorer.

**not out** *adv & adj* (of a batsman) remaining undismissed, for example after the fielding side has made an appeal or after the end or declaration of one's side's innings:

'In a series of intercolonial matches in Jamaica, George
[Headley] made, out of 356, 203 not out; out of 151 for five, 57
not out; out of 456, 79 retired hurt' (James 1963, p 146).

'Bird consulted with Don Oslear, who had no hesitation in
giving me not out' (Brearley 1982, p 82).

In recording the score of a team or individual, an asterisk is conventionally used to indicate that a batsman has not been dismissed, thus: England 358 (Botham 149*).

**nudge** *n* **1** a gentle pushing movement of the bat by which the ball is deflected and 'helped on its way', usually into the area backward of square, its effectiveness depending on timing rather than on force:

> 'He . . . began to time his drives and nudges and glances in what became a typically efficient Fletcher innings' (Henry Blofeld, Guardian 31 May 1983).

~ *vb* **2** to play the ball with a nudge:

> 'With more than usual relief I nudged a single to square-leg' (Brearley 1982, p 148).

**NZCC** *abbr* New Zealand Cricket Council

**obstructing the field** *adv* a mode of dismissal in which the batsman is given out 'if he wilfully obstructs the opposite side by word or action' (Law 37 § 1). The relevant section of the Laws elaborates on the two cases in which an appeal is most likely to be made, namely an attempt to prevent a catch being taken and an attempt to prevent a run-out being made; and in all cases the umpire must be satisfied that the obstruction was intentional. A dismissal under this law is entered in the scorebook as 'obstructing the field', and the wicket is not credited to the bowler. Obstructing the field is one of the few modes of dismissal that remain valid even in the case of a no-ball, but it is doubtful whether this clause will ever be put to the test, given that only 12 first-class players have *ever* been dismissed for obstructing the field.

At a more primitive stage of the game, the art of batsmanship seems to have included the skill of preventing the fielders from taking catches, at least within the immediate vicinity of the wickets. The original (1744) code of Laws spells out the circumstances in which either batsman may legitimately hinder a catch; for example, if the ball is hit up to the other end of the pitch, 'the other Player may place his Body any where within the Swing of the Bat, so as to hinder the Bowler from catching it'. But even under this code the batsman was out if he left his ground to obstruct a catch. The first MCC code (1788) brought an end to this rather rustic feature of the early game, with a ruling to the effect that 'if under pretence of running a Notch, or otherwise, either of the Strikers prevent a

Ball from being caught, the Striker of the ball is out'. The law was subsequently extended (1888) to cover any tactics by the batsmen that are intended to hinder the fielding side.

**obstruction** *n* **1** the act of OBSTRUCTING THE FIELD (qv).

**2** the act of obstructing a batsman who is taking a run: intentional obstruction by a fielder constitutes 'unfair play' under Law 42 and in such circumstances the umpire calls 'dead ball' and allows the batsmen any runs completed or attempted.

**occupation of the crease** *n* the playing of a cautious defensive innings with the emphasis on avoiding dismissal rather than scoring runs:

> 'In a series where occupation of the crease has been of prime importance, Downton fully justified his choice' (Michael Carey, *Daily Telegraph* 15 August 1984).

**off** *n* **1** that side of the pitch on which the striker does not stand when receiving the ball, separated from the leg-side by an imaginary line passing between the two wickets, bounded at its outside edge by the third-man, extra-cover, and long-off boundaries, and constituting half of the entire playing area. See FIELDING POSITIONS.

~ *adj & adv* **2** on, towards, or relating to the off-side:

> 'A bowler very often bowls wide of the off stump . . . merely to make the hitter reach after it' (Boxall 1800, p 35).

> 'These balls may be played straight off, or between the point of the bat and the middle wicket' (Nyren 1833 in *HM*, p 25).

Often used in combination, as in 'off-break', 'off-drive', etc.

This use of the word 'off' originates in the old distinction between the 'off side' and 'near side' of a horse or carriage, the off side being *opposite* the one on which a driver walks or a rider mounts; the *OED* has several quotations referring to the off side of a horse which long predate the earliest cricketing uses. Some early cricket writers also use its antonym 'near' in referring to the leg-side, but this usage did not survive:

*'If the ball is directed to the legs of the Striker, or near stump, it is frequently hit to the hip'* (Lambert 1816, p 13).

See also LEG, ON.

**off-break** *n* **1** a relatively slow ball that deviates from off towards leg after pitching. Technically, the term can apply to any ball breaking in towards the batsman, such as a googly bowled to a right-handed batsman. But for practical purposes off-break generally denotes the 'stock' ball of a right-arm finger-spinner (see FINGER-SPIN). The term off-break formerly embraced balls of any pace that broke back from off: describing Tom Richardson, the great England fast bowler of the 1890s, Pelham Warner observes:

> *'He seldom bowled short, aiming at clean bowling the batsman with a good-length off-break'* (Warner 1934, p 58).

In current usage it describes a slower ball, and the 'fast off-break' is nowadays called an 'off-cutter' or 'break-back'.

**2** deviation of the ball from off towards leg after pitching, as a result of spin imparted by the bowler; off-spin:

> *'Leg-break is artificial rather than natural, and is much more difficult to produce than off-break'* (Ranji 1897, p 78).

**off-cutter** *n* a relatively fast ball that deviates from off towards leg after pitching, produced by 'cutting' the ball (see CUT 4) rather than by finger-spin:

> *'V. W. C. Jupp . . . one of the most prolific and colourful all-rounders between the wars, could adapt to conditions with either nippy off-cutters or slow off-spin'* (Frith 1984, p 95).

Compare OFF-BREAK.

**off drive** *n* a form of drive, played to a ball pitching on or just outside off stump, by which the ball is sent into the area between cover and mid-off. See DRIVE.

**off-drive** *vb* to strike the ball when making an off drive:

> *'In the seventy-ninth over he off-drove a no-ball by Underwood for four'* (Berry 1982, p 115).

**offer** *vb* to attempt to play a stroke, rather than deliberately leaving the ball alone:

'The post-lunch session was almost siesta-like in its calm, with neither batsman offering at anything that did not demand a stroke' (Michael Carey, Daily Telegraph 15 December 1982).

**off play**  *n* the technique or skill of playing balls towards the off:

'His off play was distinctly weak, but his hooking and forcing shots past mid-on were magnificent' (Headlam 1903, p 121).

**off-side**  *n & adj* (on or towards) the side of the pitch away from that on which the striker stands when receiving the ball:

'Walter Hammond, for instance, finding his cover-driving checked by a slow left-arm bowler accurate enough to bowl to a packed offside field and contain him, would go down on one knee and sweep . . . to square-leg or finer' (Arlott 1983, p 63).

See OFF.

**off-spin**  *n* the practice or technique of spinning the ball so that it deviates from off towards leg after pitching; especially, the bowling of off-breaks by means of FINGER-SPIN (qv):

'Even he was outshone by the charmingly-named Jack McGoon, who bowled 10 overs of very nifty offspin' (Matthew Engel, Guardian 4 January 1984).

**off-spinner**  *n* **1** an exponent of off-spin bowling:

'It used to be said, falsely, but, for Australian batsmen, valuably, that English off-spinners could never succeed in Australia' (Arlott 1983, p 44).

**2** an off-break:

'To his rugged batsmanship he added a crisp off-spinner bowled with a muscular arm after a short, unelaborate run-up' (Frith 1984, p 168).

**off-theory**  *n* a form of attack in which most of the fielders are stationed on the off-side, many of them in close catching positions, and the ball is bowled on or outside the off stump with the primary aim of inducing the batsman to hit a catch; a typical off-theory field would include three slips, a gully, point or cover, mid-off and perhaps a third man, leaving only two fielders on the leg-side:

*'Larwood had set his field for off theory with four men in the slips and Leyland covering them on the boundary'* (*Melbourne Argus* 11 February 1933).

Off theory is in fact the standard, basic field setting for many types of bowling, and is so well-established that the term is rarely used nowadays; it is usually only the non-standard 'leg-theory' that is singled out by name.

In the very early days of cricket, when the object was to slog the ball and the 'straight bat' had not yet evolved, there were probably more fielders on the leg-side than on the off. By the early 19th century, however, field-settings already show an off-side bias, and the basic principles of off-theory seem to be understood: 'A bowler very often bowls wide of the off stump, and a little faster than his common pace, merely to make the hitter reach after it' (Boxall 1800, p 35). But the refinement of this form of attack, with the ring of fielders in close-catching positions, came only towards the end of the century:

*'George Lohmann who played for Surrey from 1884 . . . was one of the first to put the "off-theory" so much into practice. When a man like Lohmann bowls four out of five balls on the off-side and crowds the fielders on that side . . . you may hit it, but it would not be long before you hit it into a fielder's hand'* (Pullin 1900, p 129).

Though heartily disapproved of by the older generation – 'I call bowling off the wicket wasted energy' says George Wootton (Pullin 1900, p 203) – off-theory quickly became the norm. Like so many developments in this period, it is closely associated with the great improvement in playing surfaces characteristic of the time (see WICKET²). As Ranji says:

*'Wickets are so good and true . . . that to clean bowl a good batsman is next door to impossible. So bowlers have adopted almost universally what is known as the off-theory'* (Ranji 1897, p 180).

**old enemy** *n* from an English point of view, Australia; from an Australian point of view, England:

*'As in 1977, and again in 1978–9, we had won three Tests in a row against the old enemy'* (Brearley 1982, p 131).

Australia and England are the oldest Test-playing countries and the rivalry between them dates back to 1877.

**old-fashioned point** *n* a close fielding position (or the player occupying it) square of the wicket on the off-side; a 'short' variety of point, distinguished from 'silly' point by being squarer on to the wicket. The position of point itself was generally closer to the wicket in the 18th and 19th centuries than it is nowadays (see POINT), and it is to this older position that the term old-fashioned point refers.

**on** *n* **1** the side of the pitch on which the striker stands to receive the ball; LEG (qv).

~ *adj & adv* **2** on, towards, or relating to the on-side:

> 'On-balls have a greater tendency to turn in towards the wicket' (*New Sporting Magazine* July 1836).

See also LEG, OFF.

Although roughly synonymous, the terms 'on' and 'leg' are not completely interchangeable. 'Leg' originally denoted a fielding position square of the wicket on the leg-side, and cricket terminology retains some vestiges of an old distinction – implied rather than explicit – whereby 'leg' indicates the area bounded by an arc from deep square leg to deep fine leg, while 'on' denotes the area in front of the wicket on the leg-side. Hence mid-on is in front of the wicket, but fine leg and leg slip are behind it; similarly, the on drive goes in front of the wicket but the leg glance goes behind it. The difference is most clearly shown in the terms long on and long leg, which are of course in no way synonymous.

~ *adv* **3** in or into the position of being the bowler:

> 'A bowler should never be kept on if he is not getting wickets, and if the batsmen are playing him with ease' (*Badminton* 1888, p 208).

> 'At 247, Benaud brought himself on for Rorke, but persevered with Lindwall' (Peebles 1959, p 168).

**on-break** *n* (obsolete) a LEG-BREAK:

> 'One thing I am certain of, which is that there was an on-break from Farmer Miles' bowling' (*Badminton* 1888, p 282).

**on drive** *n* a form of drive, played to a good-length ball pitching on or just outside leg stump, in which the ball is sent into the area between mid-on and mid-wicket. Described by John Arlott (1983, p 61) as 'the most difficult to play' of all the batting strokes, the on drive involves a rather complex movement in which the batsman's weight is shifted simultaneously forward and towards the on-side.

**on-drive** *vb* to strike the ball when playing an on drive:

> 'Colin Wells on-drove Emburey for successive sixes and Barclay moved steadily to his unbeaten half-century' (Patrick Barclay, *Guardian* 31 May 1983).

**one-day** *adj* **1** denoting a game or variety of cricket played under regulations that are designed to produce a result within a single day's play, typically involving one innings per side limited by a stipulated number of overs:

> 'It has become commonplace in one-day cricket to put the other side in on winning the toss' (Gordon Ross, *Cricketer* September 1984).

**2** (often disparaging) characteristic of the style of cricket played in one day games:

> 'In a Test match he has produced a . . . one-day shot and it is crucial' (Scyld Berry, *Observer* 2 January 1983).

**one leg** *n* the position of the bat when it is held so as to cover leg stump by a batsman taking guard. Compare TWO LEG.

**one short** *interj* the call made by the umpire in the event of either batsman taking a SHORT RUN (qv).

**on-side** *n & adj* (on or towards) the side of the pitch on which the striker stands; on-side and leg-side are virtually synonymous, but while leg-side tends to be used mainly with reference to field settings and bowling tactics, on-side is more often used to describe a batting stroke or a batsman's technique:

> 'Grimmett considers Headley to be the greatest master of on-side play whom he ever bowled against' (James 1963, p 143).

**open** *vb* **1** to begin the innings of the batting side by being the first batsman (or one of the two first batsmen) to face the bowling:

*'Jardine and Sutcliffe opened for England, and never appeared to be in the slightest difficulty with the bowling'* (*Cricketer* Spring Annual 1933, p 30).

*'No. 3 misses the occasional loosener that comes the way of the opening batsman'* (Brearley 1982, p 111).

**2** to bowl the first over or overs in an innings:

*'The Queensland fast bowler Fisher opened to Richardson down a fairish breeze from the pavilion end'* (Peebles 1959, p 55).

**opener** *n* **1** either of the first two batsmen on a batting side; an opening batsman:

*'The West Indies openers, Greenidge and Haynes . . . abandoned efforts to meet the daunting, but increasingly more plausible, challenge of scoring 323 in the final innings to win'* (Tony Cozier, *Cricketer* May 1984).

**2** either of the bowlers who bowl the first two overs in an innings:

*'Percy Fender . . . maintains that the Australians themselves precipitated events by their unease at the prospect of facing a battery of four England fast bowlers, including Larwood and his fellow Nottinghamshire opener, Bill Voce'* (Peter Deeley, *Observer Magazine*, 7 November 1982, p 28).

**order** *n* (also **batting order**, formerly **order of going in**) the arrangement of a team's batting resources, with regard to the order in which each player takes his turn to bat; the 'order' may be subdivided into the openers, the middle order, and the late order or 'tail':

*'Deep had been the consultation at supper as to the order of going in'* (Thomas Hughes, *Tom Brown's School Days* 1857, ch 8).

*'The Essex task was marginally eased by the absence of Mark Davies, ninth in the order, who could not bat because of a shoulder injury'* (John Mason, *Daily Telegraph* 15 August 1984).

**orthodox** *adj* bowling or bowled with FINGER-SPIN as opposed to WRIST-SPIN (qv):

*'Pakistan held the upper hand, not so much in the bowling of Iqbal Qasim and Abdul Qadir (though the latter's wrist-spin was an asset) but in the ability of their leading batsmen to counter the orthodox spin of Bracewell, Boock and Gray'* (WCM January 1985).

**out** *adv & adj* **1** having one's innings terminated; dismissed from batting:

> 'If a Ball is nipp'd up, and he strikes it again wilfully, before it came to the Wicket, it's out' (*Laws* 1744).

> 'Bear in mind not to leave your ground till the ball has quitted the Bowler's hand, or he will be justified in trying to put you out' (Clarke 1851 in *HM*, p 169).

See also ALL OUT.

~ *adj* **2** of or denoting the team that is fielding, as distinguished from the team that is 'in' or batting:

> 'A cricketer need only look at his scores and references to see how often the out side . . . has prevented the in side from getting the runs required' (*Badminton* 1888, p 197).

See also OUTCRICKET.

~ *vb* **3** to get a batsman or batting side out; dismiss:

> 'The home team were all outed for 153' (Headlam 1903, p 187).

> 'Back in the field, they improved this position by outing four of the opposition for 84' (Peebles 1959, p 142).

~ *n* **4** (obsolete) a decision by the umpire that a batsman is out; a dismissal:

> 'They are the sole Judges of all Outs and Inns [and] of all fair or unfair Play' (*Laws* 1744).

A batsman can be out in any of the following ten ways (all of which are defined at the appropriate places): (1) bowled (2) timed out (3) caught (4) handled the ball (5) hit the ball twice (6) hit wicket (7) lbw (8) obstructing the field (9) run out (10) stumped. Seven of these modes of dismissal (viz all except 2, 7, and 8) are included in the original (1744) code of Laws and have remained unchanged, apart from technical details. The decision as to whether a batsman is out rests exclusively with the umpires, to whom the fielding side must appeal. If the appeal is answered in the affirmative, the umpire signals his decision to the players and the scorers by raising his index finger above his head.

**outcricket** *n* the performance or skill of a team as a fielding side, as distinguished from its performance with the bat:

'In contrast to Sri Lanka's fine outcricket, Wettimuny was dropped once and Dias twice' (WCM May 1984).

**outfield** *n* **1** the area of a cricket field outside the pitch and its immediate vicinity, especially the area beyond the 'midfield' and close to the boundary, often considered in terms of the extent to which it helps or impedes the progress of a ball struck from the bat:

'A target of 201 at five an over did not seem an exacting task for Lancashire, given an easy-paced pitch and a fast outfield' (David Lacey, *Guardian* 9 July 1984).

**2** (old) a fielder stationed in the outfield; an outfielder:

'Ulyett is a very good outfield, as good a run-getting bat as Gunn, and at times a dangerous bowler' (*Badminton* 1888, p 216).

**outfielder** *n* a fielder stationed in the outfield; a 'deep' fielder:

'The crowd behaved abysmally, forcing Sunil Gavaskar to lead India off the field . . . when one of his outfielders was hit by a bottle' (Matthew Engel, *Guardian* 21 January 1985).

**outing** *n* a period spent 'in the field', as distinguished from an 'innings':

'A man even in full training invariably feels the effect of fatigue after bowling sixty or seventy overs, and fieldsmen go through the same experience during a long outing' (*Badminton* 1888, p 94).

**outside** *prep* with the bat moving along a line on the far side of the ball's line of flight, so that the ball passes the inside edge of the bat:

'Qadir played outside a slower ball from Lawson and was bowled when it came back off the seam' (Henry Blofeld, *Guardian* 31 December 1983).

Compare INSIDE.

**outside edge** *n* the edge of the bat, when held more or less perpendicularly, that is further from the batsman; the 'off-side' edge of the bat:

'Harper, after a long intelligent spell at the left-handers . . . found the top outside edge of Gower's bat' (Christopher Martin-Jenkins, *Cricketer* September 1984).

**outswing** *n* (also **outswerve**, **away-swing**) movement of the ball in the air, typically from a line around middle stump, away from the batsman so as to hit or pass just outside of off stump; though more difficult to achieve than inswing, outswing is more likely to produce problems for the batsman, especially if the ball moves late:

> *'Inswing, of course, can be more easily smothered than outswing'* (Arlott 1983, p 38).

See SWING and compare INSWING.

**outswinger** *n* (also **away-swinger**) a ball that swings away towards the off-side, especially so as to pass outside off stump, from a line initially closer to middle stump:

> *'Simpson . . . played a stylish little innings until he reached across too far and touched an out-swinger from Lindwall, sending a difficult wide chance which Langley held with clever agility'* (Cardus 1978, p 211).

**over** *n* a stipulated number of fair deliveries (now usually six) bowled consecutively by one bowler from one end of the pitch. Overs are bowled alternately from each end of the pitch, and no bowler may bowl two overs consecutively. No-balls and wides do not count in the over. The term derives from the call made by the umpire when the prescribed number of balls has been bowled:

> *'When the Four Balls are bowl'd he is to call Over'* (Laws 1744).

thereby indicating that the field will 'change over' and the ball will be bowled from the other end of the wicket.

The earliest code of Laws prescribes a four-ball over and this remained the norm for well over a hundred years. The length of the over was officially increased to five balls in 1889, but experiments with overs of five balls or more had evidently been in progress for some time:

> *'Some clubs insist upon bowling more than four balls to the over . . . Some contend for five balls, being more convenient as a submultiple of ten'* (Box 1868, p 117).

The preference for longer overs reflects an increasing tactical sophistication on the part of bowlers, who needed more than four balls in which to develop their plan of attack. At any rate the pressure continued, and the modern six-ball over was established in 1900. The 20th century has seen a number of experiments with an eight-ball over, notably in Australia where this was the norm from the end of the first world war until 1979. England, New Zealand, the West Indies, and South Africa have all at different times flirted with the eight-ball over, but in these cases the arrangement has never lasted for more than two or three years. At the present time the six-ball over is almost universal but the eight-ball variety is still permitted by the Laws, and survives in some branches of the game, such as the Lancashire leagues.

**overarm** *adj & adv* using the normal method of bowling, in which the arm is raised almost vertically above the shoulder before swinging forward and downward as it delivers the ball. Overarm bowling was finally legalised in 1864, but had been tolerated with varying degrees of resistance ever since the legalisation of roundarm bowling in 1835. See BOWLING.

**overpitch** *vb* to bowl the ball so that it pitches further down the wicket than a good length:

'Saunders was over-pitching them and Hayward drove a full toss to the track' (*Melbourne Argus* 14 December 1903).

'The really good player to lobs runs out to a certainty when the ball is overpitched' (*Badminton* 1888, p 80).

See LENGTH.

**over-rate** *n* the average number of overs bowled per hour during a given period such as a match, a series, or a season. Efforts have recently been made to reverse the trend whereby over-rates have steadily declined since the 1950s. A rate of well in excess of 20 six-ball overs per hour was quite normal in pre-war years, even at Test level, but Test match over-rates have in recent years slumped to as low as 11 or 12 overs an hour, especially in the case of teams with an all-pace attack. At the county championship level in England, a system of fines was introduced in 1978 for counties failing to reach a stipulated minimum rate (19 overs per hour in 1983). But this was abandoned for the 1984 season in favour of an arrangement whereby play would continue until 117 overs had been bowled in an uninterrupted day, which represents an over-rate of

18. At international level nothing of a statutory nature has yet been attempted, but it is now usual for the two sides in a Test series to try and reach agreement about minimum over-rates before the series begins. The figure of 96 overs per day (= 16 an hour) has proved relatively easy to enforce, and although this is regarded as quite inadequate by some of the older ex-players, the point has been well made that a higher rate – such as prevailed between the wars – would be 'incompatible with the maximum concentration of thought and effort which modern Test cricket demands' (Berry 1982, p 58).

**over the wicket** *adv* delivering the ball from the hand that is closer to the bowler's wicket; by going 'over the wicket' the bowler is able to reduce to a minimum the angle between the ball's line of flight and the line passing from wicket to wicket:

> *'It was now that Bright started to bowl over the wicket to the right-handers . . . a ploy he was to rely on for most of the remaining Tests'* (Brearley 1982, p 32).

**overthrow** *n* **1** a ball thrown in from the field that travels beyond the wicket after eluding any intervening fielders, thus enabling the batsmen to take a run or runs, or to continue taking runs if they have already started.

**2** a run made as a result of an overthrow:

> *'From 97 not out overnight he completed his century off the third ball yesterday, with the aid of four overthrows'* (The News Line 10 January 1985).

If an overthrow crosses the boundary, any runs already taken by the batsmen, *plus* the allowance for the boundary, are added to the score. The runs resulting from an overthrow are credited to the striker (and debited to the bowler) if he hit the ball in the first place; but if the original ball was a wide or resulted in a bye or leg-bye, any extra runs coming from overthrows are added to the appropriate section of the 'extras'. If a ball thrown in from the field hits the stumps while the batsman is in his ground and then continues into the outfield, the batsmen may still take runs on the overthrow.

**pace**  *n* **1** the speed at which a ball is delivered by a bowler:

> *'If a batsman misjudges the pace of the ball he often loses his wicket'* (*Badminton* 1888, p 123).

**2** the extent to which the wicket affects the speed of the ball when it pitches:

> *'He made the best use of the green, moist pitch that almost throughout was of uncertain pace'* (*WCM* April 1984).

**3** fast bowling:

> *'He* [Gavaskar] *is equally at home against pace or spin'* (Peter Hook, *WCM* January 1984).

> *'After I had seen the Australian pace trio operate, the initial selection seemed more defensible'* (Brearley 1982, p 60).

**paceman**  *n* a fast bowler:

> *'The second day, though, saw a change of fortunes as West Indies' pacemen restricted India to a further 165 runs'* (*WCM* December 1983).

**pack**  *vb* to concentrate fielders on a particular side of the wicket, especially in close catching positions:

> *'As runs came Larwood packed his leg field; and now had seven men on the leg side'* (*Melbourne Argus* 3 December 1932).

> *'This* [restriction] *was not welcomed by the off-spinning contingent on tour as we are accustomed to bowling to a packed onside field'* (Vic Marks, *Cricketer* April 1983).

**pad**  *n* **1** either of a pair of protective coverings worn by batsmen and wicket-keepers to protect their legs from above the knees to below the ankle.

**2 – off one's pads:** striking the ball smartly towards leg at a late stage in its flight, when it has almost made contact with the pads:

> *'Hutton forced Lindwall for four to the on, a glorious forearm thrust off his pads'* (Cardus 1978, p 198).

Various forms of protection for the legs were experimented with in the early 19th century, the most primitive being a single wooden board tied to the batsman's front leg. One writer describes a system involving 'longitudinal sockets' sewn into the trouser legs at half-inch intervals, into which 'long strips of Indian rubber' could be inserted (Felix 1850, p 7). The older players, predictably, were disdainful of these namby-pamby arrangements: Herbert Jenner-Fust, who played in the 1820s and 30s, reports that 'pads were not heard of in my young days, and the player would be laughed at who attempted to protect his shins' (Pullin 1900, p 6). These and similar comments are strikingly reminiscent of remarks made nowadays about the introduction of protective helmets. But apologists of the helmet would probably say the same as W. G. Grace said about pads, that 'the sense of confidence that comes from wearing them more than makes up for the slight loss of freedom' (*Badminton* 1888, p 392). Notwithstanding the scorn of the old guard, pads began to be widely adopted from the 1840s onwards, and much of the impetus for this change will have come from the major developments in the area of bowling that were currently in progress:

> *'When round-arm became "all the go", and pace was regarded as the grand object to be achieved, the bowling became often so dangerous that the legs of the batsmen needed protection, and, as necessity is the parent of invention, pads of various designs were brought into notice'* (Box 1868, p 158).

**paddings** *n* (obsolete) an early form of protection for the batsman's legs (see PAD):

> *'Always, whether in practice or whilst engaged in matches, wear paddings'* (Felix 1850, p 6).

**pad play** *n* the practice or technique of 'padding up' as a defensive manoeuvre, especially when playing spin bowling:

> 'Qadir . . . becomes frustrated at the "old pro" pad play of Bob Taylor, who thrusts his front leg forward at any ball around offstump in case it turns out to be a googly' (Scyld Berry, Observer 11 March 1984).

**pad up** *vb* **1** to put on one's pads in readiness for going out to bat:

> 'Gower, who was originally padded up to go in No. 3, held back to let Edmonds and Foster go in and slog' (Matthew Engel, Guardian 16 January 1985).

**2** (also **pad out**, **pad away**) to move the front leg down the wicket, usually outside the line of off stump, with the aim of stopping the ball either with the pad or with the bat, which is usually held a little further back:

'Before the roaring crowd had regained breath, Morris padded up without constructive ideas to Lock, and died the modern hero's death, leg before' (Cardus 1978, p 245).

'Offsetting the benefits to off-spinners of the law penalising batsmen who deliberately padded away had come the restrictions upon leg-side fielders' (Frith 1984, p 149).

'Botham had to come in with 25 minutes to go, when Mike Gatting had his second break of concentration, padding out again to another straight one from Marshall' (Scyld Berry, Observer 1 July 1984).

Padding up became especially prevalent after an alteration to the lbw rule in 1937 made it possible for batsmen to be out to balls pitching outside off stump: by moving the front leg forward and across the batsman could prevent the ball hitting him 'between wicket and wicket', and thus avoid dismissal (see LBW). But a further change in the rules in 1970, whereby a batsman could be given out even if the ball hit him *outside* off stump, provided he was playing no stroke, has made deliberate 'pad play' a distinctly more hazardous business. Even so, batsmen still occasionally take the risk, no doubt calculating that if their front foot is far enough forward or if some pretence of playing a shot is made, the umpire is likely to give them the benefit of the doubt.

**pair** *n* (also **pair of spectacles**) a batsman's score of nought in both innings of a match, so called because of the supposed resemblance of the two noughts in the scorebook to a pair of spectacles; a batsman who has scored nought in the first innings of a game is said to be **on a pair** when he goes in to bat for a second time:

'In a conversation after net practice he confessed that he had made a pair of spectacles only once in his life' (Cardus 1978, p 64).

'Poor Woolmer got a pair without playing a single bad stroke' (Brearley 1982, p 18).

See also KING PAIR, EMPEROR PAIR.

**palm-break** *n* (Australian, obsolete) break applied to the ball by the movement of the palm of the hand across the seam as the ball is delivered; CUT:

'All the bowlers found it a wicket upon which the ball declined to *answer either finger or palm-break' (Melbourne Argus* 16 January 1904).

**pano** (Corfu) *lit 'up'*: the batting side. Compare KATO.

**partnership** *n* **1** a period during which two batsmen are batting together, usually measured in terms of the number of runs that are scored while they are at the wicket, and lasting either until one of them is dismissed or – in the case of an 'unbroken' partnership – until their side's innings ends while both of them are still in:

> *'Greenidge and Haynes . . . have shared in seven century partnerships, three of which have passed the 200'* (Derek Lodge, *WCM* May 1984).

**2** a pair of batsmen, especially opening batsmen, who regularly bat together:

> *'With Greenidge, he forms the most settled opening partnership in international cricket'* (Tony Cozier, *Cricketer* June 1984).

**peg** *n* (old) a stump:

> *'A loose one on the leg side was neatly turned for a couple, the next went perilously near his off peg'* (Jack Hobbs, *The Test Match Surprise* 1926, p 143).

**penalty runs** *n* runs accruing to the score as a result of no-balls, wides, a lost ball, or an instance of the ball being stopped other than by a fieldsman (eg if it is stopped by a helmet): see Law 18 § 6.

**pick** *vb* (of a batsman) to form an accurate assessment, as a ball is bowled, of the way it will behave when it pitches, and take appropriate action:

> *'Most of the Australian batsmen have told me that they can pick his leg break and play him as an off-spinner for the rest of the time'* (Henry Blofeld, *Guardian* 2 January 1984).

> *'His steep bounce, coupled with the problem of picking his length, presented more problems than his turn'* (David Green, *Cricketer* April 1983).

**pick-up** *n* the action or method of bringing the bat up from a stationary position preliminary to playing a stroke:

> *'If his wrists are cocked early in the pick-up then it should be comparatively easy for him to take the bat up higher when the*

*full swing of the bat at the ball is called for'* (Alf Gover, *Cricketer* March 1983).

**pintz** (Corfu) a yorker; origins unknown.

**pitch** *n* **1** the area of ground between the two sets of stumps. Like 'wicket' (WICKET²) the term is used both for the playing area itself and for the quality of its surface as this affects the behaviour of the ball:

*'The pitch enabled the seam bowlers to move the ball around a good deal at the start'* (Henry Blofeld, *Guardian* 21 July 1983).

The pitch is so called because it is the place where the wickets are 'pitched': see **5**, below. It measures 22 yards (20·12 metres) in length and 10 feet (3·04 metres) in width (Laws 7 § 1, 8 § 1). The length of a cricket pitch has not changed since the first code of Laws in 1744, and there is evidence to suggest that it was already well established long before then. Writing in 1833 and referring to an old manuscript that described the game in its infancy, John Nyren observes: 'It appears that about 150 years since, it was the custom, as at present, to pitch the wickets at the same distance asunder, viz. the twenty-two yards' (Nyren 1833 in *HM*, p 84). This distance is equivalent to the chain, a linear unit that is used for measuring land and was standardised at 66 feet by a Mr Gunter in the early 17th century. However, 'why twenty-two yards were originally resolved upon as the limits of distance is not more mysterious than the appointment of eleven persons necessary for playing the game' (Box 1868, p 113). In other words, nobody really knows.

**2** the point at which the ball first makes contact with the ground after being delivered by the bowler:

*'Trumper used to say that if you got to the pitch of the ball it did not matter which way it was breaking'* (James 1963, p 178).

~ *vb* **3** to deliver the ball so that it makes contact with the ground at a particular point on the wicket; also (of the ball) to strike the ground at a particular point when bowled:

*'The young Bowler should at all times strive to pitch the Ball to a good length'* (Lambert 1816, p 17).

**4** to deliver the ball so that it strikes the ground in line with a particular target; also (of the ball) to follow such a line when bowled:

*'Supposing the ball pitches on or just outside the off-stump, the batsman will assuredly play that particular ball more correctly if he moves his right leg across the wicket'* (Warner 1934, p 12).

**5** to set up the wickets in readiness for a game by driving the stumps into the ground:

*'On Mon., Aug. 7, in the field adjoining to the* Wool Pack *at Islington, London v. the County of Middlesex for £20 a side. Wickets to be pitched at one o'clock, play or pay'* (Whitehall Evening Post 1 August 1732).

**place** *vb* to hit the ball skilfully through the gaps in the field so as to derive the maximum benefit from a shot:

*'Zaheer . . . was making the most of the brief respite afforded by the off-spin of Gomes, placing the ball with deft skill and honeyed timing'* (Christopher Martin-Jenkins, *Cricketer* August 1983).

**play** *n* **1** the activity of conducting a game of cricket:

*'At the conclusion of the first day's play, the Leicester Club went in against 50 notches only'* (*Leicester Journal* 22 September 1791).

**2** the performance of an individual or team in a match:

*'The Umpires shall intervene without appeal by calling and signalling "dead ball" in the case of unfair play'* (Law 42 § 3).

**3** the style or skill of a batsman in dealing with the bowling:

*'The play of Lord Winchilsea was the conspicuous thing in the match . . . All the five bowlers tried at him in vain'* (Kentish Gazette 21–3 August 1788).

*'In offensive forward play, great care should be taken not to bend the right knee'* (Warner 1934, p 11).

**4 – in play** (of the ball) in active use according to the Laws, as distinguished from being 'dead':

*'If a Fieldsman releases the ball before he crosses the boundary, the ball will be considered to be still in play'* (Law 32 § 3 (b)).

The ball is 'in play' from the moment the bowler begins his run-up until it becomes 'dead' for whatever reason. See DEAD.

~ *vb* **5** to take part in a game of cricket:

*'Simpson-Hayward . . . had been unable to play at Pindi owing to a bruised hand'* (Headlam 1903, p 163).

**6** to include a particular player in a team:

*'We should have liked to play two spinners . . . but we could not imagine either going in with only two seamers or leaving out a batsman'* (Brearley 1982, p 80).

**7** to stage a match:

*'A three days' match was played at the Surrey Ground . . . commencing on the 1st of July, 1847, between the counties of Kent and Surrey'* (Bat 1851, p 73).

**8** to execute a batting stroke in an attempt to hit the ball:

*'By operating round the wicket and aiming at off stump, Yardley probably forced the batsmen to play more often'* (Michael Carey, *Daily Telegraph* 15 December 1982).

*'Hardly had Shah begun to play a few attacking strokes than Sandhu made one lift to have him caught behind'* (Tony Pawson, *Observer* 12 June 1983).

**9** to strike the ball when batting:

*'Dyson took two offside fours off Pringle before playing him wide of mid-on for two'* (Henry Blofeld, *Cricketer* February 1983).

**10** to deal with bowling of a particular type or from a particular bowler:

*'There is a golden rule to be carefully remembered in playing slows, and that is, never to run out to a ball that is well outside the off stump'* (Badminton 1888, p 80).

*'Harvey alone played him [Lock] well, before being bowled by a ball which pitched well outside his off stump and hit the leg'* (Peebles 1959, p 60).

**11** (of the pitch) to provide favourable or unfavourable batting conditions as specified:

*'Seven wickets had fallen for 19 runs on a pitch playing little worse than in the first innings when . . . the same batsmen had amassed 401 runs'* (Brearley 1982, p 77).

**12 – play and miss** to attempt a stroke but fail to make contact with the ball:

'He played and missed a good deal early on, but then began to time his drives and nudges and glances' (Henry Blofeld, *Guardian* 31 May 1983).

**13 – play on** to deflect the ball on to one's stumps with the bat; the resulting dismissal is entered in the scorebook as 'bowled':

'Unfortunately for Essex's immediate prospects, Gooch had played on at the start of Williams's decisive over' (Matthew Engel, *Guardian* 28 April 1984).

**14 – play oneself in** to play cautiously at the beginning of one's innings, or of a new session of play, in order to become accustomed to the bowling and the wicket:

'Fowler moreover had to play himself in six times (100 minutes being lost to bad light on the first day) before reaching 99 with an adventurous pull-drive' (Scyld Berry, WCM August 1984).

**15 – play out** to move well forward down the wicket in order to make a stroke:

'His innings was a very reformation of cricket, until at ten minutes to three he played out at Wardle, and was beaten and bowled' (Cardus 1978, p 179).

For **play across, play back, play forward, play inside, play outside**: see ACROSS, BACK, FORWARD, INSIDE, OUTSIDE.

**player** *n* **1** a participant in a match:

'They are not to order any Man out, unless appealed to by one of the Players' (*Laws* 1744).

**2** (especially in Britain before 1962) a professional cricketer, as distinguished from a 'gentleman' or amateur cricketer:

'In the year 1806, the Gentlemen first arrayed themselves against the Players at Lord's' (Box 1868, p 89).

See GENTLEMAN, PROFESSIONAL.

**plumb** *adj* **1** denotes a flat, true wicket that provides optimum conditions for batting and offers little or no assistance to the bowlers:

'I clean bowled the Old Man, W. W. Read, and A. E. Stoddart in a couple of overs with that ball, on a plumb Oval wicket' (Cardus 1978, p 30).

~ *adv* **2** clearly and indisputably lbw:

> *'In his third over, he bowled me an attempted bouncer which cut back and kept insidiously low. I was plumb* LBW' (Brearley 1982. p 89).

The first meaning of 'plumb' relates to the word's more general use in the sense of 'completely straight or perpendicular' (as determined by a 'plumb line'); while its use as an adverb – meaning 'utterly' or 'completely – is well established in the general language, in expressions like 'plumb crazy' and 'plumb tuckered'.

**pod** *n* (old) the blade of the bat:

> *'When the practice of bowling length-balls was introduced . . . it became absolutely necessary to change the form of the bat . . . It was therefore made straight in the pod'* (Nyren 1833 in *HM*, p 85).

**point** *n* **1** (formerly **point of the bat**) a fairly close off-side fielding position (or the player occupying it) between cover and gully and roughly in a line with the popping crease:

> *'Louch of Chatham behaved with his usual activity: he caught out 3 at the point of the bat* [and] *he got 29 in the second innings'* (*St James's Chronicle* 22 September 1774).

> *'The distance at which point should stand varies according to the pace of the bowling, the pace of the wicket, and the hitting powers of the batsman in point's direction'* (Ranji 1897, p 48).

The connotations of this term have changed considerably over the last 200 years. In the early days of cricket, point denoted a *very* close position, and its full name – 'the point of the bat' – alludes to the fact that the fielder stood very near to the end of the striker's bat (hence also the even older term 'bat's end'):

> *'The Point of the Bat (Slow Bowling). The young fieldsman who is appointed to this situation . . . should place himself within three yards and a half of the batsman'* (Nyren 1833 in *HM*, p 32).

Even half a century later, it was believed that 'in no case ought he to be more than eight yards away' from the wicket (*Badminton* 1888, p 263). Nowadays the 'normal' position of point for a fast bowler would be a little deeper still, and variations from this norm are shown by an appropriate adjective: thus, a very close fielder a little in front of square is at **silly point**, while a player fielding a little behind the line of the wicket is at **backward point**; a less common term is OLD-FASHIONED POINT (qv) indicating a close position square of the wicket – in fact, the position that point occupied in earlier times.

~ *vb* **2** (obsolete) to field at point:

'The bowling of Tarrant and Grundy . . . the pointing of Carpenter, was all cricket in perfection' (*Baily's Magazine* September 1867).

**poker** *n* (obsolete) a batsman with a 'pokey' style of play:

'To the poker, the man who refuses to do anything but stick his bat in front of the wicket . . . the high-dropping full-pitch is an excellent ball' (*Badminton* 1888, p 143).

**pokey** *adj* (obsolete) (of a batsman or batting style) characterised by a tendency to push or 'dab' at the ball rather than committing oneself to a proper stroke:

'Sometimes mid-off . . . is required to go "silly mid-off" with a view to catching a pokey batsman' (Ranji 1897, p 54).

**pole bowler** *n* the leading member of a side's bowling attack, so called by analogy with the motor-racing term 'pole position', indicating the leading position on the starting grid occupied by the fastest driver:

'Now Botham had acceded to the position of pole bowler; but John Lever and Graham Dilley never rose to the situation' (John Arlott, *Guardian* 31 December 1982).

**pop** *vb* **1** (of the ball) to rise steeply and unexpectedly off the wicket after pitching, usually as a result of some irregularity in the surface:

'The balls were popping about in dangerous fashion, and Champain behind the wicket was taking them above his topi or brushing them off his nose like flies' (Headlam 1903, p 163).

**2** (of a batsman) to cause the ball to rise sharply off the bat in making a defensive stroke:

'When he had made 10 Burke, in sparring at Tyson . . . popped the ball up very near to Mortimore at short-leg' (Peebles 1959, p 181).

**popper** *n* (obsolete) a ball that 'pops' up off the wicket:

> 'He defended his wicket well against "breakers" and "poppers"'
> (*Bell's Life* 19 July 1857).

**popping crease** *n* a line marked on the ground at each end of the pitch, parallel with the BOWLING CREASE (qv) and 4 feet/1·22 metres in front of the stumps; it marks the forward limit of the batsman's GROUND (qv), and although in practice it is only slightly longer than the bowling crease it 'shall be considered to be unlimited in length' (Law 9 § 2). The popping crease was already in existence at the time of the original (1744) code of Laws, which stipulated that it 'must be exactly Three Feet Ten Inches from the Wicket' (the extra two inches being added in 1819 in conjunction with an increase in the height of the wicket). However, there is evidence to show that it was a fairly recent innovation when these Laws were drawn up. John Nyren's tentative reconstruction of the game as it was played 'about 150 years since' (ie in the late 17th century) includes the following description: 'Between the stumps a hole was cut in the ground, large enough to contain the ball and the butt-end of the bat. In running a notch, the striker was required to put his bat into this hole, instead of the modern practice of touching over the popping crease. The wicket-keeper, in putting out the striker when running, was obliged, when the ball was thrown in, to place it in this hole before the adversary could reach it with his bat' (Nyren 1833 in *HM*, pp 84–5). This practice of 'popping' the bat in the hole in order to complete a run led to 'many severe injuries of the hands' and was eventually superseded – via an intermediate stage in which the batsman had to touch a stick held by the umpire – by the 'modern' method, in which the batsman's crease becomes, for the purposes of scoring a run, a symbolic vestige of the original 'popping hole'. The popping crease is also used to mark the forward limit of the bowler's territory in determining whether a delivery is fair: the umpire must be satisfied that 'some part of the front foot . . . was behind the popping crease' (Law 24 § 3). See also RUN.

**poppy** *adj* (of the wicket) liable to make the ball 'pop':

> 'Several . . . got out in hitting at balls which, off a wicket that

*was somewhat poppy, found a lodging in a very safe pair of hands belonging to Walters'* (Headlam 1903, p 71).

**post** *vb* (of a batsman, partnership, or batting side) to score the stated number of runs:

> *'Shastri and Binny were unhurried as they posted 127 for the fifth wicket'* (WCM January 1984).

**professional** *n* a person who plays cricket as a profession rather than as a pastime; specifically, in the context of first-class cricket in Britain before 1962, a player in the paid employment of one of the counties as distinguished from the 'amateurs' who played without remuneration. People were already playing cricket as a profession by the second half of the 18th century, and the first encounter between the Gentlemen (amateurs) and Players (professionals) took place in 1806. The amateur/professional distinction became institutionalised in the English first-class game, as an extension of the overall class system. There were separate dressing rooms for the two types of player, and a system of nomenclature that made everybody's status quite clear: thus, Surrey's team in the 1950s included the amateurs P. B. H. May and R. Subba Row and the professionals Lock, G. A. R. and Laker, J. C. With the abolition of amateur status in 1962 the term 'professional' lost its former social connotations. Now that all first-class cricketers are professionals, the word is perhaps most often used of those players – often overseas stars or former county players – who are employed in league cricket as the sole paid member of an otherwise amateur team. See also GENTLEMAN.

**pull** *n* 1 an attacking batting stroke in which a ball pitching on the wicket or outside the off stump is 'pulled' round towards the leg-side. The pull is usually played to a ball of goodish length, and is executed by moving the front foot slightly across towards the leg-side so that the batsman is almost chest on to the bowler, and hitting the ball on the half-volley, *across* its line of flight, sending it into the area between square leg and mid-on. By contrast with the hook, the pull is 'more in the nature of a drive' (Warner 1934, p 18) in that it is played with the bat more perpendicular than horizontal. In common with other strokes played across the ball's line of flight, the pull was regarded with great suspicion in the 19th century. To the *Badminton* book (1888, p 48) it is simply 'a bad stroke'. Ranji is slightly less censorious, at least so long as the stroke is reserved for balls pitching outside off stump. He contends, however, that 'it is never used by a good player to deal with the ball pitching on the wicket; at least if it is, the player is for the nonce a bad one' (Ranji 1897, p 192). Modern coaches are likely to take a more indulgent line, but it remains true that considerable care is needed in selecting the right ball to pull. Compare HOOK.

~ *vb* **2** to hit the ball across to the leg-side when making a pull:

> 'Then, with Australia's total still 107, Harvey committed his fatal error, pulling against Trueman with less than a great batsman's power of selection' (Cardus 1978, p 236).

**pull-drive** *n* **1** a pull, especially one that sends the ball well forward of square on the leg-side:

> 'A pull-drive by Robinson to the mid-wicket boundary was the only stroke of note in the abbreviated play possible' (Derek Hodgson, *Observer* 22 May 1983).

Though sometimes used interchangeably with 'pull', the term often describes a stroke somewhere between an on-drive, which is played more along the line of the ball, and a full-scale pull, which is played across the line.

~ *vb* **2** to strike the ball when making a pull-drive:

> 'Once, at the Oval, he [Clive Lloyd] pull-drove a ball from Robin Jackman . . . over midwicket into the yard of Archbishop Tenison's Grammar School on the far side of the road' (John Arlott, *WCM* June 1983).

**push** *n* **1** a defensive batting stroke in which a straight bat is pushed forward to meet the ball with a minimum of backlift:

> 'When he [Glenn Turner] first appeared his shots were just about limited to a forward and backward defensive push' (Jim Laker, *WCM* August 1984).

~ *vb* **2** to hit or attempt to hit the ball when playing a push stroke:

'After nearly four hours Smith's concentration faltered too: he pushed at a ball from Sarfraz that should have been driven firmly or ignored, and played on' (Matthew Engel, *Guardian* 15 March 1984).

**push through** *vb* (of a slow bowler) to deliver the ball with a relatively low, flat trajectory, with the primary aim of restricting scoring opportunities rather than of deceiving the batsman:

'The finger-spinners have virtually abandoned flight, preferring safely to "push it through" defensively flat' (Arlott 1983, p 16).

'Three times in the late 1950s he exceeded 100 wickets for the county, pushing the ball through at a pace which discouraged much forward footwork' (Frith 1984, p 124).

**put down** *vb* **1** to fail to take a possible catch:

'Though their fielding in general remains first-rate, England have made a habit of putting down critical chances in this series' (Matthew Engel, 21 March 1984).

**2** (of a fielder of wicket-keeper) to dislodge either or both bails with the ball, especially so as to cause the dismissal of a batsman:

'Sueter . . . and Hammond . . . were the two best wicket-keepers I ever saw. Both of them would put the wicket down without any flourishing or fuss' (Nyren 1833 in *HM*, p 32).

**put in** *vb* (of the captain who wins the toss) to cause one's own side or one's opponents to take first innings:

'It has become commonplace in one-day cricket to put the other side in on winning the toss' (Gordon Ross, *Cricketer* September 1984).

**put on** *vb* (of a batting side or batting partnership) to add the stated number of runs to the team's score:

'They saw England make an encouraging start after the rain in the morning, the two left-handers Fowler and Broad putting on 92 for the first wicket' (Christopher Martin-Jenkins, *Cricketer* September 1984).

**put out** *vb* to dismiss from batting, especially by means of a run-out:

'Bear in mind not to leave your ground till the ball has quitted the Bowler's hand, or he will be justified in trying to put you out' (Clarke 1851 in *HM*, p 169).

**quick** *n* (also **quickie**) a fast bowler:

> 'The rest of the batting just fell away against the cock-a-hoop
> Australian quicks' (WCM January 1984).

> 'Both Chappell and Inverarity mentioned Mike Whitney, the
> young left-arm quickie from New South Wales, as the best
> long-term prospect in Australia' (Brearley 1982, p 22).

**quilt** (obsolete) *vb* **1** to subject the bowling to aggressive
and powerful hitting:

> 'A batsman may be bowled first ball, a bowler may be quilted all
> over the field, but both can redeem themselves by good fielding
> (Ranji 1897, p 61).

~ *n* **2** a powerful hit:

> 'His drives were superb, and included one terrific quilt out of the
> ground' (Headlam 1903, p 121).

**rabbit** *n* a late-order batsman with little or no batting skill; a tailender:

> *'Nearly every eleven has a "rabbit" or two at the end'* (*Westminster Gazette* 8 May 1906).

This term was much in vogue in the earlier part of the century, and could be applied to a poor performer in any sport. Harold Larwood extends the metaphor by referring to the late-order batsmen collectively as the 'hutch': 'Short of a couple of discoveries during Australia's next season . . . Australia will surely have the hutch door open at 7 wickets down in the next season's Test matches' (Larwood 1933, p 176).

**read** *vb* to make a correct evaluation, as the ball is bowled, of the way it will behave, especially with regard to the way it will turn after pitching:

> *'Qadir was a joy to watch . . . Nobody "read" him, and of the right-handers, Bob Taylor played him better than most'* (Jack Bannister, *WCM* May 1984).

> *'The first ingredient of a good stroke, no doubt, is early reading of the ball: identification of its pace, spin and, above all, its length'* (Arlott 1983, p 62).

**replacement ball** *n* a used ball given by the umpires to the fielding side to replace a ball that has been lost or become unfit for play before it is due to be replaced by a new ball in the normal way; the replacement ball must have had roughly the same amount of wear as the ball it replaces. See also NEW BALL.

**reply** *vb* **1** (of a batting side) to score the stated number of runs when chasing a total made by the opposing team:

> *"England were on top for most of the match. This second day, when India replied with 105–2 in the last two sessions, was the only time when they were not'* (Berry 1892, p 114).

~ *n* **2** the innings of a batting side that follows that of their opponents:

> *'Kuruppu deflected a catch to Gatting's right at first slip in the second over of the Sri Lanka reply'* (Scyld Berry, *Observer* 12 June 1983).

**result wicket** *n* a wicket on which a match is unlikely to end in a draw, usually because the conditions give some assistance to the bowlers and make batting relatively difficult:

> *'Being a fluctuating, low-scoring match played out on a "result wicket" (in cricketers' jargon) it had much in common with the more breathtaking Test matches in the Ashes series the previous English summer'* (Berry 1982, p 55).

**retire** *vb* (of a batsman) to leave the field during one's innings without being dismissed and with the option of resuming the innings at a later stage. A batsman may retire 'owing to illness, injury, or any other unavoidable cause' provided he first notifies the umpire, and if capable of doing so he 'may resume his innings at the fall of a wicket' (Law 2 § 9). The most common reason for retirement is physical injury, such as results when a batsman is hit by a fast short-pitched ball, and if the injured batsman is unable to complete his innings he is marked down in the scorebook as 'retired hurt', but is not regarded as having been dismissed.

**return** *vb* **1** to throw the ball in to the batsman's or bowler's wicket after fielding it:

> *'It is necessary to be able to gather in the hands a ball hit along or on to the ground and to return it equally surely and swiftly to either wicket'* (Ranji 1897, p 16).

**2** to achieve the stated bowling analysis in a match or spell of bowling:

> *'He returned, too, the best first-class figures of any of the famous*

*quartet, 9 for 72 for Mysore v Kerala in 1969–70'* (Frith 1984, p 174).

~ *n* **3** an instance of the ball being thrown into the wickets by a fielder:

*'Simpson-Hayward . . . had been unable to play at Pindi owing to a bruised hand – an injury received in the last over of the match from a very hard return'* (Headlam 1903, p 163).

**4** the bowling analysis achieved by a bowler in a match or spell:

*'His 8 for 103 was the best return by an England bowler in a home Test match against West Indies'* (WCM August 1984).

**return catch** *n* a catch made by a bowler off one of his own deliveries:

*'Richardson, meeting a ball that may have stopped a little, gave Willis a return catch so simple that he stood in disbelief'* (Michael Carey, *Daily Telegraph* 1 June 1984).

**return crease** *n* either of two lines marked on the ground at each end of the bowling crease and at right angles to it, extending at least 4 feet/1·22m behind the wicket and (usually) as far forward as the popping crease, but considered to be of unlimited length. The return creases mark the lateral limits of the bowler's territory for the purposes of determining whether a delivery is fair: the umpire must be satisfied that 'the Bowler's back foot has landed within and not touching the return crease' (Law 24 § 3). The return crease makes its first appearance in the second major code of Laws, dated 1774.

**reverse sweep** *n* **1** an unorthodox batting stroke in which – just as in a conventional sweep – the batsman adopts a half-kneeling position with the front foot well forward and strikes the ball with a long sweeping movement of a horizontal bat, with the important difference that the wrists are turned over and the bat is swung from leg towards off, sending the ball into the third-man area. Though popularised in recent years by Ian Botham, this hazardous shot dates back at least as far as E. M. Grace and has figured in the repertoire of a number of well-known players, such as Percy Fender and more recently Mushtaq Mohammad.

~ *vb* **2** to strike the ball into the off-side area when making a reverse sweep:

> 'He swung the first ball of this new over for two, and reverse-swept the next for four more' (Berry 1982, p 146).

**rib-roaster** *n* (old) a fast ball that rises sharply from the pitch, especially so as to put the batsman in danger of physical injury:

> 'Both "rib-roasters" and shooters were frequent at head-quarters, and many a lion on the Cambridge lawn . . . has proved a veritable lamb when placed on a fiery Lord's wicket' (Ranji 1897, p 343).

**ring** *n* (old) the boundary of a cricket field:

> 'There are few better moments at cricket than when one has forced a good-length ball through the fielders on the off-side, standing well balanced where one is, and the ball speeding to the ring' (Warner 1934, p 11).

The term harks back to the period before the 1860s, when boundaries as such did not exist but were simply formed by the 'ring' of spectators at the edge of the playing area. In such circumstances it was obviously important for the fair conduct of the game that the spectators maintained their positions in an orderly way:

> 'As very considerable sums are depending not only upon the game but upon Small, Miller and Minshull's notches, the company are earnestly requested to keep a good ring' (Morning Post 3 August 1776).

**rough** *n* a worn or roughened area on the pitch produced by the repeated impact of the bowlers' feet as they 'follow through' after delivering the ball:

> 'The selectors were disappointed that Emburey had not taken more wickets when bowling into the rough at Lord's (Brearley 1982, p 50).

**roundarm** *adj & adv* using a bowling action in which the arm, extended more or less horizontally, is brought round from behind the bowler in a plane between the level of the elbow and the level of the shoulder. Roundarm bowling, which was pioneered by John Willes at the beginning of the 19th century, 'marked the transition from the old order to the new' (Ranji 1897, p 100). Its legalisation in 1835 – by a law stating that the hand must not go *above* the shoulder – was in reality a rearguard action intended to halt any further development towards a full overarm delivery. But as noted by a contemporary, 'umpires were commissioned to watch with a keen eye the elevation of the arm, but notwithstanding their vigilance it rose and rose' (Box 1868, pp 118–9). Consequently, roundarm bowling had already become fairly uncommon by the time overarm bowling was legalised in 1864. See BOWLING.

**round the wicket** *adv* delivering the ball from the hand that is further away from the bowler's wicket; a right-arm bowler going round the wicket has the wicket on his left and is thus able to slant the ball across a right-handed batsman at a considerable angle:

> '*Marshall usually switches to round the wicket if his first spell has been wicketless, and it makes an awesome sight too*' (Scyld Berry, *Observer* 4 December 1983).

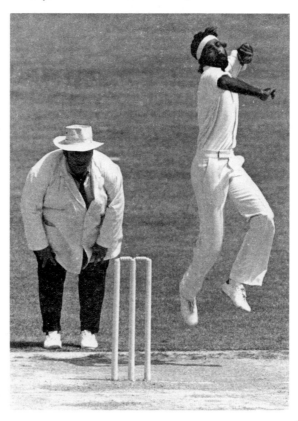

**rubber** *n* a series of Test matches or other games at international level. The word 'rubber' has been used to denote a set of games – for example, in whist, backgammon, or bowls – for almost 400 years, but its use in a cricket context is very much more recent. In its earliest sense it denoted the *deciding* game in a set of three or five, and this may conceivably account for its derivation – meaning the game that eliminated, or 'rubbed out', one of the contestants.

**run** *n* **1** an act of running from one popping crease to the other by both batsmen simultaneously, each batsman reaching the other end of the pitch without his wicket being broken by the fielding side; completion of this act results in a score of one being added to the batting side's total:

> *'Each Umpire is the sole Judge of all Nips and Catches; Inns and Outs; good or bad Runs, at his own Wicket'* (Laws 1744).

> *'Gatting committed himself to the run and was run out by about a foot'* (Matthew Engel, *Guardian* 24 March 1984).

**2** any of the scoring units that are credited to the total score of a team or individual and are gained in any of the following ways: (a) by the completion of a 'run' (see 1); (b) by the ball crossing the boundary while in play; (c) by the awarding of penalties such as those for a no-ball or wide. The runs of a batsman comprise all those made as a result of actual hits, while the runs of a team comprise all those made by any legitimate means.

**3** a bowler's running approach to the bowling crease prior to delivering the ball; run-up:

> *'Willis, off his short run, quickly wrapped up the innings by taking the last four wickets'* (Andrew Longmore, *Cricketer* April 1984).

~ *vb* **4** to cross from one wicket to the other in order to score a run:

> *'There are no set rules as to how to run . . . but there are certain points pretty generally accepted and followed'* (Ranji 1897, p 200).

**5** to obtain a stated number of runs by actually running, rather than by hitting a boundary:

> *'Bailey . . . was hit into the deep by Davidson, at which the*

*batsmen once again ran four, quite a common occurrence on this immensely long ground'* (Peebles 1959, p 55).

**6** to act as a runner to an incapacitated batsman:

*'Tyldesley came in with Rhodes to run for him, his leg still being painful'* (*Melbourne Argus* 17 December 1903).

**7** to deflect the ball off an angled bat so that it goes along the ground into the area backward of square, usually on the off-side:

*'Greenidge, trying to run one wide of slip, was caught by Downton'* (John Thicknesse, *WCM* September 1984).

In order to complete a run the batsmen, after crossing, must each ground 'some part of his bat in his hand or of his person . . . behind the line of the popping crease' (Law 29 § 1). This procedure was already operating when the original (1744) code of Laws was drawn up, but had probably not been established for very long. An earlier method is described in a narrative poem by William Goldwin, written in Latin in 1706 (*'In Certamen Pilae'*). In Goldwin's poem there is an umpire at each wicket 'leaning on his staff', and in order to score a valid run the batsman had to touch this staff with his bat. This arrangement was apparently still in force as late as 1727, for the 'Articles of Agreement' govering two games to be played in that year between the Duke of Richmond and a Mr Brodrick include the provision: 'The Batt Men for every one they count are to touch the Umpire's stick'. However, this method of completing a run was only a transitional stage from the still earlier procedure by which the batsman had to 'pop' his bat into a hole dug between the stumps: see POPPING CREASE. See also EXTRAS, SHORT RUN.

**runner** *n* a player who is allowed to take runs on behalf of an incapacitated batsman. The job of runner is performed by another member of the batting side, usually one who has already batted and got out. The injured striker faces the bowling in the normal way while the runner stands out from the wicket, usually on the off-side, and takes runs when appropriate. When the injured batsman is at the non-striker's end he is considered to be 'out of the game' and the runner takes his place at the bowler's wicket (Law 2 § 5–7).

**running ground** *n* (obsolete) the area between the two popping creases which the batsmen cross in making a run, as distinguished from the batsmen's 'home' ground. An old regulation allowed the batsmen to obstruct a fielder attempting a catch within this area – 'When the Ball is hit up, either of the Strikers may hinder the Catch in his running Ground' – but it seems to have dropped out of the code by the end of the 18th century.

**run out** *adv* **1** a mode of dismissal in which either of the batsmen may be given out if 'in running or at any time when the ball is in play . . . he is out of his ground and his wicket is put down by the opposite side' (Law 38 § 1); the dismissal is not credited to either the bowler or the fielder and is entered in the scorebook as 'run out'. If the batsmen have already crossed, the one running towards the wicket that is put down is out, but if they have not crossed, the batsman who has left the wicket that is put down is out. The dismissal remains valid even in the case of a no-ball. With regard to the run-out Law, there are two borderline areas which occasionally cause confusion. The first is the case of

the striker hitting the ball straight on to the opposite wicket when his partner has already left his ground: in this case, neither batsman is out *unless* the ball has been touched en route by a member of the fielding side. Secondly there is the more contentious problem of the bowler attempting to run out the non-striker when he is backing up too far before the ball is actually bowled. According to a strict interpretation of the Laws the bowler is within his rights to do this: the ball ceases to be 'dead' – and is therefore in play – 'when the Bowler starts his run up or bowling action' (Law 23 § 3), and either batsman can be run out so long as the ball is in play (see above). In practice, however, this is something of a grey area. There is a general reluctance among bowlers to exercise this right (any attempt to do so would be regarded as 'unsporting'), while batsmen for their part are deterred from exploiting the situation by a further regulation to the effect that attempting to steal a run during the bowler's run-up constitutes 'unfair play' (Law 42 § 12). The likeliest scenario, if a bowler felt that the non-striker was deliberately and consistently backing up too far, would be for the bowler to remove the bails as he reached the wicket, as a warning to the non-striker not to exceed his rights.

~ *vb* **2** to cause the dismissal of a batsman in this way:

> 'Wettimuny should have been run out, but a poor throw from Tavaré let him off' (David Frith, WCM October 1984).

**3** to gain runs by actually running, rather than as a result of a boundary hit:

> 'Up to about 100 years ago it was customary for all hits to be run out, and this resulted in some most productive strokes, such as the Hon Fred Ponsonby's hit to leg for nine . . . in 1842' (Gerald Brodribb, WCM December 1983).

**4** to leave one's crease and advance down the wicket when playing a stroke:

> 'I do not think that batsmen run out enough at slow bowling or at lobs' (Ranji 1897, p 172).

**run-out** *n* a dismissal in which a batsman is run out:

> 'Australia recorded their first World Series win yesterday when two crucial run-outs denied Pakistan victory in their one-day match in Sydney' (Guardian 11 January 1984).

**run rate** *n* the average number of runs scored by a team within a given period or number of balls; run rates are usually expressed as runs per over or runs per 100 balls.

**run-saving** *adj* denoting a field setting or fielding position primarily intended to prevent the batsmen from scoring runs; third man and long leg are among the typical 'run-saving' positions found in a defensive field setting:

> 'He obviously considered the time was come to check a situation which might become dangerous, and for a spell Davidson and Mackay bowled defensively to deep-set, run-saving fields' (Peebles 1959, p 135).

**run-up** *n* the bowler's approach to the wicket prior to delivering the ball:

> 'The object of the run-up is to bring the bowler to the bowling crease completely balanced and with the momentum necessary to bowl . . . at his normal, designed pace' (MCC 1952, p 28).

> 'With Willis and Botham operating off shortened run-ups, England managed to capture the last four wickets in eight overs' (David Frith, WCM April 1984).

**SACB** *abbr* South African Cricket Board: the ruling body for non-white cricket in South Africa.

**SACU** *abbr* South African Cricket Union: the official body controlling cricket in South Africa.

**save** *vb* to be in a position to prevent the batsmen from taking the stated number of runs; for example, a player stationed to 'save the two' is intended to deter the batsmen from going for a second run after they have run a single:

> *'Suppose the fieldsman to be standing out to the hip, for the purpose of saving two runs, and the wicketkeeper draw him in by a motion of his hand, to save the one run'* (Nyren 1833 in *HM*, p 29).

**score** *n* **1** the number of runs made by an individual or team in an innings or at a particular point in the innings:

> *'In looking over carefully the list of matches for twenty years, we shall find no scores on the average at all approaching those of the elder Walker and Beldham'* (Mitford 1833 in *HM*, p 129).

> *'The scores were level . . . and if no run came from the last ball Kent were the winners, having the higher score after 30 overs'* (Graeme Wright, *WCM* October 1984).

**2** the record of all the runs made in a match:

> *'The score was kept by notching each individual run on a stick'* (*Encyclopaedia Britannica* 1877, vol VI p 578).

**3** (obsolete) a mark or 'notch' made on a tally as a primitive way of recording the making of a run:

'It is called a run, and one notch or score is made upon the tally towards the game' (J. Strutt, *The Sports and Pastimes of the People of England* 1801, p 84).

~ *vb* **4** (of an individual or team) to gain a run or runs; make the stated score:

'*Botham started fairly quietly, scoring 39 in 87 minutes before tea*' (Brearley 1982, p 68).

'*Both players* [Bradman and Gavaskar] *in fact scored a large proportion of their hundreds against the leading opposition of the day*' (Richard Lockwood, *Cricketer* January 1984).

'*The record is held by India's Chandrasekhar, who four times was out without scoring in both innings of a Test*' (WCM October 1984).

**5** to add a run or runs to the total made by an individual or team; record as part of the score:

'*A penalty of one run for a no ball shall be scored if no runs are made otherwise*' (Law 24 § 8).

**6** to record the score in a match; act as the scorer:

'*The great thing in keeping score, after keeping it correctly, is to score neatly*' (W. G. Grace in *Outdoor Games and Recreations* 1891, p 14).

**7** (obsolete) to cut a mark or 'notch' in a tally as a way of recording the making of a run:

'*They are sole Judges of all Hindrances . . . and in case of Hindrance may order a Notch to be scor'd*' (*Laws* 1744).

The original meaning of the word 'score' is 'to cut an incision', and in the earliest phase of the game the scores were kept by cutting notches on a stick. This was a perfectly practicable system at a time when low scores were the norm and it was fairly unusual for batsmen even to reach double figures. (In the earliest major match for which the full scores are known – the encounter between Kent and All England in 1746 – the highest individual score was 18, and the aggregate total of all four innings was 221.) But the increasing sophistication of the game from the late 18th century onwards led to the development of more complex scoring methods. In contemporary cricket, the scores of the teams and players, as well as other details, are kept by the scorers on a standard SCORESHEET (qv) and the salient features are also displayed on a scoreboard.

This much is standard at almost every level of the game, but in the realm of professional cricket scoring has been elevated to something like a combination of high art and exact science: scoring systems of great complexity and refinement can now provide a comprehensive description of everything that happens on the field of play on a ball-by-ball basis, while the advent of the computer has made it possible for TV viewers to be regaled with detailed statistical analyses of players' achievements while they are still in the process of achieving them.

**scoreboard** *n* a device used for displaying a concurrent record of the score of a game which will be visible to both players and spectators. In the early days of cricket, before the introduction of scoreboards, it was traditional for the scorers to stand up when the scores of the two sides drew level, as an indication to players and spectators that the batting side needed only one run to win; this convention apart, the public were left to their own devices as far as the scores were concerned. Scoreboards – originally known as 'telegraph boards' – began to appear at major grounds in the mid-19th century (Lord's got one in 1846, the Oval in 1848) but the early versions conveyed only a bare minimum of information. The simplest type of scoreboard – still often seen in school and club cricket – consists of a board on which movable metal plates are hung or mounted, showing three rows of figures: the top row gives the score of the team, the middle row the number of wickets down, and the bottom row the score of the last man out. The traditional mechanical scoreboards used at first-class grounds show a good deal more information, including the scores of the batsmen at the crease, the mode of dismissal of the last man out, and the score at which each wicket has fallen. The 'state-of-the-art' electronic scoreboards now seen at some major Test grounds, notably in Australia, not only provide a wealth of statistical detail but can also show instant replays of the action in the middle.

**scorebook** *n* a book containing the scoresheets used in keeping the score of a cricket match.

**scorecard** *n* a printed card, produced and issued for sale at a cricket ground, showing the names of the players on each side listed in their batting order and giving details of the scores, dismissals, and fall of wickets up to the time at which the card was printed. Scorecards of some kind were already in existence before the end of the 18th century, but it was Fred Lillywhite, touring the major grounds with his portable printing press from 1848, who made the continually-updated scorecard one of the institutions of the game.

**scorer** *n* **1** a person appointed to keep a concurrent record of the scores in a match. The Laws do not stipulate the number of scorers needed, but it is normal practice for each side to appoint its own scorer, and 'where there are two Scorers they shall frequently check to ensure that the score sheets agree' (Law 4 § 1).

**2** – **without troubling the scorers** (of a dismissed batsman) having scored no runs. See DUCK.

## Match *Shelford* v *Walford*  Played at *Walford*  Date *29th June* 1985

### 1st INNINGS OF *Shelford*

| ORDER OF GOING IN | BATSMAN'S NAME | SCORE | HOW OUT | BOWLER'S NAME | TOTAL RUNS |
|---|---|---|---|---|---|
| 1 | M. Stevens | 2 1 1 4 1 2 1 / | c Altham | Jones | 12 |
| 2 | T. Jeffries | 1 3 2 4 1 1 2 1 6 4 1 1 4 1 / | lbw | Thomas | 32 |
| 3 | H. Hardinge | 1 / | c & b | Thomas | 1 |
| 4 | D. Browne | 4 1 2 1 1 | | | |
| 5 | C. Hales | 1 3 | | | |
| 6 | S. Burrows | | | | |
| 7 | M. Hendry | | | | |
| 8 | B. O'Kill | | | | |
| 9 | S. Magee | | | | |
| 10 | A. Smith | | | | |
| 11 | R. McKee | | | | |

BYES *111*  LEG BYES *1*  WIDE BALLS *1*  NO BALLS *111*

| RUNS AT THE FALL OF EACH WICKET | 1 FOR 24 | 2 FOR 35 | 3 FOR 50 | 4 FOR | 5 FOR | 6 FOR | 7 FOR | 8 FOR | 9 FOR | 10 FOR | TOTAL |
|---|---|---|---|---|---|---|---|---|---|---|---|

## Bowling Analysis

| BOWLER'S NAME | WIDES | NO BALLS | NUMBER OF OVERS AND RUNS MADE FROM EACH BOWLER 1 2 3 4 5 6 7 8 9 10 11 12 13 14 15 16 17 18 19 20 | TOTALS OVERS MAIDENS RUNS WIDES NO BALLS WICKETS |
|---|---|---|---|---|
| A. Wilson | / | / | | |
| G. Jones | | // | | |
| M. Thomas | | | | |

w  wicket
+  wide ball
⊚  no ball

M  maiden
Ŵ  wicket maiden

**scoresheet** *n* a printed form, typically occupying a double page spread in a scorebook, on which details relating to the score of a match are entered by the scorer as each ball is bowled so as to form a complete tabulated record. The traditional scoresheet is in two parts, the first giving details of the batting side's innings (including the runs scored by each player, the way in which each player was dismissed, and the side's total at the fall of each wicket), and the second providing a detailed analysis of the bowling during that innings, with a record of every ball bowled and final bowling figures for each bowler.

**scout** (obsolete) *n* **1** a fielder:

'It fell upon the tip of the bat and bounded far away over the heads of the scouts' (Dickens, *Pickwick Papers* 1837, ch 7).

Like 'fag', scout can also denote a boy whose job is to retrieve balls during net practice.

~ *vb* **2** to field, or act as a scout retrieving balls:

'The small boys of the neighbourhood gather to field (or scout, as they call it) for the members at the nets' (*Daily Chronicle* 14 August 1908).

**scratch** *n* (obsolete) a crease, especially the popping crease:

'Your skill all depends upon distance and sight
Stand firm to your scratch, let your bat be upright'
(Rev R. Cotton, 'Hambledon Song' 1778 in *HM*, p 52).

This term was formerly used in a variety of sporting contexts to denote a line or starting point at which a participant stood; for example, a line drawn across a prize-fighting ring at which the contestants stood at the beginning of a bout.

**screw** *n* (obsolete) rotary motion, or 'break', imparted to the ball by the bowler, causing it to change direction on pitching; the term is borrowed from the vocabulary of billiards:

'The next ball, very swift, with lots of screw on, is snicked into the slips' (W. G. Grace in *Outdoor Games and Recreations* 1891, p 13).

**seam** *n* **1** the ridge formed by the rows of stitching that join the two halves of the leather outer case of a cricket ball:

'Neil Foster . . . created a favourable impression with his straightforward approach, pace, and ability to move the ball awkwardly off the seam' (John Arlott, *WCM* December 1983).

**2** (also **seam bowling**) a style of bowling, typically practised by bowlers of fast or medium pace, characterised by deviation of the ball off the wicket as its seam makes contact with the ground:

'The first hour, though, had been a different story, when the pitch was helpful to swing and seam' (*WCM* February 1984).

'Alan had scored 100 runs in the low-scoring match, and played our strong seam attack with skill' (Brearley 1982, p 110).

~ *vb* **3** to cause the ball to deviate after pitching by using its seam to produce movement, rather than by means of spin:

*'Selvey played three times for England but has sustained a reputation as an economical new-ball bowler with ability to swing and seam the ball either way'* (Alan Lee, *Cricketer* December 1982).

**4** (of the ball) to deviate after pitching on the seam:

*'Barlow's dogged 38 . . . did most to save them as the ball swung and seamed through a muggy morning'* (Patrick Barclay, *Guardian* 1 June 1983).

**5** (of the wicket) to be conducive to movement off the seam:

*'An exciting morning's cricket is promised on Headingley's seaming wicket where West Indies . . . will be striving to keep a fingerhold on the Prudential World Cup'* (Derek Hodgson, *Observer* 12 June 1983).

The use of the term seam to describe one of the major 'schools' of bowling is a fairly recent development in the language of cricket. In its narrowest sense it indicates the movement off the pitch that results when a ball of medium or fast-medium pace hits the ground with its seam at a slight angle to the surface. More generally, the term is often used to denote a type of bowling that is neither slow nor very fast and combines movement off the pitch with movement in the air, or 'swing'. It is a style especially well adapted to conditions often found in England – a damp, overcast atmosphere and a well-grassed or 'green' wicket. In recent years the economical, stroke-inhibiting seam bowler has tended to be preferred to the spinner for the role of 'stock bowler' and, as John Arlott laments, 'there is now a vast army in English cricket of practitioners of "military medium"; bowling briskly, seam up, achieving a little movement but, above all, striving for sufficient precision to avoid punishment' (Arlott 1983, p 41). The relative decline in slow bowling is at least partly attributable to the increasingly prominent role taken by 'seam', and this development has in turn been accelerated by the tactical demands of one-day cricket.

**seamer** *n* **1** an exponent of seam bowling; in practice 'seamer' has a wide application, and is used as a coverall term to distinguish the faster bowlers of a side's attack from its slow bowlers or 'spinners':

*'There were times not only on Monday but even on Saturday when Hughes would have been delighted to have a fourth seamer rather than his spinner'* (Brearley 1982, p 60).

**2** a ball bowled by a seam bowler:

*'On English wickets you can usually get away with bowling little seamers to a defensive field'* (Bob Willis, *Observer* 3 June 1984).

**seam-up** *n* a style of seam bowling in which the ball is held with the seam more or less straight (rather than at an angle to the line of the fingers) and bowled at medium pace so that it may swing either way in the air (though not dramatically) and deviate in either direction as the seam grips the pitch:

*'In an age of long-drawn-out overs of fast bowling . . . or the seemingly endless procession of fast-medium "seam-up", cricket needs the kind of spectator-stimulus that wrist-spin affords'* (John Arlott, *WCM* May 1984).

**seamy** *adj* (of a wicket) helpful to seam bowling; conducive to movement off the seam:

*'The wicket was green and seamy'* (Matthew Engel, *Guardian* 31 May 1983).

**seeker out** *n* (obsolete) a fielder:

*'Four times from Hodswell's arm it skims the grass. Then Mills succeeds. The seekers out change place'* (James Love, *Cricket: an Heroic Poem*, 1746).

**seek out** *vb* (obsolete) to field; be a fielder:

*'The man who is in, must strike the ball before these limits, or boundary lines; and it must be returned in the same direction by those who are seeking out'* (Nyren 1833 in *HM*, p 38).

Many of the older terms used for fielding, such as 'seek out', 'look out', and 'scout', would have originated at a time when the game was played without boundaries on rough, often undulating terrain, and the ball would often have to be literally 'sought out'.

**semicircles** *n* an arrangement of lines bounding an area within which, according to the rules governing certain limited-overs competitions, at least four fielders (not including the bowler and wicket-keeper) must be stationed at the moment that the ball is delivered; the rule is intended to prevent captains from setting wholly defensive fields with every available man out in the deep, and in the event of an infringement the square-leg umpire calls 'no-ball':

> *'An oversight by Bob Willis cost a no-ball when he posted only three men, one short of the legal minimum, within the white semi-circles'* (Scyld Berry, *Observer* 19 June 1983).

The area in question is formed by two semicircles, one centred on the striker's wicket, the other centred on the bowler's wicket, and each having a radius of 30 yards. They are joined by a pair of parallel lines which go down each side of the pitch, and the entire configuration is marked not by lines but by white dots painted on the pitch at five-yard intervals.

**send back** *vb* (of a bowler) to dismiss a batsman, and thus send him back to the pavilion:

> *'In the space of seven balls, he sent back Tavaré, Gower and Randall without conceding a run'* (Andrew Longmore, *Cricketer* April 1984).

**send down** *vb* (of a bowler) to deliver a ball or balls:

> *'A good deal of short stuff was sent down but the two batsmen coped admirably'* (Henry Blofeld, *Cricketer* February 1983).

**session** *n* any of the three periods of play that make up a full day's cricket at first-class level, separated by the intervals for lunch and tea:

> *'In the pre-lunch session 157 runs were added for the loss of Harper'* (David Frith, *WCM* August 1984).

**set** *adj* **1** having played oneself in so as to be confidently established at the crease and able to play the bowling without difficulty:

> *'Here was a state of things to which Australian enthusiasts had long looked forward . . . Hill and Trumper in on a perfect wicket, both well set, and the bowlers tiring'* (*Melbourne Argus* 16 January 1904).

'He is . . . able to play all the shots except the hook and not averse to the odd straight six when really set' (Matthew Engel, *Guardian* 9 July 1984).

~ *n* **2** (old) the target that must be reached by the side batting last in order to win the match:

'The grand total of 288 left Oxford with a "set" of 331' (Ranji 1897, p 362).

**shape** *vb* to get oneself in position to play a particular stroke, but without necessarily executing the shot successfully:

'A brutal ball from Miller reared shoulder-high, Denis shaped to hook it, but slipped on the wet grass, and fell on the stumps' (Cardus 1978, p 105).

'I have seen a bunch of short-legs cower when a batsman shaped at a loose one, but kept my eye on Tony Lock and saw him bend at the waist a little and face it' (James 1963, p 91).

**sharp** *adj* **1** (of a ball coming off the striker's bat) potentially catchable, but only with considerable difficulty; a 'sharp chance' is one that is difficult to hold:

'Mohsin . . . had failed to get his hand round both a sharp one and a sitter at slip to Qadir' (Robin Marlar, *Sunday Times* 25 March 1984).

~ *adj & adv* **2** (obsolete) relatively close to the line separating leg and off behind the striker's wicket; fine:

'The old-fashioned long-leg hitting of George Parr is almost a thing of the past; so that long-leg should stand too square, rather than too sharp' (*Badminton* 1888, p 258).

**shine** *n* the smoothness and polish characteristic of a new ball, which is gradually impaired as the ball is struck by the batsmen:

'May joined Graveney, and both batsmen exercised due caution until the shine was lessened' (Peebles 1959, p 56).

A high degree of shine keeps friction to a minimum and is generally felt to assist the faster bowlers, as well as being conducive to movement in the air; on the other hand, as the ball loses its shine and the surface becomes rougher, it is more likely to respond to break imparted by the slower bowlers.

**shirtfront** *n* (also **shirtfront wicket**) a good, true batting wicket with an even bounce, offering little assistance to either seam or spin bowling. It is hard and flat, like the starched, well-ironed front of an old-fashioned dress shirt:

> '*As those who knew it best had prophesied, the "googly" possessed few terrors on the "shirt-front" wickets of Adelaide and Sydney*' (H. S. Altham, *History of Cricket* 1926, p 348).

> '*On another "shirtfront" in Hyderabad, he made an unbeaten fifty-five in three and a half hours*' (Berry 1982, p 97).

**shock bowler** *n* a fast bowler used very sparingly in a purely attacking role:

> '*I recalled Willis's early Test experiences under Illingworth, when he was used solely as a shock bowler*' (Brearley 1982, p 67).

**shoot** *vb* (of the ball) to keep low and come rapidly on to the bat after pitching, usually because of some irregularity in the wicket:

> '*When you see the ball shoot, play the bat back as near to the wicket as possible, taking care not to knock it down*' (Nyren 1833 in *HM*, p 23).

> '*There were signs later in the day that there could be more of the low shooting deliveries that have made the MCG a batsman's nightmare in recent years*' (Ian Brayshaw, *The Times* 27 December 1983).

**shooter** *n* a ball that fails to rise normally after pitching and comes rapidly on to the bat; shooters were a regular feature of the game until playing surfaces began to improve in the second half of the 19th century:

> '*Not a great many years ago Lord's used to be celebrated for shooters, owing to its rough condition*' (Badminton 1888, p 184).

**shoot out** *vb* to dismiss a batsman or team quickly and for a low score:

> '*His career as an opener was brought to a rough ending when his old adversary Lindwall shot him out for a pair at Melbourne*' (Peebles 1959, p 205).

> '*English cricket took a long time to recover from this pair's*

*demolition of a strong MCC side at Lord's in 1878, when the
premier club were shot out for 33 and 19'* (Frith 1984, p 33).

**short**  *adj & adv* **1** indicating a position relatively close to the
batsman's wicket; the term is often used in combina-
tion to indicate a modified fielding position that
would normally be somewhat further from the striker,
such as third man, mid-wicket, or extra cover:

> *'Wessels and Dyson took their opening stand to 39 before
> Wessels pulled one from Willis to Botham at a short and rather
> wide mid-on'* (Henry Blofeld, *Cricketer* February 1983).

Compare DEEP and see FIELDING POSITIONS.

**2** pitching at a point on the wicket somewhat closer to
the bowler than a ball of good length but further down
the wicket than a long hop (see LENGTH):

> *'Holding produced a vicious rising short ball to have Gavaskar
> caught at slip when 10 runs more would have given the batsman
> a unique 30th Test century'* (WCM January 1984).

> *'There is also the question of whether the wearing of a helmet,
> especially by the lower order batsmen, gives fast bowlers a
> licence to bowl short even at batsmen incompetent to deal with
> the bouncer'* (Christopher Martin-Jenkins, *Cricketer*
> September 1983).

**3** – **short of a length** closer to the bowler than a good
length:

> *'The Pakistan first innings was finished off by Rackemann, who
> took 5 for 32 in eight overs and bowled extremely well, making
> the ball lift from only just short of a length'* (Henry Blofeld,
> *Cricketer* January 1984).

**short leg**  *n* a close leg-side fielding position (or the player
occupying it) anywhere in an arc between leg-slip and
silly mid-on: see FIELDING POSITIONS. As the MCC
coaching book observes, 'it is impossible to lay down
any fixed rule as to the "normal" position of short-leg'
(MCC 1952, p 24), since, like slip, it is not a single
position but a general area that may be occupied by a
ring of fielders. While a forward short leg is used in a
variety of attacks, the use of a ring of short legs 'can
only be justified for a bowler who, whether by swing
or spin, is bringing the ball into the batsman' (MCC
1952, p 24) – for example, an off-break bowler on a

turning wicket. Harold Larwood's fast leg-theory attack was based on a packed leg-side field that included up to four short legs and a silly mid-on, but the more extreme form of 'bodyline' field is now ruled out by modern legislation to the effect that 'the number of on-side fieldsmen behind the popping crease at the instant of the Bowler's delivery shall not exceed two' (Law 41 § 2).

**short-pitched** *adj* (of a ball) pitching before it reaches a full length; SHORT 2:

> 'The bowling of short-pitched balls is unfair if . . . it constitutes
> an attempt to intimidate the Striker' (Law 42 § 8).

The connection between short-pitched bowling and the deliberate intimidation of batsmen is a relatively modern one. In the 19th century it was believed that 'a short ball is the worst ball a man delivers' because 'a batsman can hit it almost where he chooses' (Clarke 1851 in *HM*, p 159). Clarke's view is typical of his generation, and indeed of much later writers too. The inference seems to be that wickets in the 19th and early 20th century were not as lively as they later became, and their relatively lower bounce would tend to turn a short-pitched ball into an innocuous long hop rather than a vicious bouncer. At the height of the Bodyline crisis an article by J. W. Trumble discussed the allegation that 'old-time fast bowlers' had not resorted to the ploy of bowling short, and made the telling point that 'on the old-time turf wickets . . . as it did not rise, short-pitched bowling was in those days looked upon as rubbish, and generally had heavy punishment' (*Melbourne Argus* 23 January 1933). Trumble's point seems to be corroborated by the gradual shift in meaning of the terms 'bumper' and 'bouncer': these were originally used to describe a ball that rose steeply off the pitch because of some irregularity in the surface, and only later came to be exclusively applied to the fast short-pitched ball used to unnerve the batsman.

**short run** *n* **1** (also formerly **short notch**) a run which either or both of the batsmen fail to complete properly (by grounding the bat or part of the body over the popping crease) before turning to take another run. In the case of a short run the umpire, once the ball is dead, calls 'one short' and signals to the scorer by bending one arm upwards and touching the shoulder. The incomplete run is not credited to the score, but the batsmen do not – as might be expected – cross back to the opposite wickets. The regulations governing short runs were introduced in 1774 and have remained essentially unchanged. There was a proposal in 1835 that two runs be deducted rather than one, on the grounds that the batsman 'not having run home in the first instance, cannot have started in the second from the proper goal'. This suggestion was not, however, incorporated in the revision of that year, and the modern code specifically states that 'although a short run shortens the succeeding one, the latter, if completed, shall count' (Law 18 § 2).

**2** a quickly-taken run off a ball that only travels a short distance from the wicket:

> 'A safe field is generally a slow one . . . and, as batsmen get to know this, the short run is attempted with impunity' (Badminton 1888, p 248).

**short-slip** *n* (obsolete) an off-side fielding position (or the player occupying it) equivalent to what would now be called slip:

> 'On no occasion should short-slip be dispensed with . . . The object of short-slip is to pick up snicks which just miss the wicket-keeper' (Badminton 1888, p 179).

Compare LONG SLIP.

**shoulder** *n* **1** the slightly concave upper edge of the blade of the bat, close to where it joins the handle:

> 'When Watkinson had Boon caught at gully off the shoulder of the bat . . . Leicestershire had slumped to 73 for six' (David Green, Daily Telegraph 15 August 1984).

~ *vb* **2** – **shoulder arms** (also **shoulder up**) to raise the bat high above the shoulders so as to avoid playing a shot:

> 'The first ball brought another two to the on, but as the second pitched the batsman covered up and shouldered arms' (Peebles 1959, p 158).

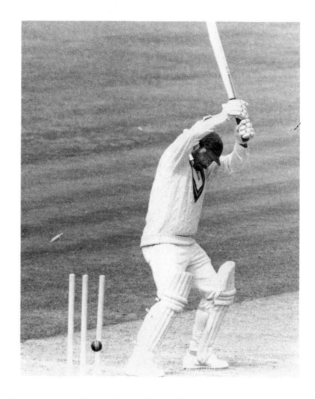

**shout** *n* an appeal made against a batsman:

> 'Botham had one convincing shout against Richards and then
> beat him with a ball of exquisite beauty' (Robin Marlar, 1 July
> 1984).

**shuffle across** *vb* to move across towards the off-side but without
committing oneself to a shot, thereby making oneself
vulnerable to an lbw dismissal:

> 'Howarth was bowled by a plain delivery, the shock
> compounded when Crowe was fourth out at 47, shuffling
> casually across' (Christopher Wordsworth, *Observer*
> 19 June 1983).

**shutters** *n* – **put up the shutters** to adopt a purely defensive
style of batting, especially after a period of batting
more freely:

> 'One can fault Gower for not having switched to the attack then
> . . . for only diffidently did he bring his fielders in once Sarfraz
> put up the shutters' (Scyld Berry, *WCM* May 1984).

**sight** *n* a sense of confidence in one's ability to judge accurately the flight, pace, and length of the ball, developed by a batsman as his innings progresses:

> 'Once he has had a sight of the ball and judged the pace and bounce of the ball off the pitch, he should start thinking about scoring opportunities' (Alf Gover, *Cricketer* March 1983).

**sightboard**  *n* (Australia) a sightscreen:

> 'The cheering and waving of hats was inspiring when Trumper stepped out and lifted a ball from Rhodes straight over the sight-board for five' (*Melbourne Argus* 5 January 1904).

**sighter**  *n* a ball bowled early in a bowler's spell or early in a batsman's innings, that does not force the batsman to play a stroke but gives him the opportunity to become accustomed to the bowling without any risk to his wicket:

> 'Subba Row was bowled off his pad before he had got a sighter, and MCC were once again off to a bad start' (Peebles 1959, p 56).

**sightscreen**  *n* a large white movable structure, usually wooden but occasionally made of other materials (such as canvas), which is placed close to and outside the boundary directly behind either of the wickets in order to assist the batsman by enhancing the visibility of the bowled ball.

**silly**  *adj & adv* (of a fielder or fielding position) extremely close to the batsman; very short:

> 'Gatting took two catches at short-extra and forward short-leg, positioned some yards farther from the bat than the "silly" helmeted situations now in favour' (Robin Marlar, *Sunday Times* 28 August 1983).

The term is normally used in combination to indicate a modified fielding position in front of the wicket that would otherwise be considerably further from the striker, specifically point, mid-off, and mid-on: see FIELDING POSITIONS. The word simply alludes to the 'silliness' of exposing oneself to such danger, though the *OED* does record a now obsolete – but rather appropriate – use of silly to mean 'defenceless'. 'Silly' fielding positions were popularised, if not actually invented, by the Australian team that toured England

in 1878, and had been made possible by the recent improvements in playing surfaces (see WICKET[2]). According to H. S. Altham (*History of Cricket* 1926, p 148) 'it was a revelation when on the sticky wickets of 1878 Boyle proceeded to take up his position at silly mid-on, often no more than 6 or 7 yards from the bat'. The silly fieldsman's dual role – of taking close catches and unsettling the batsman – seems to have been appreciated from an early stage:

> '*Sometimes mid-off . . . is required to go "silly mid-off" with a view to catching a pokey batsman or putting him off his stroke*' (Ranji 1897, p 54).

Since the advent of the helmet, it has become fashionable to station heavily armoured fielders in very silly positions, and the fairness of this practice is currently a matter of debate.

**single**  *n* one run added to the score, obtained by the batsmen actually running:

> '*He hurled the ball wide from short cover when the last pair of Englishmen dashed for the single which brought a one-wicket victory at Melbourne*' (Frith 1984, p 83).

> *'Gomes on Tuesday was the perfect foil once again, taking the singles England somewhat carelessly offered, in the knowledge that Greenidge would continue to crash the ball for four'* (Robin Marlar, *Sunday Times* 8 July 1984).

**single wicket** *n* a variety of cricket in which there is only one set of stumps, with a single stump at the other end of the pitch from which the ball is always bowled. Only one batsman is in at any given time and in order to score a single run he has to run up to the bowler's stump then back to his own ground. The game can be played between teams ranging in size from one to six players, but if there are fewer than five men on each side the whole area behind the batsman's wicket does not 'count' and the ball immediately becomes dead if struck or bowled behind the stumps.

The single wicket version of the game seems to have existed since the earliest days of cricket, and in the 18th and early 19th century 'single-wicket matches . . . were played nearly as often as double-wicket games' (*Badminton* 1888, p 383). These contests included not only games between the foremost sides of the day (such as those between 'five of Hambledon' and 'five of All England' in 1773 and 1781) but also one-to-one encounters between great all-round players like Alfred Mynn and Tom Marsden. By 1850, however, single wicket was 'practically dead' (*Badminton* 1888, p 387), and despite various attempts to revive the single-wicket game in some form or other (notably in the contests sometimes staged between leading international all-rounders) it is unlikely ever to be more than an occasional entertainment at the margins of the game.

**sitter** *n* an easy catching chance offered to a fielder:

> *'He had not been at his best, but would I think have been retained if he had not dropped a "sitter" from Border when he had scored only 10'* (Brearley 1982, p 20).

**six** *n* a shot by the batsman that sends the ball over the boundary without bouncing, resulting in an addition of six runs to the batsman's score. A ball caught by a fielder and then carried over the boundary also counts as a six and in this case of course, the striker is not out. Presumably a ball going straight over the boundary from an overthrow or as a bye would also be a six, though such cases are – it is to be hoped – purely hypothetical. A ball that hits a sightscreen full pitch when the sightscreen is on or inside the boundary only counts as four, not six. The umpire signals a six to the scorers by raising both arms above his head. The allowance of six runs dates only from 1910, before which the ball had to be hit right out of the ground to score six. See BOUNDARY.

**sixer** *n* (old) a six:

> *'Hammond rounded off this noisy series with a smashing sixer off O'Reilly'* (Larwood 1933, p 161).

**skid** *vb* (of a fast ball) to come quickly on to the bat or wicket with a lower than expected bounce and an (apparent) increase in pace off the pitch:

> *'Statham was soon recalled, and for the moment checked the dashing young man, who had a narrow escape when what was intended to be a bouncer skidded'* (Peebles 1959, p 87).

> *'A couple of overs later he made a mess of Phillips's wicket, the ball skidding through'* (Dilip Rao, *Guardian* 12 April 1984).

**skimmer** *n* a ball struck by the batsman that follows a low flat trajectory:

> *'In the 53rd over, John Carr, fielding as substitute, caught a skimmer at deep mid-on to send back Turner'* (Robin Marlar, *Sunday Times* 24 July 1983).

**skittle** *vb* to dismiss a batting side cheaply and quickly:

> *'Previously, if you could dismiss Amiss early, you might hope to skittle Warwickshire'* (Peter Roebuck, *Cricketer* November 1982).

**sky** *vb* to hit the ball very high into the air; 'loft' the ball:

> *'Two runs later Hookes was out when he tried to pull Cowans and skied the ball towards mid-wicket where Willis . . . judged the catch beautifully'* (Henry Blofeld, *Chricketer* February 1983).

**skyer** *n* a ball hit high into the air:

> *'After almost four hours of familiar devastation, one of New Zealand's fielders finally accepted a chance from Botham – a*

*monstrous skyer that nobody felt like going for but was finally
taken at cover'* (Scyld Berry, *Observer* 22 January 1984).

**sky-rocket**  *vb* (obsolete) to sky the ball:

> *'At times it's enough to make you bite your thumbs to see your
> best balls pulled and sky-rocketed about'* (Clarke 1851 in *HM*,
> p 162).

**slant**  *vb* to deliver the ball so that it comes into the striker
(from off to leg) or moves across him (from leg to off) at
a fairly sharp angle to the line of the wickets; the effect
is achieved by movement in the air or off the pitch,
especially when combined with a fairly 'wide' bowling position which maximises the angle of the ball's
line of flight relative to the line of the wickets:

> *'Often in the past fast bowlers have switched their line of attack
> from over to round the wicket, in order to slant the ball across a
> right-hand batsman and get him edging into the slips'* (Scyld
> Berry, *Observer* 4 December 1983).

**sledge**  *vb* to attempt to unsettle a batsman by means of
'sledging':

> *'Last season Edmonds was ticked off by the umpire . . . for
> allegedly "sledging" the Indian batsman Dilip Vengsarkar at
> Lord's and generally overdoing the overt aggression at forward
> short-leg'* (Christopher Martin-Jenkins, *Cricketer*
> December 1982).

**sledging**  *n* a form of gamesmanship in which a close fielder
attempts to unsettle the batsman at the crease, as by
chatting to him or 'needling' him:

> *'Throughout this period many English players . . . were
> disturbed by the highly developed Australian "sledging",
> usually aimed at them when they were trying to concentrate on
> an innings'* (John Arlott, *WCM* January 1985).

The term seems to have originated in Australia, and
perhaps alludes to the idea of 'breaking down' the
batsman's concentration, as if with a sledgehammer.
The practice of 'sledging' is covered by a section in the
unfair play law, to the effect that the umpire 'shall call
and signal "dead ball" if, in his opinion, any Player of
the fielding side incommodes the Striker by any noise
or action while he is receiving a ball' (Law 42 § 6). An

almost identical clause appears in the original (1744) code of Laws, suggesting that this form of gamesmanship had already been perfected over 200 years ago. Nyren also warns the wicket-keeper against annoying the batsman 'either by noise, uncalled-for remarks, or unnecessary action' (Nyren 1833 in *HM*, p 12), and sixty-odd years later Ranji observes:

> '*I heard the other day of another way of getting out – viz. being talked out . . . Batsmen are quite within their rights in requesting conversational fieldsmen to hold their tongues*' (Ranji 1897, p 206).

All of which goes to show that although 'sledging' is a new word it is certainly not a new phenomenon.

**slice** *n* **1** a batting stroke in which the bat is swung across the line of flight of the ball with the face at a sharp angle, often resulting in a dangerously high trajectory as the ball flies off the bat, usually into the area between point and slip; the stroke may be played deliberately, as a rather risky form of cut, but it is just as likely to be the result of a more orthodox shot that has been mistimed. The term is borrowed from the vocabulary of golf, where it has a much longer history.

~ *vb* **2** to strike the ball with a slice:

> '*He had only one rampant phase, when swinging Snedden over square leg for six, slicing Martin Crowe high over the slips, and pulling both for four more*' (Scyld Berry, *Observer* 22 January 1984).

> '*But Botham was unable to capitalise, caught in the gully off a searing sliced drive*' (Christopher Martin-Jenkins, *Cricketer* September 1984).

**3** (or the ball) to fly uppishly off the angled face of the bat:

> '*He is not the type of cricketer who guffaws when his cover drive slices over third slip for four*' (Vic Marks on Chris Tavaré, *Cricketer* December 1982).

**slip** *n* **1** an off-side fielding position behind the batsman's wicket, between the wicket-keeper and gully; slip is a close catching position, but like the position of wicket-keeper its 'depth' increases in direct proportion to the pace of the bowling:

'In backing up, he should take care to give the man at the slip sufficient room' (Lambert 1816, p 41).

'Greenidge, trying to run one wide of slip, was caught by Downton' (John Thicknesse, *WCM* September 1984).

**2** a fielder occupying this position, or any of several fielders occupying positions in an arc between the wicket-keeper and gully and called collectively **the slips**; when there is more than one slip they are called **first slip**, **second slip**, and so on, first slip being the one closest to the wicket-keeper:

'The best slips I have ever seen are Chapman, Lohmann, Hammond, and Constantine' (Warner 1934, p 82).

'I remember facing him [Lillee] in the Centenary Test at Melbourne . . . bowling with six slips, a square cover, short leg, and deep fine-leg' (Brearley 1982, p 65).

See FIELDING POSITIONS.

~ *vb* **3** (obsolete) to 'run' the ball towards slip off the angled face of a straight bat:

'Strokes behind the wicket were the chief features of his game; his cutting and slipping, leg-hitting and leg-gliding being safe and brilliant always' (Headlam 1903, p 219).

The origins of this term are hinted at in Nyren's description of the long stop, who 'is required to cover many slips from the bat' (Nyren 1833 in *HM*, p 34).

The slip's job is to catch balls that glance off the bat, and most balls that do so are the result of a batting error, or 'slip'. Early writers identify two slip positions, a 'short-slip' (equivalent to the modern first or second slip) and a 'long-slip' (equivalent to a shortish third man or fly-slip), but in certain conditions – 'in particular when the ground is hard' – a 'Second Short-Slip' may also be needed (Boxall 1800, p 54). By the turn of the present century an attacking field would usually have two slips (in the modern sense), which were called 'first-slip' and 'cover-slip' or 'extra-slip'; and 'sometimes for very fast bowling a third slip is added' (Ranji 1897, p 42). The growing importance of the slips, especially to fast bowlers, reflects the development of the modern 'off-theory' attack in the late 19th century (see OFF-THEORY). Nowadays, three slips are the norm for a fast bowler's attacking field, four would not be unusual, and in exceptional circumstances even more may be used.

**slog** *n* **1** a powerful, usually cross-batted stroke in which the bat is swung forcefully and often blindly at the ball, regardless of its length or direction.

~ *vb* **2** to hit the ball powerfully and often indiscriminately, especially with a horizontal bat:

> 'Clift slogged vigorously for a while, once striking Watkinson for six over cover, but finally skied one to third man' (David Green, *Daily Telegraph* 15 August 1984).

**slow** *adj & adv* **1** denoting a bowler, a ball, or a style of bowling characterised by a complete absence of pace; 'slow' is one of the three basic types according to which bowlers are conventionally categorised (the other two being fast and medium-pace) and bowlers of this type rely on flight, turn, accuracy, and deception, rather than on speed through the air:

> 'The gradation of a day's cricket, begun with new-ball thrills as athletic fast bowlers operate and continued as the slow men take over, knows no parallel in terms of entertainment value' (Frith 1984, p 12).

~ *adj* **2** (of the wicket) providing conditions that are unhelpful to the faster bowlers, in that the ball is likely to lose pace and life after pitching; a 'slow' pitch will often also assist the spin bowlers:

'The pitch was the slowest of the four so far, and being bare of grass and brittle, held something for the spinners on each day' (John Thicknesse, *WCM* September 1984).

~ *n* **3** a slow ball or slow bowler:

'There is a golden rule to be carefully remembered in playing slows, and that is, never to run out to a ball that is well outside the off stump' (*Badminton* 1888, p 80).

**slow left-arm** *adj & adv* practising or denoting a style of slow bowling characteristic of some left-arm bowlers, in which break is imparted to the ball by means of finger-spin, causing it to turn from leg towards off when bowled to a right-handed batsman:

'Although he [M. J. K. Smith] could stroke the ball through the covers as handsomely as anyone, he considered that to be uneconomic against the normal packed off-side field-setting for slow left-arm spin' (Arlott 1983, p 15).

'Hadlee sent down one delivery slow left-arm to Chris Smith on the fourth day' (*WCM* April 1984).

Slow left-arm bowling is the left-armer's equivalent of the off-spin bowling of an 'orthodox' right-arm spinner, in that it depends on the use of finger-spin rather than wrist-spin, and the slow left-armer's stock ball is in effect a leg-break. A wrist-spin bowler who happens to be left-handed is more likely to be called a 'left-arm wrist-spinner' than a 'slow left-armer'.

**slow left-armer** *n* an exponent of slow left-arm bowling:

'Another slow left-armer who must have rued often the existence of Rhodes and Blythe was George Dennett of Gloucestershire' (Frith 1984, p 73).

**smother** *vb* to bring the bat well forward so as to meet the ball as soon as possible after it pitches, thus precluding the possibility of the ball rising steeply or turning sharply:

'The deviation of the ball from its original line of flight makes forward-strokes rather unsafe unless the ball is completely smothered at the pitch' (Ranji 1897, p 204).

**sneak** *n* (obsolete) an underhand ball that pitches very short and travels mostly along the ground:

*'It is as certain as anything can be at cricket that a good forward
straight bat cannot miss a "sneak"' (Badminton* 1888, p 185).

**snick** *n* **1** a very slight hit in which the ball only just makes
contact with the edge of the bat instead of meeting the
full face; a 'thin' edge:

> *'A snick to long-leg may bring more runs than a hard hit
> straight' (Badminton* 1888, p 307).

~ *vb* **2** to hit the ball lightly with the very edge of the bat;
'edge' the ball:

> *'Border and the luckless Kim Hughes put together a fourth
> wicket stand of 62 but Marshall forced the captain to snick a slip
> catch and the West Indies wrapped up the Australian tail'* (Tony
> Cozier, *Cricketer* June 1984).

**spectacles** *n* (obsolete) a batsman's score of nought in each
innings of a match; a pair:

> *'Unlucky enough to make spectacles for his side against
> Middlesex' (Whitaker's Almanac* 1893, p 613).

See PAIR.

**spell** *n* a period of bowling by a particular bowler, consisting of a number of overs bowled 'consecutively' from
one end of the pitch, allowing of course for another
bowler operating from the other end in alternate
overs:

> *'Hogan, spinning the ball, kept the pressure on the batsmen in a
> spell of 25 consecutive overs, ending with four for 56'* (Tony
> Cozier, *Cricketer* May 1984).

**spill** *vb* to fail to take a possible catch:

> *'Richards was missed knee-high by Allott at mid-on off Cook,
> Gower having spilt Gomes at slip off Pringle'* (David Frith,
> WCM September 1984).

**spin** *n* **1** a rotary motion imparted to the ball as it is
delivered by the bowler, causing it to change pace or
deviate from its original line of flight after pitching:

> *'The wickets were coconut matting on hard clay . . . but they
> took all the spin you put on the ball and there was always some
> lift'* (James 1963, p 60).

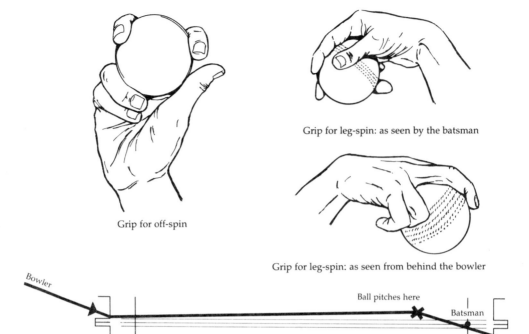

Grip for leg-spin: as seen by the batsman

Grip for off-spin

Grip for leg-spin: as seen from behind the bowler

Ball pitches here

Batsman

**THE OFF-BREAK**

Ball pitches here

Batsman

**THE LEG-BREAK**

**2** the practice or technique of imparting spin to the ball when bowling; spin bowling:

*'It is often possible nowadays to watch much of a day's cricket – certainly in over-limit games – without seeing much worthwhile spin'* (Arlott 1983, p 41).

~ *vb* **3** to impart spin to the ball when bowling:

*'Allan, a left-hander, spun the ball a lot and made it curl in the air before hopping towards first slip'* (Frith 1984, p 32).

**4** (of the ball) to change direction after pitching as a result of spin:

*'In the Test against India in 1979 Phil Edmonds made several balls spin sharply on the Saturday evening, but on Monday the ball went straight on'* (Brearley 1982, p 80).

Spin is applied by the movement of the bowler's fingers or wrist at the moment of delivery (see FINGER-SPIN, WRIST-SPIN) and, to a large extent, depends for its effect on the responsiveness of the playing surface; on 'crumbling' or 'sticky' wickets, for example, the spin imparted to the ball is converted to lateral deviation to a very high degree. Although bowlers of any pace can put spin on the ball, the term is normally only used to describe the technique of the slower bowlers; faster bowlers are said to 'cut' the ball rather than spin it (see CUT 4). Spin bowling was already a feature of the game in the days of underarm bowling. Until the late 18th century bowlers who spun, or 'twisted', the ball generally made it turn from leg to off, for 'it is as natural to bowl leg-spin underarm as it is to bowl off-spin overarm' (Frith 1984, p 13). Consequently the Hambledon bowler Lamborn tied his opponents in knots when he pioneered the art of spinning the ball the other way in about 1780. Half a century or so later, with the arrival of overarm bowling, off-spin came to be the norm: in overarm bowling, a certain amount of clockwise rotation tends to be almost automatically imparted to the ball in the course of a right-arm bowler's delivery (see ACTION-BREAK) and the technique of off-spin is thus, as a rule, more easily learned than the somewhat 'artificial' leg-spin. For a variety of reasons, all forms of spin-bowling are in a state of long-term decline, if not – in some cases – under threat of actual extinction. The factors contributing to this development include: new legislation governing the covering of pitches, which has virtually eliminated the old 'sticky' wicket; the advent and increasing importance of limited-overs cricket, in which the overriding imperative is to restrict scoring rather than to take wickets; the tendency of modern balls to retain their shine for longer; and the tendency of groundsmen to prepare 'greener' wickets that favour medium-pace or fast-medium seam bowling. See also LEG-SPIN, OFF-SPIN, SEAM.

**spinner** *n* **1** a bowler who specialises in spinning the ball; broadly, any slow bowler:

*'If boundaries were extended, no second new balls were permitted, and outfields were made less lush, the spinner could come back into his own'* (Frith 1984, p 186).

**2** a ball bowled with spin on it:

> 'He got an undeniable spinner past the stubborn bat of the Lancashire man' (*Westminster Gazette* 2 March 1895).

**splice** *n* the wedge-shaped bottom end of the handle of the bat, which fits into a corresponding mortice in the top of the blade.

**spoon** *vb* to hit the ball high in the air but without much force, especially as a result of a mistimed stroke:

> 'Shahid, too, in leaden boots, spooned a simple catch to short midwicket against a ball he never saw' (Richard Streeton, *The Times* 23 June 1983).

**sporting** *adj* denotes a wicket, typically one that is hard and dry, that gives considerable assistance to the faster bowlers and makes it unlikely that the batsmen will ever be in command:

> 'There are, of course, some good wickets left in England, but there are far too many of this 'sporting' variety, and we are now paying the price' (Peebles 1959, p 199).

**square** *adj & adv* **1** close to or along an imaginary line extending outwards to the left and right of the batsman's wicket:

> 'For Lillee, Hughes took Dyson from the slips and put him at squarish third man' (Brearley 1982, p 67).

> 'Woolmer . . . was content to wait for the ball which could be punched square of the wicket, especially on the offside' (Norman Harris, *Sunday Times* 10 July 1983).

See FIELDING POSITIONS.

~ *n* **2** the imaginary line extending outwards from the batsman's wicket:

> 'The ploy worked nicely, Hughes timing his hook perfectly so that it carried all the way to Emburey fielding a few yards in from the edge just behind square' (Brearley 1982, p 93).

**3** the closely-mown area in the middle of a cricket ground, on which all the pitches used for playing matches are laid out:

> 'The Oval square is one of the largest in the country. There are

*27 pitches altogether, 20 of them for first-class matches'* (Harry Brind, *WCM* December 1983).

**square cut** *n* a cut made by bringing a more or less horizontal bat sharply down on a short-pitched off-side ball at the moment that it passes the batsman, usually sending the ball slightly backward of square, between point and third man. See CUT 1.

**square-cut** *vb* to strike the ball when making a square cut:

> *'Then Zaheer irrationally tried to square-cut a straight ball and dragged it on to the stumps'* (Matthew Engel, *Guardian* 7 March 1984).

**square drive** *n* a form of drive, played to a good-length ball pitching just outside off stump, in which the ball is sent into the area between cover and point. See DRIVE.

**square-drive** *vb* to strike the ball when making a square drive:

> *'After lunch Viswanath displayed the only commanding strokeplay of the entire match when he twice drove Willis for four and square-drove a three in the same over'* (Berry 1982, p 60).

**square leg** *n* a leg-side fielding position (or the player occupying it) roughly in a line with the batsman's wicket and usually close enough in to save the single; if closer to the boundary it becomes **deep square leg**. It is one of the 'standard' positions shown in all the early 19th-century cricket manuals, but is probably used rather less often in the modern game.

**square-leg umpire** *n* the umpire who usually stands in a position equivalent to that of a shortish square leg: see UMPIRE.

**squat** *vb* to fail to rise significantly after pitching; keep low:

> *'With some deliveries squatting and others lifting it was clear that survival would be difficult'* (Paul Fitzpatrick, *Guardian* 3 August 1983).

**squatter** *n* a ball that keeps low after pitching; a shooter.

**squirt** *vb* to propel the ball along the ground, usually into the area in front of square; the word suggests a minimum of activity on the part of the batsman, and often describes a blocking movement of the bat:

*'There had not been enough bounce to justify having a short square-leg with the old ball; better, we agreed, to stop him squirting a single out on the leg-side'* (Brearley 1982, p 88).

**st** *abbr* STUMPED: used in the scorebook, following the name of a batsman and preceding the name of the wicket-keeper, to indicate the manner of the batsman's dismissal and the player responsible for it. In earlier times dismissals by stumping were usually credited to the wicket-keeper alone, but since the early 19th century it has been usual to mention the bowler as well (thus 'st Kirmani b Kapil'). See STUMPED.

**stance** *n* the position adopted by the batsman as he stands at the wicket to receive the ball:

*'That incident ended a promising partnership between Vengsarkar and the in-form Amarnath who, from an unclassical square-on stance, plays most of the strokes with vigour and courage'* (Matthew Engel *Guardian* 16 June 1983).

**stand** *n* **1** a period in which two batsmen are batting together, considered in terms of the runs that are scored while they are at the wicket; 'stand' is used interchangeably with 'partnership', but perhaps carries an added suggestion of defiance in adverse circumstances, and so is often used to describe partnerships involving late-order batsmen:

*'The Baptiste-Holding stand for the ninth wicket was worth 150'* (David Frith, *WCM* August 1984).

~ *vb* **2** (of an umpire) to officiate in a match:

*'Rhodes . . . became a first-class umpire after retirement as a player at the age of 43, stood in eight Test matches, and coached both Oxford and Cambridge Universities'* (David Frith, *WCM* December 1983).

**stand out** *vb* (obsolete) to act as a fieldsman; field:

*'No substitute shall in any case be allowed to stand out or run between wickets for another person without the consent of the opposite party'* (*Laws* 1854).

**stand up** *vb* (of the wicket-keeper) to take up a position immediately behind the stumps, typically for a slow bowler, rather than several yards back from the wicket:

> *'Botham, off a short run with Taylor standing up, was difficult to get away'* (Henry Blofeld, *Cricketer* February 1983).

**star** *vb* (obsolete) to offer a potential catch to the fielding side:

> *'Hollins . . . proceeded to give chance after chance that was not accepted. He starred 7 before being finely caught and bowled for 28'* (Headlam 1903, p 157).

**steeple** *vb* (of the ball) to rise to a considerable height at an unusually steep angle often because of unevenness in the wicket:

> *'John . . . was a consistent danger. So was the inconsistent bounce. Rumesh Ratnayeke had one steepling from a length and Wright's nose was broken'* (Dick Brittenden, *Cricketer* May 1983).

**steepler** *n* a ball that 'steeples', either off the pitch or off the striker's bat:

> *'Catching nearer the wicket is all over in a moment and there is no time to think, except in the case of a steepler near the wicket'* (Ranji 1897, p 60).

**steer** *vb* to deflect the ball off the face of the bat so that it travels close to or along the ground, usually into the area just in front of or just behind square; the word suggests careful placing and minimal use of force:

> *'I brought Botham on for Emburey and Willis for Old, Bright having steered two fours between slips and gully'* (Brearley, 1982 p 85).

**stick** *vb* (of a possible catch) to be successfully held by a fielder:

> *'If these two catches had stuck Australia would have been 32 for three'* (Henry Blofeld, *Guardian* 10 December 1983).

**sticker** *n* (old) a cautious defensive batsman whose main objective is to stay at the crease rather than to score runs:

'Sometimes, when the ground is very bad, it is good to have a sticker, but taken altogether cricket would be very much better off if the whole race of stickers occasionally adopted a somewhat freer style' (Badminton 1888, p 200).

**sticks** *n* the stumps; the batsman's wicket:

'In these particular games [the Bodyline Tests] it is noticeable that our bowlers have hit the sticks so often' (Cricketer Spring Annual 1933).

**sticky** *adj* denotes the kind of wicket that is produced when the ground is drying out in warm sunshine after a heavy downpour. The soft, glutinous quality of the pitch provides ideal conditions for the slower bowlers because the ball can really 'bite' the turf and will often turn quite alarmingly, making batting a nightmare. With the added attraction of variable bounce, the 'sticky' wicket is 'liable to bring about the ignominious downfall of the most powerful side imaginable' (Ranji 1897, p 88). In such circumstances, batsmen have traditionally been advised to 'throw careful play to the winds, and hit, pull, and slog in every direction' (Badminton 1888, p 152). But modern regulations on the covering of pitches (see COVER 3) have to all intents and purposes eliminated the sticky wicket from contemporary cricket – a situation which, though no doubt agreeable to batsmen, has taken away one of the game's traditional features and, incidentally, done nothing to alleviate the already embattled position of the slow bowler.

**sticky dog** *n* (old) a 'sticky' wicket:

'We did not like the look of the sky with the possibility of having to get over 100 against O'Reilly and Ironmonger on a sticky dog in the fourth innings' (Larwood 1933, p 146).

**stock ball** *n* the type of delivery that forms the standard part of a bowler's repertoire, as opposed to other types of ball that are bowled as an occasional variation to take the batsman by surprise:

'Lillee and Alderman . . . both swing their stock ball away, but can bowl an inswinger' (Brearley 1982, p 65).

'The other three had the leg-break as a stock ball with the hard-to-pick googly as a lethal wicket-taker' (Frith 1984, p 65).

**stock bowler** *n* a bowler whose primary function is to bowl accurately and defensively for long spells in order to restrict the opposition's scoring opportunities, rather than to take wickets:

> 'It was not to be expected that he would turn the ball to any extent, but he proved a most useful stock bowler' (Peebles 1959, p 23).

> 'Gibbs toiled away predominantly as a stock bowler through series after series . . . tying batsmen down for hours without necessarily reaping great harvests' (Frith 1984, p 162).

In earlier years finger-spinners were often used in the role of stock bowler (see quotations). But the contemporary stock bowler is more likely to send down medium-pace inswingers. Compare STRIKE BOWLER.

**stonewall** *vb* to bat extremely defensively, with the intention of remaining at the crease rather than scoring runs:

> 'Later Roberts, stonewalling at first but hitting out towards the end, made the highest score of his career and posted a ninth-wicket stand of 161 with Lloyd' (WCM February 1984).

**stonewaller** *n* a player who 'stonewalls'; a totally defensive batsman:

> 'The stonewallers of our cricket fields have a great deal to answer for in the heavy indictment against modern players of leaving so many unfinished matches' (Badminton 1888, p 199).

**stop** *n* 1 (obsolete) = LONG STOP:

> 'In laying out your field, you should be careful in selecting good men for your principal places, such as wicket-keeper, point, stop, short-slip' (Clarke 1851 in HM, p 160).

~ *vb* 2 (obsolete) to field as long stop:

> 'No substitute in the field shall be allowed to bowl, keep wicket, stand at the point or middle wicket, or stop behind to a fast bowler, unless by consent of the opposite party' (Laws 1830).

3 to block the ball defensively:

> 'I would strongly recommend the young batsman to turn his whole attention to stopping: for, by acting this part well, he becomes a serious antagonist to the bowler' (Nyren 1833 in HM, p 22).

**4 – stop and look at you** to rise quite steeply off the wicket with a significant loss of pace, often as a result of back spin:

'Both Briggs and Jack Hearne, when helped by the wicket, are very skilful at making balls of apparently similar flights either "stop and look at you" or whip along like lightning' (Ranji 1897, p 81).

**straight** *adj & adv* close to an imaginary line separating the off and leg sides of the pitch in front of the batsman; the term is used especially in describing fielding positions in front of the wicket, such as long-on or mid-off, but can also denote a ball struck by the batsman that goes back past the bowler or over his head:

'The pace of the pitch is indicated by the setting of the field. If it is fast, mid-on, mid-off and cover-point will be set straighter than usual; if slow, they will be more square' (Arlott 1983, p 21).

'His 150, reached in 333 minutes, included a delightful straight six off Matthews' (Ian Brayshaw, *The Times* 27 December 1983).

**straightarm** *adj & adv* (obsolete) using a bowling action in which the arm remains unbent at the moment of delivery; roundarm or overarm:

'The straight-arm bowling, introduced by John Willes, Esq., was generally practised in the game' (Box 1868, p 73).

**straight bat** *n* a bat held in a perpendicular position so that, in the execution of a stroke, it moves straight down the ball's line of flight rather than across it:

'The fundamental principle of good safe batting is playing with a straight bat' (Ranji 1897, p 152).

Compare CROSS BAT.

**straight drive** *n* a form of drive, played to a good-length ball pitching around middle or off stump, by which the ball is sent back down the pitch (or over the bowler's head) into the area directly behind the bowler's wicket.

**straight-drive** *vb* to strike the ball when making a straight drive:

'Botham added 35 more runs to his overnight score in better than even time, straight-driving a second six to add to his 22 fours' (Scyld Berry, *Observer* 22 January 1984).

**streaky** *adj* (of a batting stroke) causing the ball to glance off the edge of the bat into the area behind the wicket:

> *'Almost every batsman I have seen play this strange attack has made one or more streaky strokes through these leg-side fieldsmen'* (James 1963, p 207).

> *'Viswanath cut a straight ball past second slip for four, off the meat too and along the ground, not streaky at all'* (Berry 1982, p 103).

**strike** *n* the position of being the batsman who is actually facing the bowling; the facing batsman is said – somewhat confusingly for the uninitiated – to be **on strike**:

> *'Once into his eighties, he proceeded quietly, with Randall (of all people) telling him to keep concentrating and pinching most of the strike'* (Scyld Berry, *Observer* 22 January 1984).

**strike bowler** *n* a 'frontline' bowler who bowls in fairly short spells to an attacking field, especially with the new ball or to a new batsman, and whose primary function is to take wickets rather than simply to restrict scoring opportunities:

> *'The emergence within a few days of Frank Tyson as a magnificent strike bowler and his partnership with Brian Statham transformed England'* (John Arlott, *WCM* September 1984).

Compare STOCK BOWLER.

**striker** *n* **1** the batsman who is facing the bowling, as distinguished from the batsman at the bowler's end (the 'non-striker'); the batsman who is 'on strike':

> *'When the ball is hit in front of the wicket the striker calls'* (Ranji 1897, p 200).

**2** (obsolete) either of the two batsmen at the wicket:

> *'When the Ball is hit up, either of the Strikers may hinder the catch in his running Ground'* (*Laws* 1744).

**striking rate** *n* any of several measures of the average rate at which a bowler or bowling attack takes wickets, or at which a batting side scores runs:

> *'His Test total of 242 wickets placed him next to Bedi, his striking rate of 4·17 per Test being best of them all'* (Frith 1984, p 174).

Striking rates for bowlers can be calculated by dividing the number of wickets taken by the number of games played (as in the example above) or as a figure showing the number of balls bowled per wickets taken. This last method is used in Britain's Benson and Hedges Cup competition, in which a side's striking rate – calculated by dividing total balls bowled by total wickets taken – is used as a tie-breaker when two teams in the same zonal group finish with an equal number of points. The striking rate of a batting side, for which sponsors of the game sometimes award prizes, is usually calculated on the basis of runs scored per 100 balls received.

**strip** *n* the area between the two sets of stumps, especially when considered in terms of its qualities as a playing surface; the wicket:

> 'The Australians toiled hard in the field but after the first hour or so found the wicket losing its sting and flattening out to a goodish batting strip' (Ian Brayshaw, *The Times* 27 December 1983).

**stroke** *n* **1** an act of striking the ball, especially one from which runs are scored; by contrast with the word HIT (qv), 'stroke' tends to suggest a gracefully executed, well-timed shot in which maximum effect is achieved by minimum force, rather than an unorthodox shot of unrestrained aggression.

**2** (obsolete) a run; a notch marked on the scorer's stick to indicate that a run has been scored:

> 'On Tues., May 22, on Blackheath, London beat Greenwich by 15 strokes; London went in first and got 112 strokes the first hands' (*Whitehall Evening Post* 26 May 1733).

~ *vb* **3** to play the ball with good timing and a graceful swing of the bat:

> 'When the New Zealanders took the new ball on Thursday, Randall stroked four extraordinary boundaries in the first two overs' (Robin Marlar, *Sunday Times* 28 August 1983).

**strokeless** *adj* unable to play scoring strokes freely, especially because the bowling gives no opportunity to do so safely:

> 'For the first two hours of his innings he was virtually strokeless

against *Garner and Botham'* (Vic Marks, *Cricketer* December 1982).

*'Crowe, troubled by a damaged left arm, was all but strokeless'* (John Mason, *Daily Telegraph* 15 August 1984).

**strokeplay** *n* batting characterised by skilful, well-timed, and often graceful hitting:

*'At times the attack was directed at the leg stump, with as many as six fielders to the on side, which was not conducive to free stroke-play'* (Peebles 1959, p 78).

*'Those who stayed away missed some elegant strokeplay of old-fashioned correctitude'* (David Frith WCM October 1984).

**stroke sheet** *n* a chart that provides a record of all the scoring strokes played by a batsman in the course of one innings, showing for each shot the direction taken by the ball and the number of runs scored.

**stump** *n* **1** one of the three upright wooden rods which, with the two bails laid across their tops, form one of the two wickets used in a game of crieket. The stumps are 28 inches/71·1 centimetres high (excluding the part below the ground) and 'of equal and sufficient size to prevent the ball from passing between them' once they are in position (Law 8 § 2); the individual stumps can be further distinguished, with reference to the position of the batsman defending them, as off stump, middle stump, and leg stump. The term 'stump' itself is a remarkable survival of a far-off time when the very earliest cricketers used a tree-stump as a target to bowl at. The original (1744) code of Laws prescribes two stumps with a height of 22 inches, and the height of the stumps gradually increased as the dimensions of the wicket were periodically altered (see WICKET[1]), reaching their present size in 1931.

~ *vb* **2** (of the wicket-keeper) to dismiss the striker by putting down his wicket if he is out of his ground when receiving a ball from the bowler:

*'If the Striker should move off his ground . . . the Wicket-Keeper will then do his best, and endeavour to put down the wicket, which is called* stumping out' (Lambert 1816, p 38).

No part of the wicket-keeper's body should be in front

# A BATSMAN'S 100 AT LORD'S

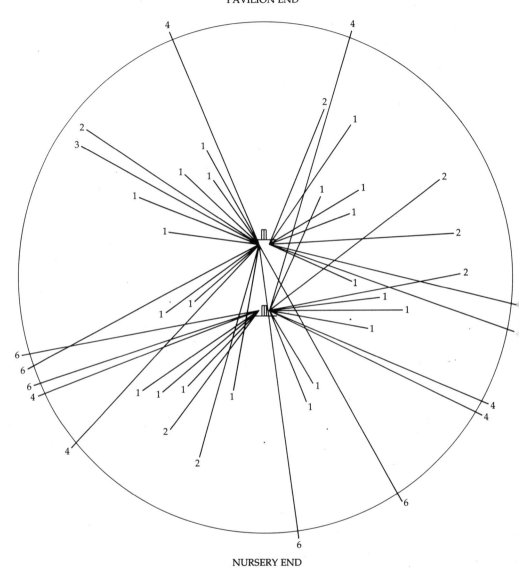

A TYPICAL STROKE SHEET

of the wicket as the ball is taken, unless the ball has already touched the batsman's bat or body. If any other fielder is involved, or if the batsman is out of his ground because he is attempting a run, the dismissal counts as a run-out rather than a stumping. Stumping seems to have been a feature of cricket since the very early days of the game and it is one of the modes of dismissal listed in the 1744 code: 'If in striking, both his Feet are over the Popping-Crease, and his Wicket put down, except his Bat is down within, it's out'. On the decline of stumping in the modern game, see STUMPER.

**stumped** *adv* a mode of dismissal in which the batsman is given out if the wicket-keeper stumps him (see STUMP 2). The dismissal is credited to the bowler and is entered in the scorebook as 'st [wicket-keeper] b [bowler]'. A batsman cannot be out stumped off a no-ball.

**stumper** *n* a wicket-keeper:

> '*I had almost forgot, they deserve a large bumper;*
> *Little George the long-stop, and Tom Sueter, the stumper*'
> (Rev R. Cotton, 'Hambledon Song' 1778 in *HM*, p 52).

The word 'stumper' has been used interchangeably with wicket-keeper since the 18th century, but in recent years it has begun to sound dated. Its decline as a word is no accident: it reflects the decline of stumping itself as a feature of the wicket-keeper's job. The slow bowler, once an indispensible member of any attack, has seen his position steadily eroded, and those that remain are more likely to bowl for containment than deception: consequently, opportunities for stumping have been dramatically reduced. Just how dramatically is illustrated by the contrasting achievements of two of the great modern wicket-keepers: Les Ames, one of the leading English 'stumpers' in the inter-war period, ended his career with a total of 1113 dismissals, made up of 698 catches and 415 stumpings. In striking contrast, Australia's Rodney Marsh, the game's most successful wicket-keeper at international level, ended his Test career in 1984 with a record total of 355 dismissals – but only 12 of them were stumpings.

**stumps**  *n* the time when stumps are drawn; close of play:

> 'His dismissal – for 59 – ten minutes before the close brought Australia back almost to even terms with the score 191–4 at stumps' (Brearley 1982, p 28).

**sub**  *abbr & n* **1** a substitute:

> 'Akram, the sub, held Marks off the fourth chance' (Robin Marlar, *Sunday Times* 25 March 1984).

The abbreviation is used in the scorebook when recording a catch made by a substitute fielder, who is never mentioned by name (thus 'c sub b Lillee').

~ *vb* **2** to field as a substitute:

> 'Subbing for Broad on the long-leg boundary, he clung on left-handed to Marshall's hook . . . but teetered over the rope' (Scyld Berry, *WCM* August 1984).

**submarine**  *vb* (of the ball) to beat the batsman by keeping very low and passing underneath his bat:

> 'Botham later paid the penalty for trying, submarined by an offbreak that almost bounced a second time before it bowled him' (John Thicknesse, *Cricketer* August 1983).

**substitute** *n* a player who takes the field in place of another who, in the course of the match, has become unable to play owing to illness or injury. Any player may be fielded as a substitute – it need not be the twelfth man – and the law no longer gives the opposing captain any rights over what position the substitute may field in, 'although he may object to the Substitute acting as Wicket-keeper' (Law 2 § 2). In practice, however, substitutes are unlikely to be posted in specialist close-catching positions and will usually field in the deep or in one of the midfield positions. Substitutes are not normally allowed to bat or bowl, but the rules governing the English county championship make provision for a special case in which this restriction does not apply: 'In the event of a cricketer currently playing in a Brittanic Assurance Championship match being required to join the England team for a Test match' the substitute appointed in his place does have the right to bat and bowl. This singular situation did in fact arise in 1982, when Gladstone Small was called away from a Warwickshire v Lancashire game to stand by for Test duty: his substitute David Brown not only bowled but took a wicket before Small, who was not after all chosen for the Test, came back and continued the game.

The earliest (1744) code of Laws specifically ruled out the possibility of substitutes, with a clause to the effect that umpires 'are not to allow a fresh Man to play, on either Side, on any Account'. The revised code of 1774 makes no mention of this rule and in 1798 there is a new regulation stating that if a player is hurt 'some other Person may be allowed to stand out for him, but not go in'. So far, there are no restrictions on the substitute's freedom of movement, but twenty or so years later a new clause outlined a number of limitations on the position of a substitute fielder: not only could he not bowl, but he was not to keep wicket or field at point, cover point, or long stop. This was later modified (1854) by a general rule that effectively gave the opposing captain a veto over where a substitute could field. The 1947 code gave opposing captains the right to 'indicate positions in which the substitute shall not field', and this regulation applied until very recently. The current latitude enjoyed by substitutes with regard to their position in the field was established in the 1980 version of the Laws, and marks a return to the situation that existed when substitutes were first introduced.

**sundries** *n* (Australia) = EXTRAS

**sweater** *n* – **take one's sweater** (of a bowler) to conclude a spell of bowling; a bowler will often give his sweater to the umpire while he is bowling and take it back again at the end of a spell:

> 'When Hadlee took his sweater . . . Rice began with a wide to symbolise his rare appearance in the attack nowadays' (Scyld Berry, *Observer* 9 September 1984).

**sweep** *n* **1** a batting stroke in which the ball is struck into the area between square leg and long leg with a long sweeping movement of a horizontal bat. It is typically played to a slower ball pitching around leg stump, and is executed by advancing the front foot down the wicket and bending the other leg so as to assume a half-kneeling position:

*'He stretched his left foot down the wicket and, with a sweep*
*that seemed to begin from first-slip and encompassed the whole*
*horizon, smashed the ball hard and low to square-leg'* (James
1963, p 91).

~ *vb* **2** to strike the ball when making a sweep:

*'Dujon reached his first hundred against England (234 minutes)*
*with a swept four off Cook'* (John Thicknesse, WCM
September 1984).

**sweeper** *n* a deep fielder who covers a large area close to the
boundary; the term is a recent borrowing from the
terminology of soccer, in which a sweeper is a player
who 'sweeps' the whole area behind the backs as an
extra line of defence:

*'The crowd . . . watched aghast as Yashpal flung his bat to the*
*delight of the "sweeper" on the cover boundary'* (Scyld Berry,
*Observer* 26 June 1983).

**swerve** (old) *n* **1** movement of the ball in the air; swing:

*'Hassett's gamble was enforced on him by a dread of Bedser and*
*the new ball on a moist wicket in an atmosphere likely to help*
*swerve'* (Cardus 1978, p 206).

~ *vb* **2** (of the ball) to move in the air; swing:

*'I was then bowling to a four slips field, as I invariably do while*
*the ball is shiny and likely to swerve away'* (Larwood 1933,
p 97).

**swerver** *n* (old) **1** a ball that moves in the air; an inswinger or
outswinger:

*'When about to bowl the swerver the seam of the ball is held*
*vertical, two fingers on each side of it on the top, and the thumb*
*directly underneath'* (Warner 1934, p 63).

**2** a bowler who makes the ball swerve; a swing
bowler:

*'Nowadays every cricket eleven has its "swerver" . . . and*
*almost excessive care is taken to keep the newness and shine on*
*the ball as long as possible in order that he may have every*
*chance'* (Warner 1934, p 60).

**swing** *n* **1** lateral movement of the ball while in flight
resulting in a curving rather than straight trajectory,

or the technique of imparting such movement to the ball:

> 'This time Willis, Cowans and Dilley found that speed and bounce were less important than swing and cut' (Christopher Martin-Jenkins, *Cricketer* September 1983).

~ *vb* **2** (of the bowler) to cause the ball to deviate laterally while in flight; move the ball in the air:

> 'He swung the ball out and in late enough for it not to be clear whether the movement was in the air or off the pitch' (Brearley 1982, p 150).

**3** (of the ball) to curve while in flight; move in the air:

> 'The ball was not swinging, and when they over-pitched they were driven mercilessly' (Henry Blofeld, *Cricketer* February 1983).

Swing occurs as a result of uneven distribution of pressure on the two sides of the ball as it passes through the air. It can be achieved by holding the ball with the seam 'canted' in the direction towards which the bowler intends the ball to swing – that is, towards first slip for outswing or fine leg for inswing. The angled seam produces turbulence on one side of the ball only, and the greater the resulting pressure difference, the more marked will be the degree of swing. The phenomenon of swing may have been dimly recognised back in the days of underarm bowling: it was said of the Hambledon bowler Noah Mann that 'his merit consisted in giving a curve to the ball the whole way' (Nyren 1833 in *HM*, p 62). But it was not till the late 19th century that swing began to be talked of as a potentially major development in the art of bowling. Both the *Badminton* book (1888) and Ranji's *Jubilee Book* (1897) devote considerable space to the apparent novelty of bowlers getting the ball to 'curl in the air', and both books acknowledge the influence of baseball (whose pitchers routinely 'swing' the ball) on the development of swing in cricket. Ranji, for example, mentions a Philadelphian bowler (probably J. B. King) who had completely baffled the Australian XI on its recent US tour: 'He is an excellent baseball player, and is said to have learnt to apply the methods of that game to cricket'. At any rate, Ranji concludes that 'when cricketers learn to command this curl in addition to their other devices,

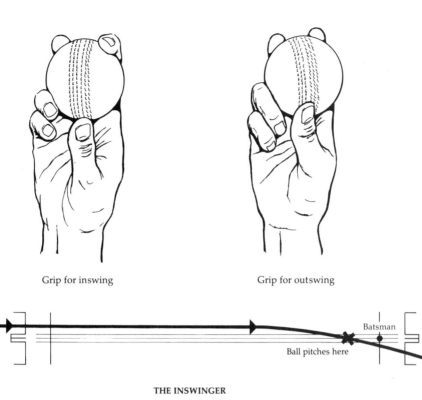

Grip for inswing   Grip for outswing

**THE INSWINGER**

Bowler

Ball pitches here

Batsman

**THE OUTSWINGER**

Bowler

Ball pitches here

Batsman

batting will become more difficult than ever' (Ranji 1897, p 108).

Swing quickly became assimilated into the repertoire of the game, though relatively few bowlers can be said to have learnt to 'command' it. While it is true that 'given certain conditions, almost every bowler . . . can make the ball swerve' (MCC 1952, p 35), the ability to do so with complete control has generally proved elusive – which is hardly surprising when one considers the complex physics of swing. The conventional wisdom is that certain conditions are particularly favourable to swing, notably a newish ball, a wind from the right quarter, and a damp, overcast atmosphere. But scientific research does not altogether bear this out. A recent paper in *Nature* (R. D. Mehta *et al*, 'Factors affecting cricket ball swing',

*Nature* 303, 30 June 1983) shows that the degree of swing is a function of several variables, especially the angle of the seam, the flow speed, and the rate of spin of the ball. Thus 'at a bowling speed of $\sim$30ms$^{-1}$ (70 mph) maximum swing is obtained at a seam angle of 20° and a spin rate of 11·4 rev s$^{-1}$. However, at lower speeds . . . and at lower seam angles . . . it is better to have a higher spin rate of about 14 rev s$^{-1}$.' In other words, complete control over swing depends on getting all the variants right – which is obviously quite a tall order. Bowlers have traditionally relied on their instincts and experience, but some lessons can be learned from the relevant physics. For example, a low seam angle (say 10°) may have the undesirable effect of making the ball swing too early, and the lower the speed of the ball, the higher the seam angle needs to be in order to avoid this. The research does confirm that genuinely fast bowling is unlikely to produce much swing, but – interestingly – it 'does not support the popular view that swing increases in damp and humid conditions'. The only explanation the authors can offer for the apparent connection between swing and humidity is that 'the varnish painted on new balls reacts with moisture to produce a rather tacky surface' – which in turn improves the bowler's grip and so produces more spin. 'So perhaps without actually realising it, the bowler just imparts more spin on a damp or humid day.' See also OUTSWING, INSWING.

**swinger** *n* a ball that moves in the air; an inswinger or outswinger:

> *'You could see that Botham didn't want to get out to Coney's gentle swingers'* (Peter Roebuck, *Cricketer* November 1983).

**tail** *n* the lower end of a side's batting order, usually consisting of players who are in the team primarily for their bowling (or wicket-keeping) skills and are not expected to contribute significantly to the team's score; if these late-order batsmen unexpectedly make a lot of runs, the tail is said to 'wag':

> 'The English tail again wagged strongly and it was not until 3 o'clock that the last wicket fell' (*Melbourne Argus* 19 January 1933).

**tailender** *n* a late-order batsman; a member of the 'tail':

> 'Tailenders are regularly greeted by a bumper first ball' (Peter Roebuck, *Cricketer* February 1984).

**talent money** *n* a bonus formerly paid by some clubs to a professional player who had made a particularly valuable contribution in a match:

> 'There is also a possibility for a man to earn what is called his "talent money", viz. 1 l. extra by making fifty runs or over' (*Badminton* 1888, p 103).

Unlike the modern 'man of the match' awards, which acknowledge an outstanding personal performance, talent money was dispensed automatically according to a scale of values fixed by each club; thus, for example, some clubs would award £1 for every 50 runs scored or every five wickets taken.

**tapetto** (Corfu) *lit 'mat' or 'carpet'*: the pitch, so called because cricket in Corfu is mostly played on matting. Like many Corfiot cricket terms it shows the strong Italian influence on the local language, dating from the period before Corfu became a British protectorate in 1815.

**TCCB** *abbr* the Test and County Cricket Board: the body that has overall responsibility for the administration of cricket in England at first-class and Minor County level. The TCCB is made up of representatives from MCC, the Minor Counties, and each of the first-class counties, and exercises general control over Test matches and one-day internationals staged in England, the county championship and the Minor County championship, and the various limited-over competitions involving first-class sides. See also ICC, NCA.

**telegraph** *n* (also **telegraph board**) (obsolete) a scoreboard:

> 'The telegraph is generally about ten feet in height and the upper portion, or face, is provided with grooves into which iron plates of about a foot square are inserted' (Box 1868, p 138).

Etymologically, the word means 'writing that can be read at a distance', but it was not applied to a cricket scoreboard until long after the invention of the 'electrical telegraph' which sent messages along a wire.

**Test** *n* **1** (also **Test match**) one of a series of international cricket matches of three or more days' duration played between representative teams from any two of the seven countries enjoying full membership of the ICC (qv):

> 'The first Test, due to start in Delhi on 22 November, will be cancelled, reducing the series from five matches to four' (*Observer* 4 November 1984).

~ *adj* **2** of or relating to a Test match or Test matches:

> 'Richie Benaud took more wickets than any other wrist-spinner in Test cricket' (Arlott 1983, p 45).

> 'The painful lesson in the end, at Lord's as at Edgbaston, was that England remain desperately short of Test class bowlers' (Christopher Martin-Jenkins, *Cricketer* August 1984).

International cricket began when an English team – not fully representative, but a strong side nevertheless – made a tour of Canada and the United States in 1859. Two years later another English party toured Australia, and opened the proceedings by defeating XVIII of Victoria by an innings. But the first match involving genuinely representative national sides meeting on even terms was played between Australia and England at the Melbourne Cricket Ground in March 1877, and ended in a victory for Australia by 45 runs. This game is now generally accepted as the first ever Test match, even though the term itself – which simply indicates that the series of games is regarded as a 'test' of the relative strength of the two sides – did not begin to be used until about ten years later.

**testimonial** *n* a special award given to a player by his county, usually in recognition of long service, whereby a sum of money is collected for the player by various forms of fund-raising activity. Whereas benefits are awarded more or less automatically in respect of a given number of years' service, the testimonial is a more occasional affair and is granted on an *ad hoc* basis according to various 'local' factors; and, unlike the benefit, the testimonial does not give its holder the right to the proceeds of a county match.

**thick-edge** *vb* to hit the ball so that it comes off the edge of the bat rather than off the face; the ball nevertheless makes fairly good contact with the bat (rather than just being finely 'snicked') and so is deflected at a considerable angle:

> 'I remember one over from Willis in which Wood thick-edged him between third slip and gully to the boundary' (Brearley 1982, p 61).

**think out** *vb* to bring about the dismissal of a batsman by some form of deception:

> 'Coney thought out Lamb with a perfect inswinger in the second innings' (Christopher Martin-Jenkins, *Cricketer* September 1983).

**third man** *n* (also formerly **third man up**) a relatively deep off-side fielding position (or the player occupying it) behind the batsman's wicket and covering the slips and gully: see FIELDING POSITIONS. The term third man originally denoted a position much closer to the wicket. It first appears in the mid-19th century to describe a position that was beginning to be used more often (with the spread of overarm bowling and the development of the 'off-theory') to supplement the more established close off-side fielding positions of point and short-slip. The new fieldsman was thus the **third man up**:

> 'The advantage of a third man up is proved to be most efficacious in the over-hand Fast-Bowling; seeing that when a man lounges out to play at a ball which he judges to be over-tossed he does not sufficiently provide for the twist and . . . becomes easy prey to this newly-formed adversary' (Felix 1850, p 48).

Indeed, the Rev Canon McCormick, who played in the 1850s and 60s, came in for criticism from opposing batsmen because he 'stood so close up at third man and caught them off the bat as they blocked the ball' (Pullin 1900, p 69). By the 1890s, with second or 'extra' slip now established as a position in its own right, third man had retreated somewhat to become 'rather a middle-slip, being long-slip placed in close enough to save the run' (W. G. Grace in *Outdoor Games & Recreations* 1891, p 26). Nowadays third man denotes a position of variable 'depth' anywhere in the quadrant bounded by point and the wicket-keeper.

**thrash** *n* (in one-day cricket) the closing stages of a side's innings, when only a few of the allotted overs remain and the main object is to score runs rather than to conserve wickets; the batsmen may be further assisted by facing a relatively weak bowling attack, in cases where their opponents' leading bowlers have already completed their full quota of overs:

> 'A further 22 overs of torrid pace . . . made a mockery of any attempt at what cricketers term the closing "thrash"' (Richard Streeton, *The Times* 23 June 1983).

**throat** *n* the central upper part of the face of the bat where the splice meets the blade:

> 'The ball looped from the throat of the bat and Athey dived forward at slip to catch the ball inches from the ground' (Paul Fitzpatrick, *Guardian* 31 May 1983).

**throat ball** *n* a short-pitched fast ball that rises steeply off the pitch towards the batsman's throat:

> 'Pocock, whose 42-minute stint as nightwatchman constituted one of the most gallant noughts of our time, Gower, Tavaré and

*Botham all went to throat balls'* (Matthew Engel, WCM
October 1984).

**throw** *vb* **1** to deliver the ball using an action that constitutes
a throw according to the Laws of cricket:

> *'A ball shall be deemed to have been thrown if . . . the process of
> straightening the bowling arm, whether it be partial or
> complete, takes place during that part of the delivery swing
> which directly precedes the ball leaving the hand'* (Law 24 note
> (a)).

In the early 19th century players of the old school like
Nyren condemned the roundarm and overarm in-
novations as 'throwing bowling', and the early exponents of these styles were often no-balled in accordance with contemporary definitions of a throw. The
legalisation of both types of action led to a narrower
definition of the term, but even so major controversies
have flared from time to time. See BOWLING, NO-BALL.

**2 – throw the bat** to bat with unrestrained aggression;
slog:

> *'Even then Sri Lanka hadn't escaped the left-handed lash as
> Gould, then Dilley, threw the bat'* (Scyld Berry, *Observer*
> 12 June 1983).

**throw out** *vb* (of a fielder) to run out a batsman by means of a
throw resulting in a direct hit on the stumps:

> *'Twelve runs later Greg Chappell played Azeem to Qadir at
> mid-on and was thrown out at the bowler's end'* (Henry
> Blofeld, *Guardian* 14 December 1983).

**tice** *n* (obsolete) a ball of full length that pitches close to the
popping crease; a yorker:

> *'There is a ball that in these days more frequently than any other
> succeeds in bowling people out, and that is the familiar "tice" or
> "yorker"'* (*Badminton* 1888, p 58).

It is so called because its aim is to 'entice' the batsman,
who, in moving forward to play it as a full toss, may be
yorked as the ball passes under his bat.

**tie** *n* the result of a match that ends with the scores exactly
level, provided that the side batting last has completed its innings (Law 21 § 4).

> '*A three days' match was played at the Surrey Ground,*
> *Kennington Oval, commencing on the 1st of July, 1847, between*
> *the counties of Kent and Surrey; each side scored 272 runs in the*
> *two innings, thus making it a tie*' ('Bat' 1851, p 73).

Ties are extremely rare in first-class cricket, and the only tie in a Test match was in the game between West Indies and Australia at Brisbane in 1960. In one-day cricket, however, ties are not especially uncommon, and in many one-day competitions (though England's John Player League is an exception) a game ending in a tie is awarded to the side that has lost fewest wickets or, if an equal number of wickets has fallen, the side with the higher scoring rate.

**timed out** *adv* a mode of dismissal in which an incoming batsman may be given out 'if he wilfully takes more than two minutes to come in' after the fall of a wicket (Law 31 § 1). A dismissal under this law is entered in the scorebook as 'timed out' and the wicket is not credited to the bowler. 'Timed out' is the newest form of dismissal and has never actually occurred in first-class cricket. Before its introduction there had always been a provision in the Laws (dating back to the original code of 1744) for a maximum interval of two minutes for each fresh batsman to come to the wicket, but a breach of this time allowance did not carry the threat of dismissal. In theory, it could entail the even more dire consequence of the match being awarded to the other side, if the umpires were satisfied that 'the delay of the individual amounts to a refusal of the batting side to continue play' (1947 code). In practice, however, this draconian penalty was rarely if ever exacted.

**ton** *n* a batsman's score of a hundred runs; a century:

> '*Allan Lamb . . . rescued England from disaster by becoming the*
> *first batsman to take two tons off the tourists this summer*'
> (Chris Morgan, *Sun* 13 July 1984).

**top** *n* **1** = TOP-SPIN:

> '*Inasmuch as every bowler should . . . try to reach the highest*
> *standard, he should do his best to acquire a command of*
> *off-break and leg-break, "top" and "hang"*' (Ranji 1897, p 81).

**2 – over the top** over the heads of the closer fielders

and out into the deep or over the boundary (as when a batsman hits a 'lofted' drive):

*'I decided to hit Botham over the top, seeing no mid-on or a man deeper, but only one in the country between long-on and deep mid-wicket'* (Sunil Gavaskar, WCM February 1984).

**top-bailer** *n* (obsolete) a well pitched-up ball that rises to the height of the bails; a BAIL BALL (qv):

*'He soon became sensible of the safety and excellence of the practice [of advancing to the pitch of the ball]; which saves alike the fingers and the wickets from a first-rate top-bailer'* (Mitford 1833 in *HM*, p 128).

**top-edge** *vb* **1** to hit the ball with the upper edge of the bat, especially when hitting across the line of flight (as in making a hook or pull) and misjudging the height of the ball; the top-edged ball loses pace and lobs upwards off the bat, often creating a chance for the fielding side:

*'Marsh, too, tried to hook Willis, top-edged, and Dilley judged an awkward catch perfectly'* (Brearley 1982, p 77).

~ *n* **2** a ball coming off the upper edge of the bat; a top-edged ball:

*'Although in hooking at 16 he was fortunate that Dujon did not pick up a top-edge, Gavaskar raced surely to his 50 in only 37 balls'* (WCM December 1983).

**top-score** *vb* to make the highest score of one's side's innings:

*'As it transpired, Amerasinghe top-scored his side's first innings as he and John shared a rousing last-wicket stand of 60'* (WCM May 1984).

**top-spin** *n* a variety of wrist-spin in which the direction of the spin imparted to the ball is the same as the direction in which the ball is travelling, causing it to 'hurry' off the wicket after pitching, with a significant increase in pace but with little or no deviation:

*'The ball comes off the wickets faster in comparison to its pace through the air . . . the reason being that it is possible to impart more top spin with a low delivery than with a high one'* (Warner 1934, p 35).

**top-spinner** *n* a ball delivered with top-spin; its unexpected change of pace and failure to turn after pitching make it a useful surprise ball for the wrist-spinner:

> 'Despite hands so small that he could not hold the ball comfortably, he bowled the leg-break, googly, and top-spinner' (John Arlott on Tich Freeman, WCM May 1984).

**toss** *n* **1** the flipping of a coin by one of the two captains as a way of deciding which team shall bat first; the toss takes place not more than quarter of an hour before the match is due to start, and 'the winner of the toss shall notify his decision to bat or to field to the opposing Captain not later than 10 minutes before the time scheduled for the match to start' (Law 12 § 4). It is important to note that the captains must nominate their teams *before* making the toss, and no changes in personnel can be made subsequently.

~ *vb* **2** to flip a coin in order to decide which team shall bat first:

> 'As Hughes and I walked out to toss in the bright sunshine, there was already an eager air of anticipation around the ground' (Brearley 1982, p 82).

In the very early days of cricket the winner of the toss not only had the choice of innings but could also decide the location of the pitch:

> 'The pitching of the first Wicket is to be determined by the Toss of a Piece of Money' (Laws 1744).

The toss fell into abeyance when the revised code of 1774 introduced a new and rather chivalrous clause to the effect that 'the Party which goes from home shall have the choice of the innings and the pitching of the wickets'. But a further adjustment of the law about 35 years later brought it more or less to its present shape, removing the choice of pitch from the captains and leaving them to toss for choice of innings.

**track** *n* the pitch; the term is used either with reference to the quality of the playing surface as it affects the game or, in phrases like 'go down the track', to describe the action of an attacking batsman who advances out of his ground, usually to a slower bowler:

> 'Like Rhodes before him, he had defied popular opinion that an English slow left-arm bowler would be murdered on hard Australian tracks' (Frith 1984, p 97).

'Botham was in finery mood; hooking the short stuff . . . and then marching down the track to hit Harper over the top' (Matthew Engel, *Guardian* 13 July 1984).

**trial ball**  *n* a ball bowled by a fresh bowler before beginning his spell and not counting in the game. Trial balls were introduced in about 1817 by a rule allowing a new bowler two such deliveries, with the proviso that he was then committed to bowling an over immediately afterwards: 'In the event of a change of Bowling no more than Two Balls to be allowed in practice. The Bowler who takes the Two Balls, to be obliged to bowl Four Balls'. According to R. S. Rait Kerr (*The Laws of Cricket* 1950, p 78), trial balls were discontinued in 1838, but the 1920 edition of the *Badminton* book mentions 'the abolition of trial balls in 1911' (p 66), and this later date seems to be supported by a match report from 1903:

> 'At 103 Saunders relieved Armstrong. In his trial ball he bowled the wicket down, and Hirst laughed at the thought of what might have happened' (*Melbourne Argus*, 17 December 1903).

**trimmer**  *n* a fast ball of exceptional quality, especially one that narrowly misses the stumps:

> 'Graveney received another real trimmer from Davidson, fast, lifting, and perhaps moving a shade away from the off stump' (Peebles 1959, p 72).

**trull**  *n* (obsolete) a delivery of the ball:

> 'On the second day rain prevented play until 3.30, when T. Walker went in and made 5 runs in 230 trulls (at one time 1 in 189)' (*Kentish Gazette* 21–23 August 1788).

The term clearly belongs to the earliest cricketing vocabulary since it comes from the verb 'troll', meaning to roll a ball along the ground as in bowls, ninepins, and (in its original form) cricket.

**trundle**  *vb* (obsolete) to bowl:

> 'Just to show that I was supposed to be able to trundle a bit, I might mention that in 1865 . . . playing for the All-England Eleven, I got all the 10 Yorkshire wickets in one innings' (George Wootton in Pullin 1900, p 199).

**trundler**  *n* 1 (obsolete) a bowler:

'The two greatest Australian batsmen were seen playing the balls of England's two most famous trundlers' (*Westminster Gazette* 1 March 1895).

**2** (modern) a defensive, usually medium-pace, 'stock' bowler:

'India had nothing to offer except trundlers – even Kapil Dev was uninspired and looked little different to all the others' (Matthew Engel, *Guardian* 16 June 1983).

**tuck up** *vb* to restrict a batsman's freedom of movement, typically with a ball that moves sharply in from off to leg, giving him no room to play either an attacking or defensive stroke:

'Early on he got tucked up by a short ball from Botham and received the benefit of the doubt when Gower dived to claim a splendid catch in the gully' (Michael Carey, *Daily Telegraph* 10 August 1984).

**turn** *vb* **1** (of the ball) to change direction after pitching, especially as a result of spin imparted by the bowler; break:

'Bracewell made the next breakthrough with his off-spinners, which were sometimes turning though never lifting' (Robin Marlar, *Sunday Times* 28 August 1983).

**2** (of the wicket) to be conducive to spin:

'All critics agree that his sixty-odd on a turning wicket in the last Test against Pakistan in 1958 was batting at the peak' (James 1963, p 223).

~ *n* **3** movement of the ball off the pitch as a result of spin imparted by the bowler:

'There were also fine cracks in the pitch, and one could move the earth between the cracks with one's hand: this suggested both uneven bounce and the chance of turn later' (Brearley 1982, p 81).

**turner** *n* a 'turning' wicket, providing conditions favourable to spin:

'The Australians, by winning the played-to-a-finish final Test, took the series by two to the one Verity won for England on a turner at Lord's' (John Arlott, *WCM* January 1984).

**tweaker** *n* (old) a spin bowler:

*'Once the shine was lessened . . . the wicket was very good and the left-handed tweakers found little help against such powerful opposition'* (Peebles 1959, p 57).

**twelfth man** *n* an additional player acting as a reserve member of a team. The usual procedure is to name twelve players in advance of a match and then – on the morning of the game – to choose eleven of them to play, after considering the state of the wicket. The twelfth man may be used as a substitute and is subject to the restrictions applying to such players. See SUBSTITUTE.

**twist** (obsolete) *n* **1** movement imparted to the ball by the bowler, causing it to change direction after pitching:

*'According as the axis of rotation . . . is horizontal or oblique, so it will have, upon reaching the ground, the bias, or "twist", as it is called'* (Felix 1850, p 2).

~ *vb* **2** to spin the ball, or (of the ball) to change direction after pitching as a result of spin:

*'For a Bowler to twist the Ball: when the ball goes out of a bowler's hand he must endeavor to make it twist a little across, then after it hits the ground it will twist the same way as it rolls when it goes from the hand'* (Boxall 1800, p 17).

**twister** *n* (obsolete) a ball that changes direction after pitching; a spinner:

*'"Mr Pinder, you're a sinful man." "How so Mr Craven?" "You bowl twisters; twisters are intended to deceive; and all deception is sin"'* (Pullin 1900, p 218).

**two leg** *n* the position of the bat when it is held so as to cover the middle and leg stumps by a batsman taking guard. Compare ONE LEG.

# U

**umbrella field** *n* an attacking field deployed for a new-ball bowler, packed with close catchers and typically including four slips, point, and gully on the off-side, and two short legs on the on-side.

**umpire** *n* **1** either of the two officials whose function is to ensure that a cricket match is conducted in accordance with the Laws of the game and to adjudicate on any point submitted to them by the players:

> 'Each Umpire is the sole Judge of all Nips and Catches; Inns and Outs; good or bad Runs . . . and his Determination shall be absolute' (*Laws* 1744).

~ *vb* **2** to act as umpire in a cricket match:

> 'More often, when feelings ran high umpiring was the cause' (John Woodcock, *Wisden* 1984, p 50).

The umpire at the bowler's end stands behind the stumps, to be in the best possible position for judging lbw appeals, while the umpire at the striker's end ('the square-leg umpire') *usually* stands in the position of a shortish square leg but 'may elect to stand on the off instead of the leg side' (Law 3 § 10). Appeals by the fielding side are in most cases answered by the umpire at the bowler's end, but the square-leg umpire has the last word in cases of stumping, hit wicket, or run-outs at the striker's wicket. At the end of each over the umpire at the bowler's end moves out to square leg at the same end of the pitch, while his counterpart moves in to the wicket to become the 'main' umpire.

The term 'an umpire' first appears in English as 'a

Out      Six runs      Four runs

Bye      Leg-bye      Wide

No ball      Dead ball      One short

noumpere' (= a 'non-peer' or 'unequal') indicating an 'odd man' or third party called in to adjudicate between two contestants. As far as cricket is concerned however, there have always been two umpires – an arrangement presumably dating back to the origins of the double wicket game. Early illustrations corroborated by William Goldwin's narrative poem on a cricket match ('*In Certamen Pilae*' 1706), show an umpire standing at each wicket and holding a staff which – under an arrangement that had already died out when the first code of Laws was drawn up in 1744 – the batsmen had to touch with their bats in order to complete a run (see RUN). The umpires' sphere of authority has always been exceptionally wide. In addition to the usual functions of counting the ball in an over, answering appeals, calling no-balls and wides, and signalling extras or boundaries to the scorers, the umpires are also 'the sole judges of fair and unfair play', and thus responsible for dealing with any infringements of Law 42 (see UNFAIR PLAY). The fitness of the pitch, the light, the weather, and the ball are also subject to the umpires' jurisdiction. The exceptional power wielded by umpires is well illustrated by the law stating that 'If an Umpire miscounts the number of balls, the over as counted by the Umpire shall stand' (Law 22 § 4). But the umpires' job, always exacting, has become more difficult than ever with the arrival of the action-replay and the players' increasing unwillingness to accept bad decisions as readily as earlier generations did (or are supposed to have done). Not surprisingly, therefore, the idea of providing umpires with some form of electronic back-up for certain types of decision is currently under debate.

**unbeaten** *adj* (of a batsman's score) made without the loss of one's wicket:

> 'By virtue of his unbeaten 127, Gavaskar became the first Indian batsman to carry his bat through an innings' (Z. H. Syed, *Cricketer* March 1983).

**underarm** *adj & adv* 1 (also **under-hand**) using a bowling action in which the arm 'is swung nearly pendulum-wise very much as it is at the game of bowls' (Ranji 1897, p 94). Originally all bowling was underarm, but with the acceptance of roundarm bowling in 1835 'the under-hand delivery tapered down in a few seasons to such small dimensions as to become kinsman to a curiosity' (Box 1868, p 75). The only real survivor of this change was the lob-bowler, who could still be found even at the highest levels of the game until the beginning of the first world war (see LOB). For the time being underarm bowling remains perfectly legal (provided the bowler informs the umpire of his intentions) but proposals for banning it have been aired at recent meetings of the ICC. The underarm delivery was used as recently as 1981 at international level, on the notorious occasion when Australia's Trevor Chappell bowled a daisy-cutter as the last ball of a one-day game against New Zealand, in order to ensure that New Zealand could not get the six runs they needed to tie the match. See BOWLING.

~ *vb* **2** to throw the ball with an underarm action when fielding:

> 'When the last ball was bowled, Carl Rackemann was tardy in starting for the bye to win the game as wicketkeeper Jeff Dujon underarmed the ball into the wicket for the run out' (Phil Wilkins, *Cricketer* April 1984).

**underedge** *n* a hit coming off the bottom edge of the bat:

> 'Gower, missed at 2, was caught behind off an underedge soon after tea' (David Frith, *WCM* August 1984).

**unfair play** *n* any behaviour that contravenes the 'spirit of the game', including: obstruction of the batsman in running, sledging, time wasting, persistent bowling of bouncers or beamers, deliberate damage to the pitch or ball, and failure to accept the decisions of the umpire. The clause in the Laws that makes the umpires the 'sole judges of all fair or unfair play' has survived intact from the original (1744) code, and the most recent (1980) code assembles all the various offences against fair play under the heading 'Unfair Play' (Law 42).

**unsight** *vb* to make a player, especially a batsman, unable to see the ball:

> 'One day at Lord's he was bowled by an unplayable ball. "Bad luck" I said, as he walked down the Long Room. Sutcliffe was clearly surprised at this comment. "I was unsighted by a man moving in the Pavilion", he said' (Cardus 1978, p 91).

**up** *n* **1** – **on the up** as the ball rises off the pitch from a good length:

> 'Their defensive partnership would be punctuated by the occasional pedigree stroke, as when Vengsarkar drove "on the up", which would bring a whole stand to its feet' (Berry 1982, p 114).

~ *adj* **2** (of a catchable ball) carrying to the fielder without bouncing.

**uppercut** *n* a form of cut or slice in which the ball glances up off the angled face of a horizontal bat, usually going towards or over the heads of the slips:

> 'So many [runs] came from uppercuts over the slips that Willis eventually sent two men two thirds of the way back to the boundary to act as fly-slips' (Matthew Engel, *Guardian* 6 November 1982).

**uppish** *adj* (of a batting stroke) sending the ball dangerously high, so that it is likely to be caught:

> 'Spofforth may have bowled more men out, but Giffen certainly was the cause of more misjudged and uppish strokes' (*Badminton* 1888, p 171).

**uppishly** *adv* playing an 'uppish' stroke:

> 'Denning had perished as he had flourished – cutting uppishly and being caught in the gully' (Michael Austin, *Daily Telegraph* 1 June 1984).

**useful** *adj* good; commendable. For cricket commentators, 'useful' has become an indispensible all-purpose word that can be used indiscriminately as a way of expressing approval of any cricketing achievement: thus, for example, a ball does not have to actually have any practical effect in order to qualify as a 'useful delivery'. The extent to which this word has invaded the vocabulary of even the most accomplished writers is well illustrated by the following snippet from a well-known expert on wine:

> 'Yugoslavian Cabernet Sauvignon: a useful example of the rapidly improving Yugoslav red wines' (John Arlott, *Guardian* 22 April 1983).

**V** *n* – **the V** an area in front of the batsman's wicket into which the ball is struck, bounded by two imaginary lines going outward from the batsman so as to form a 'V' shape; the 'V' is generally thought of as including the area between extra cover and wide mid-on, but its boundaries are variable:

> *'He cuts well, but prefers to drive through the wide V between cover and mid-wicket'* (John Arlott, *Guardian* 19 November 1983).

**walk** *vb* to leave the crease and walk towards the pavilion before the umpire has actually declared one to be out, as a way of acknowledging that one has been fairly dismissed, especially in a case where there might otherwise be some doubt about the dismissal:

> 'It was good to see that Graveney started to walk before the umpire raised his finger' (Peebles 1959, p 72).

> 'In the First Test of the 1946–47 series, Bradman refused to walk, although everyone on the ground thought he was out caught except the umpire' (Matthew Engel, 13 November 1982).

**watch** *n* (obsolete) a fielder:

> 'The "watches" are placed more behind the wicket, since the introduction of Round bowling, than they were formerly' (*Practical Hints on Cricket* 1843, frontispiece).

**watch out** *vb* (obsolete) to field:

> 'Little Tom Clement is visiting at Petersfield, where he plays much at cricket: Tom bats; his grandmother bowls; and his great-grandmother watches out!!' (Rev Gilbert White, letter dated 1786, in *HM* xi).

**WCA** *abbr* Women's Cricket Association

**wheel** *vb* (of a slow bowler) to bowl for long periods:

> 'In those four innings he wheeled down 57, 56·5, 60 and 64·5 six-ball overs for a total of 87 maidens and 19 wickets' (Frith 1984, p 97).

> 'He wheeled away from the Cathedral end for hour after hour

*without finding much turn but his control of length and line was a joy to watch'* (Henry Blofeld, *Cricketer* February 1983).

**whippy** *adj* (of a bowler's action) characterised by a sudden sharp movement as the ball is delivered, rather than a continuous flowing movement:

> *'Just before lunch Watkinson . . . getting occasional steep bounce from his high, whippy action, had him caught behind off an unpleasant lifter'* (David Green, *Daily Telegraph* 15 August 1984).

**WICBC** *abbr* West Indies Cricket Board of Control

**wicket**[1] *n* **1** either of the two targets at which the ball is bowled in cricket and which the batsman defends with his bat, each consisting of three stumps set in the ground and surmounted by two bails, the whole construction measuring 28 inches (71·1 centimetres) high by 9 inches (22·86 centimetres) wide. The two wickets are set up 'opposite and parallel to each other at a distance of 22 yards/20·12m. between the centres of the two middle stumps' (Law 8 § 1). In the normal, double-wicket version of the game the ball is bowled from one wicket (the **bowler's wicket**) at the other (the **batsman's wicket**) and the bowler's and batsman's wickets alternate after each over.

**2** (old) a stump:

> *'In the following year was played a match, when the Gentleman defended three wickets, 27 inches by 8, and the Players four, 36 inches by 12'* (*Badminton* 1888, p 358).

The word 'stump' is a vestige of an ancient embryonic phase of the game when the ball was probably bowled at a tree-stump, but even at an early stage the need must have been felt for a more portable target. This presented itself in the form of the movable hurdles used by shepherds in erecting temporary pens, or of the little gate (or 'wicket') by which such pens were entered. The earliest artificial wickets would have been modelled on these structures, and consisted of two upright sticks with forked ends across which a single bail was laid. There is some evidence to suggest that 17th century wickets were low and wide (like the original tree-stumps), measuring only one foot high by two feet in width (Nyren 1833 in *HM*, p 84). But the familiar tall and narrow configuration had already become established by the time the earliest code of Laws was drawn up in 1744, prescribing a wicket in which 'the Stumps must be Twenty-Two inches long, and the Bail Six inches'. The middle stump was added in about 1775 following an incident in a Kent v Hambledon match, when 'Lumpy' Stevens bowled three balls straight through John Small's wicket without disturbing the bail. This development led in turn to the addition of a second bail in about 1786 (see BAIL) and since then the basic construction of the wicket has remained the same, notwithstanding occasional proposals for the addition of a fourth stump. The size of the wicket, however, has gradually increased, partly no doubt because the change to roundarm bowling necessitated a rather higher target. The dimensions of the wicket have been modified as follows since the original code of Laws: 1798 – to 24 × 7 inches; 1819-21 – to 26 × 7 inches; 1823-5 – to 27 × 8 inches; and 1931 – to 28 × 9 inches.

**3 – (caught) at the wicket** (caught) by the wicket-keeper:

'There were confident appeals against Sutcliffe for lbw when he was 42, and for a catch at the wicket when he had reached 51' (Cricketer Spring Annual 1933, p 30).

**4 – over the wicket** delivering the ball from the hand that is closer to the bowler's wicket.

**5 – round the wicket** delivering the ball from the hand that is further away from the bowler's wicket.

**wicket²** *n* the area of ground between the two sets of stumps, measuring 22 yards (20·12 metres) in length and 10 feet (3·04 metres) in width; the pitch, especially when considered in terms of its quality as a playing surface and the extent to which it is likely to assist the batsman or bowler:

'Barclay thought long and hard before deciding to go in first on a slow wicket which impeded brisk scoring but encouraged the quicker bowlers to move the ball off the seam' (David Lacey, Guardian 16 June 1983).

The behaviour of the ball when it pitches is affected by so many variables – rainfall, sunshine, moisture in the air and in the pitch, type of soil, depth of grass, quality of drainage, etc. – that an almost infinite

number of different types of surface may be encountered. Consequently a large vocabulary has evolved to
classify the various kinds of wicket in terms of their
pace, bounce, liveliness, and the degree to which they
favour turn or movement off the seam. Essentially,
however, 'wickets may be divided into those in
favour of the batsman and those in favour of the
bowler' (Ranji 1897, p 84), and they range between the
'plumb' batting wicket that offers no help to the
bowler, and the dreaded 'sticky' wicket on which
batting is a nightmare.

The kinds of fine distinction that can now be made
between one wicket and another could not be applied
to the pitches on which cricket was played in its
formative years. Early wickets were of such poor
quality that they were all, effectively, bowler's wickets, and the unequal contest between bat and ball is
reflected in the very low scores that prevailed until
well into the 19th century (see SCORE). Even Lord's
cricket ground, with its unpredictable bounce and its
reputation for 'shooters', was still a dangerous place
for batsmen when W. G. Grace first played there in the
1860s. But in the last 30 years of the century, serious
attention began to be paid to improving the quality of
playing surfaces, and the subsequent 'revolution in
the state of the wickets' (Pullin 1900, p 180) had a
profound effect on the character of the game. By 1888,
pundits were already complaining about the evil of
'gigantic scoring' (*Badminton* 1888, p 401) and the
tedious drawn matches that had become a regular
feature since the tremendous improvements in the
quality of wickets. See also CRUMBLE, GREEN, PLUMB,
STICKY.

**wicket³** *n* **1** the batsman's wicket considered as something that
the batting side attempts to keep and the fielding side
attempts to capture. The wicket remains 'standing'
while a batsman is in, and 'falls' or is 'taken' when a
batsman is dismissed; a team's innings is complete
when ten of its eleven wickets have fallen:

> '*Last week there was a cricket match . . . between the gentlemen
> of Shipdown and the gentlemen of Docking and Burnham,
> which was won by the latter with three wickets standing*'
> (*Norfolk Chronicle* 23 August 1777).

> '*The loss of Amarnath to an expert slip catch by Lloyd triggered*

*an inexplicable collapse as seven wickets fell for 44 runs'* (Tony Cozier, *Cricketer* May 1983).

**2** a dismissal credited to a bowler:

*'In the last of his 79 Test matches . . . he passed Fred Trueman's world Test record of 307 wickets'* (Frith 1984, p 161 on Lance Gibbs).

*'Allott gave England the advantage by taking three prized wickets in his first five overs'* (John Woodcock, *The Times* 27 July 1984).

**3** a dismissal considered in terms of the batsman who is out:

*'After Lillee had claimed the vital wicket of Mudassar, Hogg ripped through the heart of Pakistan's batting with a devastating spell of 3 for 0 in 10 balls'* (WCM January 1984).

*'An awkward final session cost England the wicket of Broad while they made 10'* (Michael Carey *Daily Telegraph* 10 August 1984).

**4** the part of a side's innings during which two batsmen are together between the fall of one wicket and the fall of the next:

*'By adding 92 for the ninth wicket Paynter and Verity did much to recover the ground England had lost on the third day'* (*Cricketer* Spring Annual 1933, p 31).

*'The second wicket produced 145 in 200 minutes'* (WCM May 1984).

**5** a team's margin of victory expressed in terms of the number of batsmen on the winning side whose innings were either not completed or had never started when the desired number of runs had been reached:

*'England won the first match at Lord's by the comfortable margin of six wickets'* (Brearley 1982, p 24).

**wicket-keeper** *n* a specialist fielder behind the batsman's wicket whose job is to stop balls that beat the bat, catch balls coming off the edge of the bat, and – when possible – effect stumpings and run-outs. The wicket-keeper usually stands, or rather squats, slightly towards the off-side ('the left foot will be behind the middle and off stumps', says the MCC coaching book) and will nowadays take up his position either right up to the wicket or well back from it, according to the pace of the bowler; the deeper position was occupied by long stop, and wicket-keepers were advised 'to avoid standing so far away as not to be able comfortably to put down the wicket without moving the legs' (*Badminton* 1888, p 254).

Although the original (1744) code of Laws includes a section on 'Laws for the Wicket-Keepers', the job of keeping wicket was not originally done by a single specialist player, but fell to the bowlers at their own end in between overs – hence the importance of long stop in the early game. The emergence of the specialist wicket-keeper seems to date from the late 18th century and, according to the Rev John Mitford, Hambledon's Tom Sueter 'was the first wicket-keeper; that part of the game not having been attended to before' (Mitford 1833 in *HM*, p 128). The cricket manuals of the early 19th century (Boxall, Lambert, and Nyren) all insist that the wicket-keeper is 'the most proper person to place the players in the field' (Boxall 1800, p 50), apparently because his gesturing to the fielders could not be observed by the batsman on strike. This rather dubious arrangement had, however, been abandoned well before the end of the 19th century. See also STUMPER.

**wicket maiden** *n* a maiden over in which the bowler takes at least one wicket; wicket maidens are represented in the scorebook by joining up the dots in the record of the over to form a letter 'W' (see illustration at SCOREBOOK).

**wide** *n* **1** (also formally **wide ball**) a ball bowled 'so high over or so wide of the wicket that . . . it passes out of reach of the Striker, standing in a normal guard position' (Law 25 § 1). When a wide is bowled the umpire calls 'wide' and signals to the scorers by extending both arms horizontally. A wide appears as a cross in the bowling analysis and does not count as one of the six balls of the over. One run is credited to the batting side, unless the batsmen actually run more runs or the ball goes to the boundary, in which case any runs scored are credited to the extras as wides. In most limited-overs competitions a more stringent interpretation of the law is applied, and the umpires are instructed to discourage 'negative bowling' by calling as wides any balls bowled sufficiently far from the stumps 'to make it virtually impossible for the striker to play a "normal cricket stroke"'. Wides first appear in the Laws in 1810–11 and, as with many such developments (cf BAT), the new regulations came in the wake of a notorious incident in which the absence of any ruling had been flagrantly exploited. In this case William Lambert had managed to retrieve a desperate situation to win a single-wicket match at Lord's in 1810, by bowling his opponent, Lord Frederick Beauclerk, a series of wides in order 'to put him out of temper'. Initially wides were not treated separately, and any runs that resulted were 'to be put down to the Byes' (*Laws* c 1810). 'The first mention of "wides" on the score sheet appears to be in a match at Brighton between Kent and Sussex' (Box 1868, p 121), probably in 1827. There is a law of 1835 to the effect that the ball becomes dead as soon as 'wide' is called, so that no further runs could be taken, but this was reversed in 1844, and since then the batsmen have been allowed to take as many runs as they can get. The recent move towards debiting wides (and no-balls) to the bowler's analysis has already become widely established. See also EXTRAS.

~ *adj & adv* **2** relatively far from an imaginary line separating the off and leg sides of the pitch in front of the batsman:

> 'Dyson took two offside fours off Pringle before playing him wide of mid-on for the two runs which took Australia to an eight-wicket victory' (Henry Blofeld, *Cricketer* February 1983).

The term is used especially to describe fielding positions in the area behind the bowler's wicket, such as long-on or mid-off. Compare STRAIGHT and see FIELDING POSITIONS.

**work** *vb* **1** to deflect the ball off a more or less straight bat, sending it along the ground into the leg-side area:

> 'Phillips . . . produced many attractive strokes, particularly sequare-cuts and off-drives, and worked the ball off his legs well' (WCM January 1984).

> 'Abrahams offered steady resistance before he was bowled trying to work Alderman behind square leg' (David Lacey, Guardian 9 July 1984).

**2** (obsolete) to change direction after pitching; break:

*'A ball that twists after pitching is said to "work" in or off as it turns either towards or from the wicket'* (G. H. Selkirk, *Guide to the Cricket Ground* 1867, p 40).

~ *n* **3** (old) spin imparted to the ball or the resulting deviation of the ball on pitching; break:

*'On a wicket where an off-break bowler can get much work on the ball, it is sure to be frequently played towards short-leg'* (Ranji 1897, p 56).

*'He appears to be a roller rather than a spinner, but is said to get a bit more work into his googly'* (Peebles 1959, p 40).

**workhorse** *n* a bowler whose main function is to bowl defensively for long spells in order to contain the batting side; a stock bowler:

*'Jackman, who was brought out here to be a workhorse, had not played in five weeks'* (Matthew Engel, *Guardian* 27 January 1983).

**wrist-spin** *n* **1** spin imparted to the ball mainly by movement of the wrist at the moment of delivery. The right-arm bowler's leg-break is achieved by means of wrist-spin, the ball usually being gripped by the first three fingers and twisted from right to left (chiefly by the third finger) as the wrist flips over; variations on this basic action produce the googly, the top-spinner, the flipper, and the chinaman, all of them forms of wrist-spin. In so far as it involves reversing the 'natural' clockwise rotation of a ball bowled by a right-arm bowler, wrist-spin is much more difficult to achieve than finger-spin, and also produces a more devious flight and a more baffling form of break: 'The ball spins off the ground quite differently from the off-break. It does not come straight from the pitch at a certain angle to its previous line of flight; on the contrary, it describes a kind of curve after pitching, or in other words, curls off the ground' (Ranji 1897, p 78). Compare FINGER-SPIN.

~ *vb* **2** to bowl a ball with wrist-spin:

*'Hobbs crouched and advanced upon the crease to whip over a wrist-spun ball that buzzed and was liable to turn either way'* (Frith 1984, p 157).

**wrist-spinner** *n* an exponent of wrist-spin bowling:

> 'The cream of English batting has been bamboozled by Abdul Qadir and Sivaram, while the Australians have included a wrist-spinner against West Indies' (Mike Selvey, WCM January 1985).

**wristy** *adj* characterised by skilful and supple movement of the wrists, as in playing a cut or delivering a ball with wrist-spin:

> 'Sri Lanka, set a moderate target of 181, scrambled home thanks largely to a third-wicket stand of 80 between two delightfully wristy batsmen, Kuruppu and Dias' (Christopher Wordsworth, *Observer* 19 June 1983).

> 'Ian Chappell was a testing proposition for Test batsmen, letting loose wristy leg-breaks and wrong'uns from a strong action' (Frith 1984, p 176).

**wrong'un** *n* a ball bowled by a wrist-spinner that turns in the opposite direction from usual; a right-arm bowler's googly or a left-arm bowler's chinaman:

> 'Lock was overwhelmed trying to cut a very good wrong'un from Philpott' (Peebles 1959, p 51).

> 'When the shine was gone, he would settle into a leg-spin attack, with perhaps one "wrong'un" every two overs' (Frith 1984, p 66).

**york** *vb* to dismiss a batsman by bowling him with a yorker:

> 'Larwood made some beautiful strokes, including a six off Ironmonger, before being yorked' (*Cricketer* Spring Annual 1933, p 31).

**yorker** *n* a straight ball that passes underneath the striker's bat, especially by pitching right up to or just inside the popping crease:

> 'A yorker . . . depends for its success upon being mistaken for a half-volley and, therefore, of being hit at' (Larwood 1933, p 190).

The bowler can *attempt* to deliver a yorker but the ball only *becomes* a yorker if the batsman takes the bait and is induced to misjudge the ball's length, playing it either as a half-volley or a full toss. It is thus quite possible for a batsman to be 'yorked' even if he is a yard or two out of his ground so long as, in failing to read the ball's length correctly, he allows it to pass beneath the bat. The word yorker seems to have come into use during the 1860s, and within less than thirty years the perennial controversy over its origins had already begun. The favoured, but really quite unconvincing explanation for its etymology – namely that this type of delivery originated in Yorkshire – was already being advanced in 1888:

> 'We can find no derivation for the word "yorker", but are told that it came from the Yorkshiremen, who were fonder of bowling this ball than any other' (*Badminton* 1888, p 133).

A more fruitful area of investigation is the well-attested connection, in 18th and 19th century regional slang, between the words 'Yorkshire' and 'york' and the notion of cheating or deception. To 'york' or 'put Yorkshire on someone' are defined in the *English Dialect Dictionary* (1905) as 'to cheat, trick, or overreach a person', while Captain Grose's *Dictionary of the Vulgar Tongue* (1811) includes the phrase 'to come Yorkshire over someone', meaning to deceive them.

Another strand worth investigating is the similarity between 'yorker' and 'jerker', which led Andrew Lang (in a manuscript paper on 'The Yorker' written in the 1890s and now in the MCC library) to speculate on a possible etymological connection. Lang rejected this idea on the grounds that the Laws said a ball should be 'bowled not jerked', but there is some evidence – also in the *English Dialect Dictionary* – for a dialectal variant *yerker* or *yarker*, indicating 'something that jerks or wrenches'; hence, perhaps, a ball that goes under the bat and wrenches the stumps out of the ground. It is impossible to rule with any certainty on the etymology of a word whose origins were already obscure within a generation of its being coined. But it is probably fair to say that the likeliest derivation is from the *york*, *Yorkshire* words, which denote the kind of deception that is indispensible to a successful yorker. See also TICE.

# Bibliography

Illustrative quotations in the text have been drawn mainly from *The Cricketer* and *Wisden Cricket Monthly (WCM)*; from a wide range of newspapers, mostly British and contemporary but some from other times and places; and from the books listed below. Most of the extracts from 18th century newspapers are taken from *Fresh Light on 18th Century Cricket* by G. B. Buckley and *Cricketing References in Norwich Newspapers 1701 to 1800* by J. S. Penny. References to the Laws of the game are taken from *The Laws of Cricket 1980 code*, published by the MCC; when earlier codes are referred to, the date is always shown.

Many of the books used as source materials are classics of cricket literature, but this was not the main criterion for inclusion. The books were chosen as a representative sample of cricket writing spanning the period from 1800 to the present day, with at least one title from each generation to ensure the fullest possible coverage of developments in the language.

| | |
|---|---|
| Arlott 1983 | John Arlott, *How to watch Cricket* 1983 |
| *Badminton* 1888 | A. G. Steel and the Hon R. H. Lyttelton (eds) *The Badminton Library: Cricket* 1888 |
| 'Bat' 1851 | 'Bat' (Charles Box), *The Cricketer's Manual* (5th edn) 1851 |
| Berry 1982 | Scyld Berry, *Cricket Wallah* 1982 |
| Box 1868 | Charles Box, *The Theory and Practice of Cricket* 1868 |
| Boxall 1800 | T. Boxall, *Rules & Instructions for Playing at the Game of Cricket as practised by the most eminent Players* 1800 |
| Brearley 1982 | Mike Brearley, *Phoenix from the Ashes* 1982 |
| Cardus 1978 | Neville Cardus, *Cardus in the Covers* 1978 |
| Clarke 1851 | William Clarke, 'Practical hints on Cricket' (from *Cricket Notes* 1851) in *HM* |
| Felix 1850 | 'Felix' (Nicholas Wanostrocht), *Felix on the Bat: being a scientific Inquiry in the use of the Cricket Bat* 1850 |
| Frith 1984 | David Frith, *The Slow Men* 1984 |
| Headlam 1903 | J. Headlam, *Ten Thousand Miles through India and Burma* (a cricket tour by the Oxford University Authentics) 1903 |
| *HM* | E. V. Lucas, *The Hambledon Men* (a selection of classic 19th century writings) 1907 |
| James 1963 | C. L. R. James, *Beyond a Boundary* 1963 |
| Lambert 1816 | William Lambert, *Instructions & Rules for playing the Noble Game of Cricket* 1816 |
| Larwood 1933 | Harold Larwood, *Body-Line?* 1933 |
| MCC 1952 | *The M.C.C. Cricket Coaching Book* 1952 |
| Mitford 1833 | Rev. John Mitford, Review of Nyren 1833 in *Gentleman's Magazine* July/Sept 1833, in *HM* |
| Moorhouse 1979 | Geoffrey Moorhouse, *The Best-Loved Game* 1979 |

Nyren 1833      John Nyren, *The Young Cricketer's Tutor* and *The Cricketers of my Time* 1833, in *HM*

Peebles 1959      Ian Peebles, *The Fight for the Ashes 1958–9* 1959

Pullin 1900      A. W. Pullin, *Talks with old English Cricketers* 1900

Pycroft 1854      Rev. James Pycroft, *The Cricket Field* (2nd edn) 1854, in *HM*

Ranji 1897      K. S. Ranjitsinhji, *The Jubilee Book of Cricket* 1897

Warner 1934      Sir Pelham Warner, *The Book of Cricket* (3rd edn) 1934